LET IT GO
AMONG OUR PEOPLE

LET IT GO AMONG OUR PEOPLE

An Illustrated History of the English Bible
from John Wyclif to the King James Version

David Price
and
Charles C. Ryrie

Ⓛ

The Lutterworth Press

The Lutterworth Press
P.O. Box 60
Cambridge
CB1 2NT

www.lutterworth.com
publishing@lutterworth.com

First Published in 2004

ISBN 0 7188 3042 3

British Library Cataloguing in Publication Data
A catalogue record is available from the British Library

Printed in Dubai
by Emirates Printing Press

Contents

PREFACE

In this book we have attempted to portray a complex topic for the non-expert: the history of the English Bible from John Wyclif to the King James Version (KJV). This study is a result of long-term, specialised research, including many years of reading the actual medieval and Renaissance Bibles. Yet, we have described this history in general terms that, we hope, are comprehensible to all.

The history of the English Bible is not widely known. This is a little surprising, given the devotion to the Bible in the English-speaking world. Virtually every speaker of German (and English, for that matter) knows the name Martin Luther and is aware that he translated the Bible. How many people know the name William Tyndale? Or even John Wyclif? Many people admire the King James Version, yet do so without realising exactly what it is or how it came to be. There is nothing particularly wrong with that manner of appreciation. The King James Version is admirable in its own right, without elucidation of any type. Nonetheless, there are many people who want to know the tumultuous political and literary history of how this masterpiece came to be. This book is for them.

English Bibles took a different path from other European vernacular Bibles. This is because, in England, unlike almost every other country, it was illegal to translate the word of God. The ban lasted some one hundred and twenty-seven years. Overcoming the political and ecclesiastical resistance to an English Bible was not an easy task. Lives were lost along the way – not only for producing English Bibles, but also for merely owning or reading them.

Another issue that burned incandescently on the English scene was partisanship in Bibles. The early Bibles originated in heretical movements that the government opposed. This tension cut in two directions. For one, the Bibles, especially the Tyndale versions, advocated theological (and therefore political) stances. For another, authorities cracked down hard on any attempt to produce an English version. Very few copies of Tyndale's Bibles printed before 1534 are extant. There are eighteen separate printings of the complete German Bible *before* Luther, the first one dating from 1466. Every one was perfectly legal and hundreds of copies of those pre-Lutheran Bibles have survived. No one attempted to print an English Bible until 1525. That first attempt was stopped in press and now only a single fragment of it survives.

When the Bible became legal in England, the government and the new Church of England encouraged neutral presentation of the text. Naturally, that is in essence an elusive goal. But one can still strive for it. Among the conscious attempts at neutral presentation are the Great Bible (1539, etc.) and the King James Version (1611, etc.). Some people even resented the Bishops' Bible because it did not offend Catholic sensibilities. Catholics and Puritans could use the King James Version, even though the original preface was not entirely free of occasional anti-Catholic and anti-Puritan statements. Yet, partisanship marred several versions. The Douai-Rheims and Tyndale's versions certainly undermined themselves by their promotion of their own views, but the Geneva version, perhaps more than any other, cut off its own – very vigorous – life. If the Geneva version had eschewed partisan theological and political notes, it is highly likely that the King James Version would never have come into existence.

In addition to accounts of the theological and political contexts, this book attempts to give a history of the rhetorical development of the Bible. No other language, save perhaps German, can boast that its vernacular translation of the Bible is a literary masterpiece in its own right. We try to give the reader a sense of the development of the literary style of the English Bible by analysing the language as a translation, by comparing important passages in different versions and by viewing the whole as literature. Such close study of the text itself is warranted because the English Bible has had a profound effect on English language, literature, politics and ideas. It has left a lasting impress on the language that we speak today.

A unique feature of our presentation is the copious use of visual illustrations. We want to narrate the history in our prose account but we also want to tell the history in pictures. Indeed we hope that a reader who only looks at the pictures and reads the captions to them will have mastered the essential aspects of the history. Moreover, we consider the images crucial for our approach. We want the reader to experience this history as well as read it. Consequently, we also quote from the various versions at some length so that the reader can experience aspects of the early versions with little mediation from us.

Naturally, the King James Version is not *the* end of the story, although in some ways it is certainly *an* end. It had no serious competition until the end of the nineteenth century. Even though the KJV is the end of *our* story, we have added an appendix with a list of subsequent English Bibles and brief descriptions of them.

Many of the issues Bible versions face today were also major considerations in the Renaissance. We will not draw parallels but this book will make the reader aware of the basic decisions that have to be faced when preparing a translation of the Bible. The history of the English Bible is fraught with controversy. We have tried to present this complex history in as clear and unbiased a way as possible. The history of the English Bible continues, of course, but the consequences of decisions made during the pivotal period we cover in this book are still being felt today.

AUTHORS TO THE READER

2004 marks the 400th anniversary of the decision, taken in January 1604 at the Hampton Court Conference, to produce a new Bible, namely, the King James Version. This occasion offers the ideal justification for reconsidering the prehistory of the KJV. The Hampton Court Conference was a momentous event in the history of the church and the history of the English language. Nonetheless, there is one strange thing about the decision – there was no pressing need for a new Bible. Several good ones as well as one distinguished Bible were widely available. However grand and significant the KJV is, it was built on the solid foundations of earlier accomplishments. The preface to the KJV, which was published in 1611, states 'Truly, Good Christian Reader, we never thought from the beginning that we should need to make a new translation'. These are not empty words.

We are grateful for the interest of several libraries in our project to study the English Bible and for their willingness to mount exhibitions that complement this study. Bridwell Library of Southern Methodist University, Princeton University Library and the John Rylands Library of the University of Manchester are among the very few institutions where readers can study this history with all the major versions from the Middle Ages to the seventeenth century at their fingertips. It also occurred to us that not everyone enjoys proximity to such distinguished collections. And yet, we want you, dear Reader, to experience the Bibles as physical objects. We have, therefore, provided numerous illustrations so that you can see for yourself the beauty and subtleties of the texts. We have identified the images with substantial explanations so that one could, in effect, follow the history of the English Bible using our study as a picture book. We have also added, here and there, information boxes to further aid the reader in filling in gaps. In a way, we have produced three complementary histories of the English Bible that you can follow simultaneously or separately through our chapters: the text, the illustrations and the information boxes.

David Price is a specialist in Renaissance Studies with a PhD from Yale University; he currently teaches at Southern Methodist University. After receiving doctorates from Dallas Theological Seminary and the University of Edinburgh, Charles Ryrie spent his career teaching Bible and Theology; the study of the history of the Bible has been a serious vocation for him for over four decades. Each author took primary responsibility for several chapters: David Price wrote Chapters 1 (Wyclif), 2 (Erasmus), 3 (Tyndale) and 7 (Douai-Rheims); Charles Ryrie is the author of Chapters 4 (Coverdale) and 6 (Bishops' Bible) and both Appendices ('Revising the King James Version' and 'The Post-King James Era'); they collaborated on Chapter 5 (Geneva) and Chapter 8 (King James Version). Working together and checking each other's work has been a stimulating experience. We believe that the process has produced a better book than either of us could have written alone. We would also like to acknowledge that Valerie Hotchkiss has helped us at every stage of writing this book. Stella Butler, Christopher de Hamel, Stephen Ferguson, Dennis Maust, Paul Needham, Peter Nockles, Ben Primer, William Simpson, Jon Speck and Eric White have helped us with the project in general, especially with plans to mount a book exhibition to commemorate the four-hundredth anniversary of the Hampton Court Conference. Megan McLemore assisted with the preparation of the final manuscript. To Adrian Brink of The Lutterworth Press we express our deep gratitude for seeing the book through press. We are also grateful for the support we received from the Highland Park United Methodist Church.

The photographic reproductions are courtesy of Bridwell Library, Southern Methodist University, Princeton University Library, the collection of Charles C. Ryrie and the Scheide Library housed at Princeton University.

The reader will notice that we refer to the same Bible of 1611 with two terms – the King James Version and the Authorised Version. The former is most familiar to Americans and also meaningful to British readers. American publishers do not ordinarily use 'Authorised Version' since this translation, despite its popularity, never had an official status in the United States. These questions of terminology, and related ones such as orthography and usage, are difficult in books that aim at reception on both sides of the Atlantic. To paraphrase Oscar Wilde, the English and the Americans have everything in common, except language. We ask for the reader's patience with our negotiation of the two forms of English.

The history of the English Bible is a fascinating and compelling story. As you learn more about the foundations of our English Bible, we hope that the knowledge gleaned will enrich your appreciation of your Bible, regardless of which English version you use. Today, there are countless versions of the English Bible, but all are dependent on the translations described in this book. The plethora of English Bibles today has fulfilled the wishes of those who struggled, on every side, in the Reformation.

Our title – *Let It Go among Our People* – is a slight adaptation of a statement attributed to Henry VIII, allegedly uttered as he considered the merits of the Coverdale Bible (1535). The title deletes Henry's ambivalence and his qualification: 'if there be no heresy in it!' Although Henry may have had second thoughts, the Bible did go out among the people, and it had a profound effect on their faith, politics, literature, art and society. Our book describes the circumstances of the launch of the English Bible.

CHAPTER ONE
SACRED TEXT IN THE PEOPLE'S LANGUAGE

The pearl of the Gospel [has been] scattered abroad
and trodden underfoot by the swine.
– *Henry Knighton*, Chronicle[1]

John Wyclif and King James are the names we associate most immediately with the English Bible. The Wycliffite version was the first and the King James was, so to speak, the crowning literary achievement in the history of the English Bible, arguably the greatest translation ever made. These two Bibles are the alpha and the omega of this history.

There is, however, an irony in the names of the stars in this constellation. In truth, neither Wyclif nor James I is known to have translated a single word of the Bibles named after them, even though both had sufficient scholarship for the task. They each exerted, in different ways, the gravitational force that attracted people to the project of translation and, with their programmes of reform, they determined the orbit of their literary followers.

John Wyclif

John Wyclif was a bold and remarkably productive theologian. For most of his life he enjoyed the privileges of success, serving both as a professor at Oxford and as advisor to the English crown in its negotiations with the papacy. Nonetheless, in the 1370s he jolted the theological world, causing political repercussions that were still being felt, especially in central Europe, when the Protestant Reformation began nearly a century and a half later. He also felt the first repercussions, for, after a distinguished career that had earned him recognition at the highest levels of society, Wyclif would die an outcast from Oxford University and the English government.

Why? He began questioning the authority of the church and several of its central doctrines. Ultimately, he qualified the individual's reliance on the teachings and ministrations of the sacraments offered by the institutional church. He insisted instead that everyone needs to know 'God's law' and adhere to it. How is everyone to know God's law? Can the church mediate that knowledge? To the second question, Wyclif's answer was a qualified 'no'. To the first, he offered a revolutionary answer: the people must have recourse – direct access – to the Bible. Thus, the English people needed an English Bible.

When Pope Gregory XI declared eighteen of Wyclif's opinions heretical in 1377, he was not acting to limit biblical access. His reason for this extreme action was not particular concern about that issue, no matter how important it may seem to us in retrospect, but rather that he wanted to stymie Wyclif's challenge to papal and clerical authority.

In the fourteenth century, the papacy had suffered a tremendous loss of prestige, initially as a result of the Avignon papacy (1309-77) – which put the church mostly under the control of the French monarchs – and then, upon the election of Gregory XI's successor, the Great Schism (1378-1415), when two and for a time three men simultaneously laid claim to Peter's see. Papal authority was particularly resented in England, since the English had no desire to obey a French-supported primate. For the English government, the corruption of simony (which means the 'selling' of ecclesiastical offices) was provocative, as were the financial obligations of the English church to Rome or Avignon. At this vulnerable moment, Wyclif further undermined the status of the papacy and clergy with his development of a new concept of dominion.

'Dominion by grace' was his primary innovation. According to Wyclif, a person can only hold an ecclesiastical office in a state of righteousness. Should anyone's un-righteousness becomes manifest, say, as a result of public immorality, removal from ecclesiastical office must ensue, even if the office is the papacy. Moreover, in response to the assertion of fundamental authority by the papacy, Wyclif insisted the Christian must be obedient first and foremost to God, not to the pope or a cleric.

Initially, this antipapalism was music to the ears of Wyclif's political patrons,[2] not least because the English were generally at war with the French. Nonetheless, while the original context of his challenge was unquestionably political, his arguments became rigorously theological. Indeed, the courage of his convictions would be apparent and inspiring to many people. Despite initial support from some official quarters, his teachings soon encountered stiff opposition from English political leaders and churchmen. Whatever the changing relationship with Rome (or Avignon) may have been at any given moment, the church was a powerful element of the English government. English churchmen resisted any diminution of power. Moreover, the Peasants' Revolt of 1381, a destructive and terrifying event, was widely blamed on confusion arising from Wyclif's intellectual and religious upheaval. In 1382, Wyclif, his ideas and his followers were declared heretics by the English council at Blackfriars, London.

The essential point for our story is that, as Wyclif deepened the substance of the anti-Roman position, he claimed that the authority of his views rested in the Bible alone. This established a paradigm for ecclesiastical reform that would re-emerge frequently in the sixteenth century: placing the authority of the Bible against the authority of the institutional church. In this regard, the Bible could function in a way analogous to that of national constitutions. Nonetheless, the Bible as the authority for religious change is one of the great paradoxes of Christianity. It contains God's timeless, eternal message. As both a Jewish and a Christian prophet said: the Word of God will last forever (Isaiah 40:8; 1 Peter 1:25). Yet, while nearly every movement of

THE BIBLE IN OLD ENGLISH

When Christianity came to England in the sixth and seventh centuries, the people spoke several dialects now collectively called Old English or Anglo Saxon. Precious little survives in Old English, but it is clear that vernacular versions of the Bible were not forbidden. Indeed, King Alfred (849-99) condones the translation of religious texts when he says:

> . . . the law was first composed in the Hebrew language, and afterwards, when the Greeks learned it, they translated it all into their own language, and also all other books. And afterwards the Romans in the same way, when they had learned them, translated them all through wise interpreters into their own language. And also all other Christian peoples translated some part of them into their own language. Therefore it seems better to me . . . that we also translate certain books, which are most needful for all people to know, into that language that we all can understand.

Much of the Bible is quoted or paraphrased somewhere in Old English prose or poetic records,[1] there is no complete Old English translation of the Bible. The first complete Bible in English is the Middle English Wycliffite Bible of the fourteenth century.

Old English biblical texts fall into three categories:

Glosses: Glosses are interlinear insertions in Latin manuscripts that offer crude word-for-word translations written near the Latin words. The Psalms and the Gospels were most often glossed in Old English.

Paraphrases: Retellings of the biblical text in prose or verse. Prose paraphrases appear in the homilies of Aelfric (955?-1025?) and as examples in other writings. A good portion of what survives of Old English poetry falls into the category of metrical paraphrases of the Bible, including the Cædmonian poems, dating from around 1000, on Genesis (Genesis A and B), Exodus and Daniel. The famous Beowulf manuscript also contains a powerful poem on the story of Judith probably composed in the ninth century.

Translations: Distinct prose translations exist for the four Gospels in the West Saxon Gospels and for a good part of Genesis through Judges in Aelfric's *Heptateuch*. King Alfred also translated most of Exodus 20-23 in the introduction to his law code. A prose translation of Psalms 1-50 has been attributed to King Alfred and in the same manuscript (the Paris Psalter) Psalms 51-150 are rendered in alliterative verse.

---

1. See the biblical index in Cook 1903 for a complete list of biblical quotations in Old English prose. See also Morrell 1965 for bibliographic descriptions of Old English manuscripts containing biblical material.

Fig. 1.1. John Wyclif († 1384) instigated the first complete translation of the Bible into English. He was a prolific theologian who addressed both philosophical and practical issues. He questioned the nature of papal primacy and even of the clergy in general. He also advocated that lay people have access to the Bible in English. Therefore, some of his followers translated the Vulgate Bible. However, since this Bible emerged from a heretical movement, the English Bible was declared illegal in 1407/09. No authentic portraits of John Wyclif survive. This fanciful image is from the Nuremberg Chronicle *(Nuremberg: Anton Koberger, 1493), folio 238.*

JOHN WYCLIF AND THE FIRST ENGLISH BIBLE

1370s	John Wyclif, Professor of theology at Oxford University, writes revolutionary theological tracts; advocates direct access of the laity to scriptures in English translation
1377	Pope Gregory XI declares some of Wyclif's tenets heretical
1381	Peasants' Revolt in England; some blame Wyclif's movement for the unrest
1382	Oxford University declares Wyclif's views heretical
1384	Wyclif dies in Lutterworth, England
c. **1380**	The first version of the Wycliffite Bible
c. **1390**	The second version of the Wycliffite Bible
1407/09	Constitutions of Oxford, legislated under the direction of Archbishop Thomas Arundel, outlaw ownership of the Bible in English
early 1400s	Lollards (the followers of Wyclif) are crushed; after 1414, they will no longer be a significant movement
1428	Wyclif's remains exhumed, burned and scattered into the River Swift
1400s and early 1500s	Despite sporadic inquests and executions of Lollards, the Wycliffite Bible continues to be copied by hand. Complete or fragmentary remains of *c.* 250 copies are still in existence.

religious innovation has claimed the authority of the Bible, each one has constructed different messages from that immutable authority.

The Wycliffite movement, with its insistence on the authority of scripture, finally provoked a reaction with dire consequences for the development of the English Bible – the Bible in English was outlawed.

In the Middle Ages, the Bible had already been translated into the language of the people in the greater part of Western Europe, with particularly wide dissemination in Italy and Germany. One of the most common misapprehensions about the history of the Bible is that Martin Luther was the first to translate the Bible for the people. This is way off the mark. Thousands of copies of German Bibles had even been pulled off printing presses before Luther posted the *Ninety-Five Theses* on 31 October 1517. Before Luther published his first translation of the New Testament in 1522, no fewer than eighteen separate printed editions of the complete Bible in German had appeared.

However, not one Bible had been printed in English by that date. Not a single English Bible would be printed until some seventy-five years after the invention of printing. Why? Ironically, the answer, in large part, is Wyclif.

In the Constitutions of Oxford (1407/ 09), Archbishop Thomas Arundel forbade creation or ownership of a Bible in English. This was a tough measure aimed at suppressing the Lollards, the popular movement that grew rapidly from Wyclif and his circle of intellectuals. Although disgraced, Wyclif passed away peacefully of old age on 31 December 1384. Nonetheless, persecution of his followers became harsh in the following decades. The English Lollards were permanently weakened in 1414 after one of the movement's leaders, John Oldcastle, led a rebellion against Henry V. It was crushed. Thereafter, Lollardy was an underground movement that suffered continuous persecutions, one of the last known being an inquest of 1521 in Lincoln that resulted in fifty abjurations and six burnings.

Elsewhere, Wyclif's ideas fuelled a successful movement – the explosive Hussite rebellion in Bohemia. More than the English scene, it was the Bohemian rebellion that prompted the revisiting of Wyclif's theology at the Council of Constance (1414-18). Again, the verdict was heterodoxy – this time pronounced by an ecumenical council. His great acolyte Jan Hus received the same verdict from the same body, but with a different sentence: he was burned at the stake in Constance on 5 July 1415. Wyclif's body, too, would be exhumed and burned in 1428.

The Wycliffite Bible

Since the people were to obey God's law, not the church's law, they had to have a copy of it in a language they could comprehend. Wyclif's simple mandate bore immediate fruit: our first complete English Bible.

The Wycliffites, or Lollards (as they are generally known), created two versions of the Bible in English.[3] The first version,

which may have been complete by *c.* 1380, was a word-for-word rendering of the Latin in English. So literal are the renderings that the translation is not only awkward and unidiomatic but also, at least in some passages, utterly incomprehensible. A revision was absolutely necessary. The second version altered, in some cases profoundly, the plodding Latinate style. This second version, which probably dates from the 1390s, is thought to be the work of John Purvey (d. *c.* 1428), Wyclif's erstwhile secretary and an ardent leader of the Lollards.

It is unlikely that Wyclif himself had much of a role in the work, even though it is probable that the first version of the translation was complete by around the time of his death in 1384. One of the oldest manuscripts, now preserved in the Bodleian Library of Oxford University, has an annotation in Baruch 3:20, which, in modernised English, is 'Here ends the translation of Nicholas of Hereford.'[4] A manuscript now at Cambridge University has a similar note in Baruch 3:19 that states 'Here ends the translation of N and now begins the translation of J and of other men.'[5] Based on this and other evidence, it is likely that Nicholas of Hereford (d. *c.* 1420), a pious priest, took the leading role in the earliest version. It is possible that an early manuscript was copied in Italy during his imprisonment in Rome, 1382-5. If this evidence is true, then Hereford's portion of the Wycliffite Bible was complete by 1382 at the latest.[6] The J of the Cambridge manuscript could have been John Wyclif himself but there is no corroboration for this view.

The Wycliffites translated the Latin Vulgate into English. They did not consult manuscripts of the Bible in the original Hebrew and Greek. The Vulgate was the

Fig. 1.2. The Wycliffite Bible is an English translation of the Latin Vulgate. It is not based on the original Hebrew or Greek. Most of its departures from modern Bibles are due to idiosyncrasies of the Vulgate version. There are, for example, several substantive differences in the Lord's Prayer. The prayer begins on the 13th line of the left column of this folio (enlarged detail below). In the following transcription, 'y' often signifies 'th'. The Wycliffite Lord's Prayer in modernised spelling can be found on page 22.

Our[er] fadir yat (i.e. that) art in hevenes halewid be yi name/
yi kingdom come/ be yi wille don:
as in hevene [and] in erye (i.e. earth)/
gyve to us yis day our breed over oyir (i.e. other) substau[n]ce/
[and] forgyve to us our dettis as [and] we forgyve[n] to our dettours/
[and] lede us not into te[m]ptaciou[n] but delyv[er]e us from yvel ame[n].

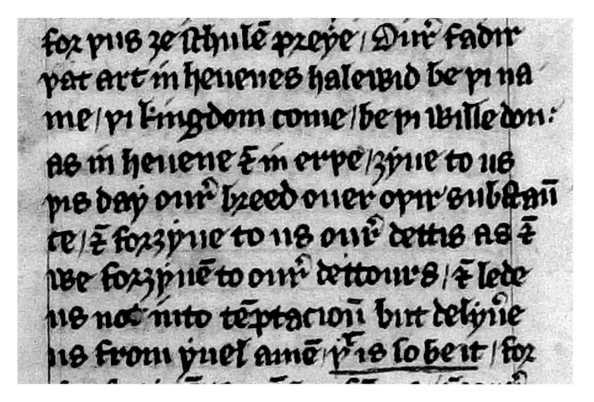

sacred text of the church in the West. Its words and formulations were memorised and held in awe; it was the source of Western theology for over a millennium. Importantly, the translators of the first version put the Latin into English word for word. This is the ultimate expression of respect for the sacred language and the ultimate insult to English. The disastrous result was immediately apparent, we can assume. The general prologue, composed for the revision, proposed that the emended translation be 'according to the sentence' and that the English must be even 'opener' (i.e. clearer) than the Latin.[7]

The General Prologue also urges a critical examination of the source text for the translation. The nature of this method may be easy to misconstrue. We might think that this is an acknowledgement that the source text, the Vulgate, is but a translation itself. After all, translating a translation is never a good procedure. But however serious this problem may be, this is not what the introduction is about. Rather, the prologue is addressing the major problem of the medieval Latin Bible – it could not be produced in a standard, uniform edition. No two manuscripts of the Latin Vulgate were identical. A comparison of the manuscripts shows a high frequency of different

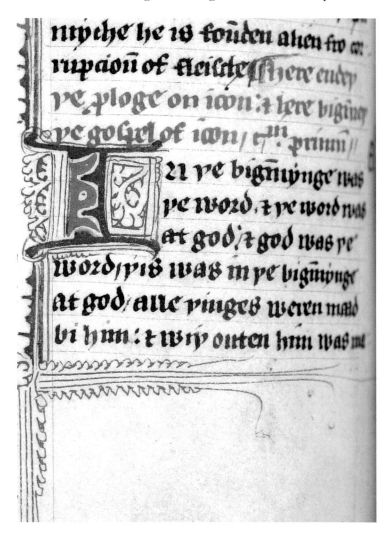

Fig. 1.3. A modest but beautiful copy of the Wycliffite New Testament. Its script is easily legible and the frequent decorations with blue and red ink give the manuscript a simple elegance. A red and blue initial marks the beginning of John's Gospel. Note that the letter 'y' often designates either 'th' or 'i'.

In ye bigi[n]nynge was ye word. [and] ye word was at god. [and] god was ye word/ yis was in ye bigi[n]nynge at god/ alle yinges (i.e. things) weren maad bi him: [and] wiy outen (i.e. without) him was not (i.e. naught). . . .

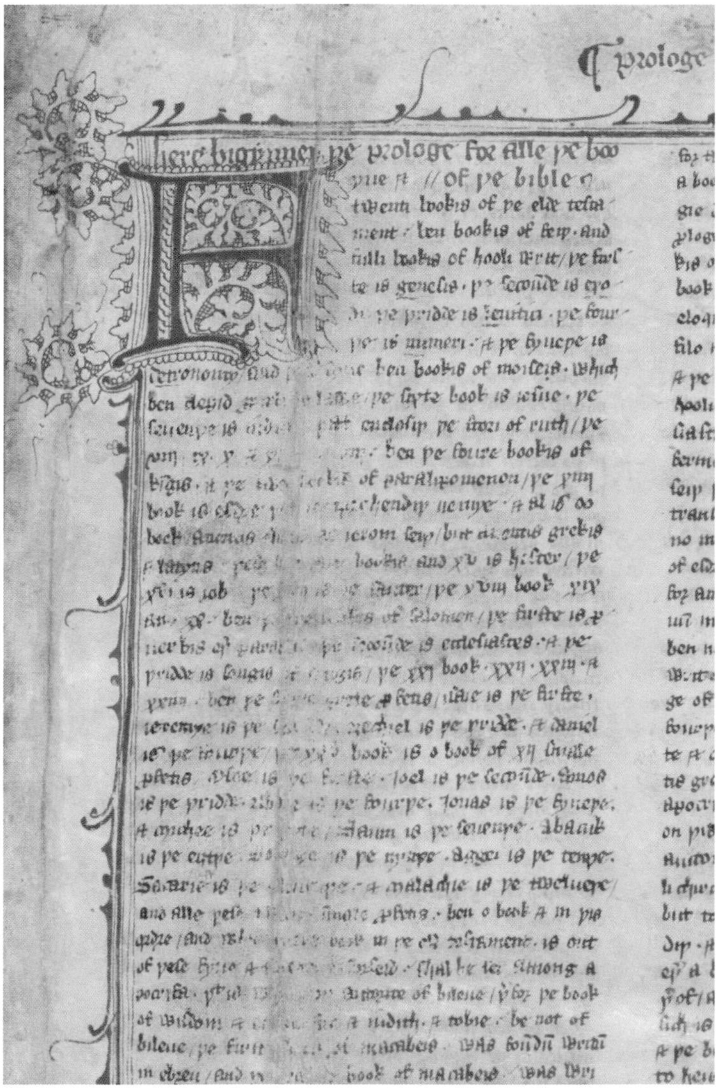

Fig. 1.4. The 'General Prologue' is a lengthy introduction for the second version of the Wycliffite Bible. It was rarely copied, however, because of its articulation of manifestly heretical views. The Scheide copy of the Wycliffite Bible at Princeton University includes not only the Old and New Testaments but the prologue also. It defines the canon of the Old Testament and provides summaries for each book. It also describes the medieval method of finding four senses (i.e. the literal, moral, allegorical and anagogic) in the Bible, and it briefly explains the method of the translation.

readings for words and phrases, even to the extent that certain clauses are present in some, while absent in others. The variations do not occur only at sentence level either; some Vulgate manuscripts even had different books of the Bible. One fraudulent book of the New Testament that occasionally crept into manuscripts of the Latin Vulgate was the Epistle to the Laodiceans. In Colossians 4:16, Paul tells the people to read the letter he sent to the Laodiceans. By the time the canon of the Bible was assembled, that letter had, un-fortunately, vanished. But one pious person, probably in the fourth century, 'supplied' the work. Some copies of the Wycliffite Bible include a translation of this spurious book.

A more common corruption came in when explanatory glosses, originally written as marginal or interlinear comments, moved into the text. This happened quite naturally. After all, scribes also wrote textual corrections in the margins or between the lines. A scribe who copied a corrected text would write the corrections into the text itself. Could one always tell the difference between a correction and a gloss? No, and recopying over the centuries offered hundreds of opportunities for such interpolations.

A notable feature of some Wycliffite Bibles is that many glosses that crept into the text are identified. The Bridwell-Prothro copy, for example, underlines phrases in red that are deemed to be glosses.[8] This marking of the text is clear in figures 1.2 and 1.5.

Passages from the Wycliffite Bible

Let us look first at the translation of the Ten Commandments, the law in its most succinct formulation.

> Thou shalt not have alien gods
>   before me
> Thou shalt not make to thee a
>   graven image . . .
> Thou shalt not take in vain the
>   name of thy Lord God
> Have thou mind that thou hallow
>   the day of the Sabbath
> Honour thy father and thy mother
> Thou shalt not slay
> Thou shalt do no lechery
> Thou shalt do no theft
> Thou shalt not speak false witnessing
>   against thy neighbour
> Thou shalt not covet the house of
>   thy neighbour

The only change we have made to the above text has been to give modern spellings. No forms, words, or syntax have been altered. Thus, the first observation we must register is astonishment. After over six centuries, the Wycliffite Bible can articulate the law to us with penetrating clarity. It is, in fact, in these imperative passages that the version exerts its greatest power. The argument could even be made that the gravity

and forcefulness of the Wycliffite English exceed that of the Latin Vulgate. The Latin does not have the powerful effect of the repetition of 'thou shalt not'. It is interesting that the Latin and the English use the unidiomatic future tense (which is a way of rendering the Hebrew verb forms here). But, in the English, the future tense used for the imperative strengthens the admonition, whereas in the Latin the phrase loses its force.

Despite the impressive intelligibility, we can feel the infelicity resulting from the closeness to the Latin original. This example, moreover, comes from the revised second version. We do not have the expression 'do no theft', and nor did fourteenth-century English. However, this is a good example of word-for-word rendering of the Latin – *non furtum facies*. Similarly, we must smile at the phrase 'alien gods', the 'alien' being more a transliteration than a translation of *alienos deos*, which really just means 'other gods'.

The austerity of the law is the Wycliffite Bible at its best. Its worst is undoubtedly in those many biblical passages of poetic flight. Where the original text is complex and elegant, the Wycliffite Bible can be dull and lapse into incomprehensibility. A good example is Elizabeth's famous greeting to the Virgin Mary, in the first chapter of Luke, immediately preceding the *Magnificat*.

> Blessed be thou among women and
> blessed be the fruit of thy womb.
> And whereof is this thing to me, that
> the mother of my Lord come to me?
> For lo! as the voice of thy salutation
> was made in my ears, the young child
> gladed [i.e. gladdened] in joy in my
> womb. (vv.42-4)

Can English prose tolerate a phrase such as 'the voice of thy salutation was made in my ears'? That is literally what the Latin says, and,

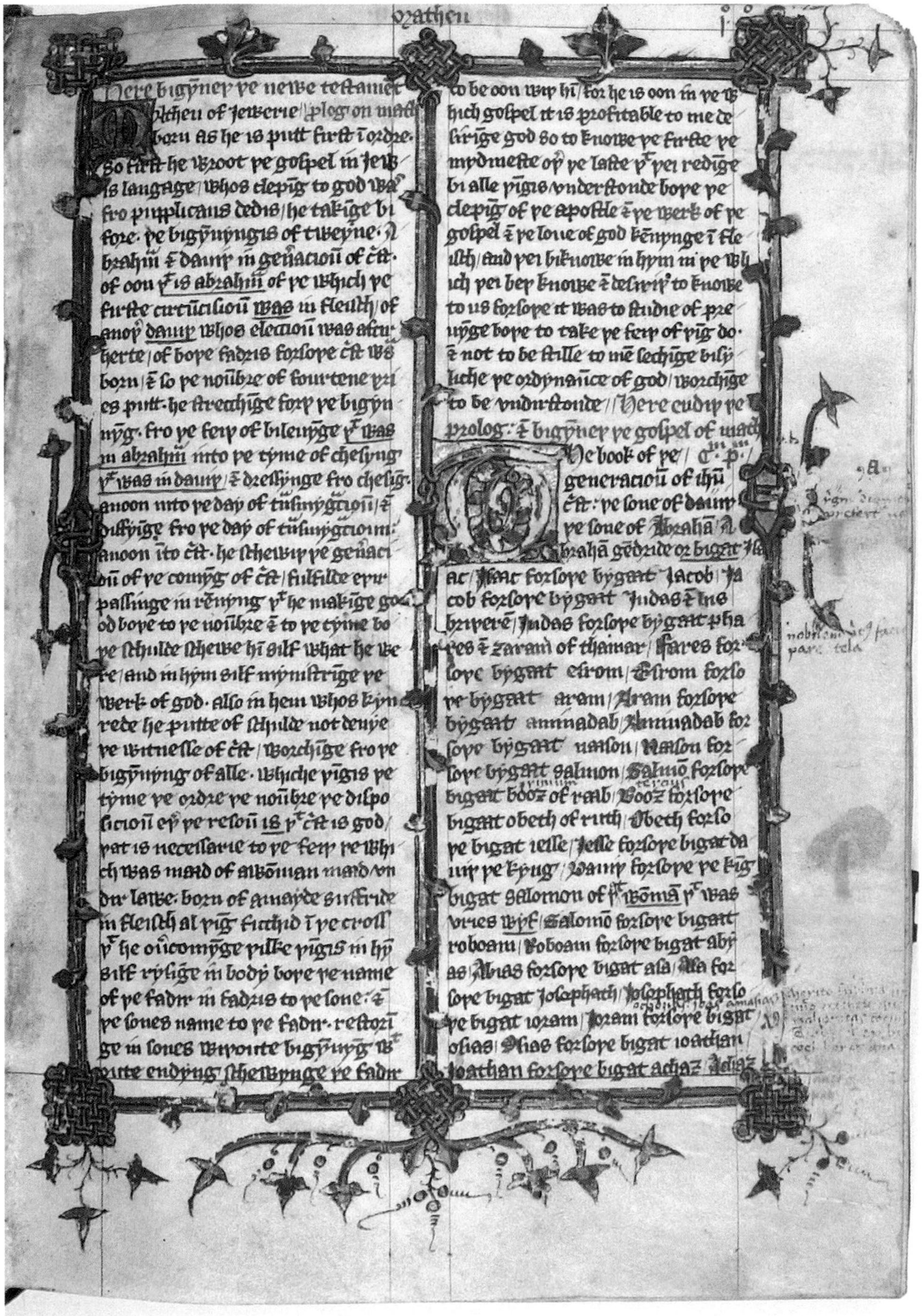

Fig. 1.5. The first page of an early fifteenth-century Wycliffite Bible manuscript. Many of the surviving Wycliffite Bibles are deluxe copies. This one has an elaborate ivy border with multicoloured paints and burnished gold leaf. The red titles (see 'Matheu' at the top centre of the page), subtitles, underlining and highlighting are called rubrication. The letters highlighted in red mark the beginning of sentences. Note that the medieval Bible did not divide the text into verses.

incidentally, that goes for the Greek original, too. Eventually, the King James Version would lift this passage to an astonishing height, respecting the original formulations (even to a degree that contradicts English usage) but also making concessions to aesthetic demands and the sentence became, 'As soon as the voice of thy salutation sounded in mine ears, the babe leaped in my womb for joy'.

All Christians know one New Testament passage by heart in one formulation or another – The Lord's Prayer.

> Our Father that art in heaven, hallowed be thy name; thy kingdom come to, be thy will done in earth as in heaven; give to us this day our bread over other substance; and forgive to us our debts as we forgive to our debtors; and lead us not into temptation but deliver us from evil. Amen.

How remarkable that today these words still sound so familiar and yet also so odd. It is the pedantic use of the preposition that disrupts the rhythm, even if so much of the prayer resonates proleptically with the elegance of the Authorised Version. 'Bread over other substance'? This is an unusual foodstuff, but wouldn't one expect the extraordinary, something beyond the physical, from God? It is a literal rendering of the Latin 'super-substantialis', which in turn is a literal rendering of the Greek 'epiousios' ('above being'). The problem is that an idiomatic sense of 'epiousios' is 'daily', something that was understood in the Middle Ages because St Jerome had translated the 'epiousios' in the parallel version of the Lord's Prayer (Luke 11:2-4) as 'daily'. In some Wycliffite manuscripts, the notes for Matthew's Lord's Prayer acknowledge

this meaning. We will see future wrestling with this difficult word in the most important prayer in the Christian tradition.

The Wycliffite Bible was for the people and it was illegal. Both of these essential qualities have some complexity. Firstly, the fact is that, even though the English Bible was illegal, no other text in Middle English survives in so many manuscripts. Nearly two hundred and fifty complete or fragmentary manuscripts of the Wycliffite Bible are recorded. More importantly, our first English Bible was 'for the people', although the manuscript copies of it were not for the average person. Literacy rates were still distressingly low and books were exceedingly expensive. With the exception of a single Psalter written on paper, all the surviving Wycliffite Bibles are on vellum. Roughly two hundred sheep would have to be slaughtered to produce the vellum for a single copy of the Bible. Paper was available in fourteenth-century England, even if it was only gradually coming into use. Nonetheless, people obviously wanted the word of God written on vellum. Many of the surviving manuscripts are, in fact, deluxe copies, commissioned by members of the high nobility. One copy was owned by King Henry VI and another by a son of Edward III. The Bridwell-Prothro copy at Southern Methodist University received very costly illumination and elegant rubrication, emphatically indicating that only a wealthy person could have commissioned or owned such a book.

The Wycliffite Bible attests to the beginnings of a cultural movement that would later advance the Bible to the centre of European life. It also reminds us that technology in the late Middle Ages made a Bible culture unfeasible. That could not happen until after the invention of printing (*c.* 1453), when the Bible would begin to be disseminated widely. The Wycliffite Bible would not be part of that development, however. It was not printed in the Renaissance, nor was it a factor in the genesis of the Renaissance English Bible. By the time William Tyndale was preparing the first printed edition of the Bible in English, scholarship on the text of the Bible had long since rendered the Wycliffite Bible obsolete. Even so, people were aware of the medieval English Bible. In his diatribes against Tyndale, no less a figure than Thomas More wrote approvingly of the old (i.e. medieval) translation of the Bible, available in manuscripts. Although the Wycliffite versions were not printed in the Renaissance, the General Prologue (the preface to the second version) was printed in 1540, at the very end of the Henrician liberalisation and again in 1550 during the Bible revival under Edward VI. The Wycliffite Bible itself was first printed in 1731 – as a curiosity.

The Renaissance did not extinguish the memory of Wyclif's heroic struggles. As Martin Luther posted the *Ninety-Five Theses*, he was aware of Wyclif and his theology and, in particular, of the history of the Bohemians inspired by Wyclif's teachings. As the leader of a revolutionary evangelical movement, Luther often thought that he would share the fate of Wyclif's most famous student, the martyr Jan Hus.

ENDNOTES TO CHAPTER ONE

1. *Cambridge History of the Bible* [1963-70] 1978-80, 2:388.
2. Bobrick 2001, 38-42, on the complex relationship with his patron, John of Gaunt.
3. The still standard edition, though woefully out of date, is Forshall and Madden 1850. Hudson 1988 is an excellent overview of Lollard writings.
4. 'Explicit translacôm Nicholay de herford'. See de Hamel 2001, 171.
5. Cambridge MS. EE. 1.10. See de Hamel 2001, 173: 'Here endith the translacioun of N, and now begynneth the translacioun of J & of othere men.'
6. De Hamel 2001, 171-3.
7. Bruce 1978, 19, and Forshall and Madden 1850, 1:57.
8. The Bridwell-Prothro copy at Southern Methodist University is available on CD-ROM (Palo Alto: Octavo, 1999) with an introduction by Fred C. Robinson.

CHAPTER TWO
RENAISSANCE OF THE BIBLE

> Only a very few can be learned, but all can be Christian, all can
> be devout, and – I shall boldly say – all can be theologians.[1]
> *– Desiderius Erasmus, in the introduction to the first edition*
> *of the New Testament in the original Greek (1516)*

We do not ordinarily associate the words 'Renaissance' and 'Bible'. Yet we should. One of the most enduring contributions of the Renaissance was the dissemination of the Bible. In the first century of printing, European presses produced hundreds of editions of the Bible in dozens of languages and formats. By 1550, millions of printed Bibles saturated European culture.

Availability is only one aspect of the Bible revolution. Texts and translations became reliable, uniform, and, as we will see particularly in the English translations, stunningly elegant. The scholarly standardisation of the printed Renaissance Bible was a major innovation over the medieval manuscript Bibles, no two of which were identical. Despite the serious efforts of many theologians, textual confusions could never be definitively rectified in medieval Bibles.

The process of laying a foundation for a reliable text begins with Desiderius Erasmus's Greek Bible of 1516, the first edition of the New Testament in the original language. This is a major break-through in Renaissance scholarship and an important milestone in the history of Christianity.

Desiderius Erasmus

Erasmus (1467-1536) was an international celebrity during his lifetime. He was one of the first contemporary authors to achieve such renown, something that became possible only as a result of the growth of the printing industry. A diverse and prolific writer, he has been heralded as one of the most influential figures in the history of education, the greatest Latin writer of the Northern Renaissance, and the most important intellectual precursor to the various reform movements.

He was born in the Netherlands, the son of a widow and a priest. Erasmus would never concede that his father was a priest at the time of his birth because children of priests were excluded from church offices. This fact was significant, as Erasmus became an Augustinian canon in 1487. Even though both his parents died while he was still a boy, Erasmus enjoyed an excellent basic education before going on to study at university.

He wrote many influential literary works – *Praise of Folly*, the *Colloquies* and *Julius Excluded* to name a few examples. These works are distinguished for their wit and erudition, especially their irony and blunt sarcasm. They also contain earnest criticism of practices and corruption in the church. *Julius Excluded*, a satire he published anonymously, portrays a conversation at the pearly gates between St Peter and Julius II, the warrior pope of the Renaissance. When St Peter denies Julius entry, the pope decides to raise an army to force his way into heaven. This and other examples of searing criticism would lead his contemporaries to blame Erasmus, at least in part, for the Protestant Reformation. His humanist challenges to the church – especially his insistence on the study of the Bible and the early church – appealed to many intellectuals and certainly conditioned initial reactions to Luther, even if it would be going too far to say that Erasmus laid the egg that Luther hatched.

He also published many scholarly works. Among his most frequently reprinted works were several manuals for humanist rhetoric. Another research speciality was editing the writings of early Christian authors. His pioneering work in that genre was the edition of St Jerome that he published in 1516. It successfully assessed the authenticity of works ascribed to Jerome in medieval manuscripts and included a biography of St Jerome that was grounded in text-historical criticism of the sources. For northern Europeans, this constituted a major breakthrough in historiography. Among his other editions of early Christian writers were Arnobius (1522), Ambrose (1528-9), Augustine in ten volumes (1528-

9), Basil (1532), Chrysostomos (1530, 1536), Hilary (1523) and Lactantius (1529). These books formed the beginning of a reliable library for research into the early centuries of Christianity.

His greatest accomplishment was the first edition of the New Testament in Greek, a work that shook the edifices of Latin Christianity to their foundations.

Although he may have inspired many who would become Protestants, Erasmus remained a devout Roman Catholic. He dedicated his edition of the Bible to Pope Leo X. He spent many of the early years of the Reformation in the city of Basel, Switzerland, where his printer, Johann Froben, operated one of the most scholarly publishing houses in Northern Europe. In 1528, however, Erasmus decided to move from Basel to Fribourg. Tremendously destructive iconoclastic riots blazed in Basel in February 1528, leading the city council to outlaw the celebration of the Catholic Mass. This necessitated Erasmus's departure, but he continued to visit the city frequently in order to continue his collaborations with Froben. It was in Basel, at Froben's house, that Erasmus died on 11 July 1536.

Despite his loyalty, ultimately the Roman Catholic Church would place all Erasmus's works on the index of forbidden books at the conclusion of the Council of Trent (1545-63).

One of his last major works was *On Mending the Harmony of the Church* (1533; *De sarcienda ecclesiae concordia*), an interpretation of Psalm 83 that proposed a way to end the religious rancour of the times. It attracted much attention, as did everything Erasmus published, but nothing short of force – something Erasmus abhorred – could have reunited the fractured church in the sixteenth century.

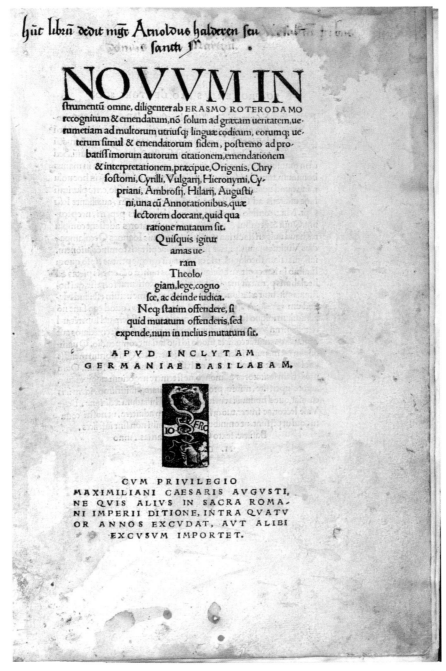

Fig. 2.1. *The first edition of the New Testament in Greek appeared in 1516. It was the crowning achievement in the career of the scholar and writer Desiderius Erasmus. This work was both influential and controversial for several reasons, one of which is that it offered a new authoritative text for Western Christianity. The long title, a typical feature in Renaissance books, narrows in the centre of the page to emphasise a challenge: 'If you love true theology, read this [the New Testament in Greek], understand it, and then pass judgment' [Quisquis igitur amas veram Theologiam, lege, cognosce, ac deinde iudica].*

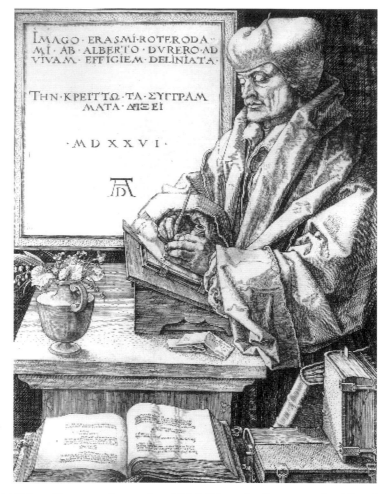

Fig. 2.2. Albrecht Dürer, Erasmus *(engraving, 1526). When the German artist Albrecht Dürer executed this engraved portrait, Erasmus was an intellectual celebrity, renowned for his Latin literary works and his edition of the New Testament in Greek. The motto, in Greek, states that [Erasmus's] 'writings will show his image better', an echo of Erasmus's contention, as expressed in the Introduction to the New Testament, that Christ's words, i.e. the Bible, represent him better than could any physical relic.*

The New Testament in Greek

Producing an edition of the New Testament in the original Greek was not a simple task. Good manuscripts of the Bible in Greek were scarce in Western Europe. In fact, Erasmus's efforts suffered somewhat from the inferiority of the textual witnesses that he could turn up. His manuscripts were not of notable antiquity – none predated the twelfth century – and several were somewhat defective.

Most of the work comparing medieval manuscripts was done in the Swiss city of Basel, and in considerable haste. Even though he had studied four Greek manuscripts in England, including a complete work, the Leicester Codex, there are reasons to believe that it was the printer Johann Froben who encouraged Erasmus to create the first edition of the Greek text. This was, as Froben must have stressed, the logical conclusion to his decade-long research on the text of the New Testament. Froben employed other scholars who could aid in such a demanding project, in particular the learned sons of the deceased printer Johann Amerbach and the budding scholar Johannes Oecolampadius. Erasmus and his team collated some five Greek manuscripts on site at the press in Basel. These manuscripts are now at the University of Basel Library and show some curious signs of wear and tear – Erasmus's handwritten notes in some margins (in the Renaissance, as now, scholars were known to write notes directly on the pages of library books!). Erasmus's text would not quite satisfy modern standards – and was even superseded in the Renaissance. All of Erasmus's manuscript sources derive from what scholars refer to as the Byzantine recension, a family of manuscripts no longer in favour. The now standard editions of the New Testament (the Nestlé-Aland editions) prefer readings from a western family of manuscripts (often called the Hesychian or Egyptian recension).

Nonetheless, with few exceptions, it is a remarkably adequate edition. Its most infamous lapse is the end of the Book of Revelation. His only manuscript for Revelation (the Codex Capnionis, which was borrowed from the great Hebrew scholar Johannes Reuchlin) was so defective that Erasmus had to translate six verses – the final verses of the Bible, Revelation 22:16-21 – from Latin back into Greek in order to fill the gap. Obviously, this was not a satisfactory solution; even though Erasmus has been ridiculed for it, it is only fair to mention that he openly admitted the problem in the first edition.

Erasmus's edition would undergo a series of revisions. He re-edited it himself four further times, his last version appearing in 1535, just months before his death. Probably the most influential edition was the second (1518-19), which was a major improvement on the first. This became the basis of Luther's revolutionary translation of 1522.

Naturally, the Greek New Testament attracted the attention of many other scholars. The most notable of the post-Erasmian editors of the Greek New Testament was Robert Estienne. Estienne was originally the scholarly printer to the King of France. As of 1550, he fled Paris for a refuge in Calvin's Geneva. Just before leaving, he produced his masterpiece, the Greek New Testament of 1550 – often called the 'received text'. This edition set the standard for the rest of the Renaissance. Among Estienne's improvements are a carefully printed listing of variant readings in the Greek manuscripts (such a list is traditionally called an 'apparatus') and the use of the ancient Codex Bezae, a Greek and Latin manuscript of the New Testament that probably dates from the fifth century. Estienne's *textus receptus* would be the principal foundation for the New Testament in the King James Version.

Controversy

The appearance of the new Bible ignited many theological controversies. After all, with the publication of Erasmus's edition in 1516, the very word of God changed for Western Europeans. Even more unsettling, Erasmus's research made it clear that the original formulation of the word cannot always be unequivocally known. The manuscript traditions of the Greek New Testament were sufficiently heterogeneous to cause uncertainty. And even today – it is a most uncomfortable fact – we cannot always be sure what the original words were in some passages of the New Testament.

The immediate question posed by Erasmus's Greek Bible concerned the status of the Vulgate Bible. That was a huge question, however, because St Jerome's Latin translation of the Bible had served as the basis for doctrine in the West for over a millennium. The church considered his Vulgate an inspired translation. Yet what should one make of passages in the Vulgate that could not be found in the Greek manuscripts? How accurately did the Vulgate render the original Greek? Had misunderstandings conveyed by the Vulgate translation unduly informed the development of some points of doctrine? The Vulgate, of course, still does have importance for the textual criticism of the Bible. It provides many clues about the state of the text at the end of the fourth century and helps us assess the reliability of the Greek manuscripts.

Consequently, a controversial part of this book is Erasmus's fresh translation of the Bible from the Greek into Latin, the language of the church and of scholarship. He included the new translation as an aid to scholars, few of whom had yet been able to learn Greek. But the unmistakable implication was that Jerome's ancient translation did not convey the sense of the original Greek as well as Erasmus could. Especially bitter objections were raised when Erasmus, in the second edition, translated the beginning of John's Gospel as 'In principio erat sermo', a rough translation of which would be: 'In the beginning was the discourse'. This new word was jarring to those accustomed to *verbum* (word). He felt that *sermo*, which has a slightly broader range of meanings than *verbum*, better captured the complexity of

logos, which, in addition to 'word', connotes 'thought' and 'concept'.

Indeed criticism immediately rained down on Erasmus from all quadrants of the heavens. How could some scholars oppose such a benign undertaking as the first publication of the New Testament in Greek? The unspoken reason for the anti-Erasmian storms was his fierce assault on scholastic theology, the complex, speculative theology, grounded in Aristotelian logic, that then dominated Europe's universities. The truth of the matter is that Erasmus fashioned the edition as part of a wider campaign against scholasticism. When Erasmus declared the centrality of the 'philosophy of Christ' for Christians, by which term he meant Christ's teachings as recorded in the Bible, he was implicitly rejecting the hegemony of the actual philosophy of his time – scholasticism. The Bible and not Aristotle, was the source of the *'philosophia Christi'*. This theology was accessible to every pious Christian, and not just to intellectuals. As Erasmus put it, 'Therefore, I believe, one should not consider himself to be a Christian because he disputes about instances, relations, quiddities and formalities with an obscure and irksome confusion of words, but rather because he accepts and exhibits what Christ taught and showed forth.'[2] Despite his deserved reputation as an advocate of preserving peace and unity in the church, Erasmus knew how to throw down the gauntlet. These are fighting words. Even more importantly, Erasmus's competing concept of theology, as we can see so dramatically in the epigraph to this chapter, urges one of the most significant developments of the Renaissance: the deep penetration of European culture by the Bible.

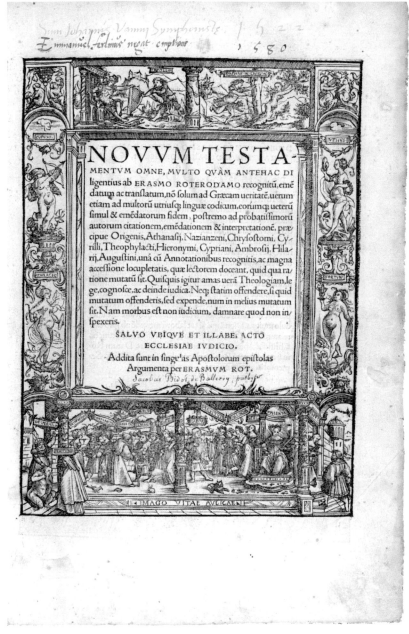

Fig. 2.3. *Title page of the second edition of Erasmus's Bible (1518-19). The woodcut borders are attributed to Ambrosius Holbein, the brother of Hans Holbein the Younger. Johann Froben of Basel, Switzerland, was the publisher of Erasmus's editions of the New Testament (and of many other works by Erasmus). Froben operated an academic publishing house and had excellent scholars on his staff to see projects such as this through press.*

This new title page, designed for the second edition – now called the Novum Testamentum (New Testament) – might appear rather unusual for a Bible. The left border shows Cupid, while the right border is dominated by a nude Venus; the top border depicts, on the right, the myth of Apollo and Daphne; the lower border depicts the 'Calumny of Apelles'. These motifs remind us that Erasmus's Bible was a Renaissance phenomenon, part of the effort to recover the heritage of antiquity.

Doctrine

Many difficulties arose from comparisons of St Jerome's Latin translation with the original Greek text. Christian theology had developed in the West without the benefit of scripture in its original languages. Erasmus's editions remedied that deficiency for the New Testament. Theologians experienced a shock when Erasmus showed that a proof text for the Trinity, 1 John 5:7-8 ('For there are three that bear record in heaven, the Father, the Word, and the Holy Ghost: and these three are one'), was in the Vulgate but not in any of the Greek manuscripts. This verse is called the 'Johannine phrase' (*comma Johanneum*). Most scholars nowadays concur with Erasmus's initial decision to delete it as an interpolation in the Vulgate.

Nonetheless, a manuscript, now in Trinity College, Dublin, was reported to include the Johannine phrase, and it was restored to the Greek text by Erasmus in the third edition of 1522. The Dublin manuscript was almost certainly produced in the sixteenth century as an attempt to forge a Greek attestation of the heavenly witnesses. Erasmus suspected as much, but restored the text so as to put an end to the bitter assaults on that issue.[3] Striking a similarly conciliatory note, he printed the Vulgate as a third version (in addition to the Greek text and his own Latin translation of the Greek) in his fourth edition published in 1527. This is important as it shows Erasmus bowing to pressure concerning the significance of the Vulgate and also embracing it as a valuable early textual witness. Indeed, probably the most principled criticism of Erasmus's first edition questioned the status he accorded the Vulgate, an issue raised vociferously by Diego López de Zúñiga, editor of a rival scholarly Bible, the Complutensian Polyglot Bible of 1514-17. The Greek manuscripts, after all, really were defective and could not necessarily be declared the panacea for all of the Vulgate's woes. Zúñiga, for instance, held that the Vulgate's authority was adequate for justifying the inclusion of the Johannine phrase on the Trinity.

Only a few people would question the doctrine of the Trinity in the Renaissance, and Erasmus was most definitely not among them. But many, in the aftermath of Erasmus, would question the established doctrine of the sacraments. The problem was that the sacraments of the church appeared to lose some textual grounding when one consulted the original Greek rather than the Latin translation. The very word for sacrament in Greek, *mysterion* (as in Ephesians 5:32), from which we have the English word 'mystery', was shown to have a significantly different sense from that of the Latin *sacramentum*.

The most important example of this problem was St Jerome's rendering of *metanoeite* as *agite poenitentiam* ('do penance'), John the Baptist's charge in Matthew 3:2, which Jesus repeated in an expanded formulation in 4:17. When divorced from the Greek original, the words *agite poenitentiam* came to be the proof text for the Roman Catholic sacrament of penance. As Erasmus pointed out in 1516, *metanoeite* does not quite mean '*do* penance', but rather 'turn your mind', or, as it is usually translated into English, 'repent'. Following Erasmus's lead, Luther translated this as 'Bessert Euch!' ('improve yourself'). Luther, in fact, defined the meaning of Matthew 4:17 in the very first thesis of the *Ninety-Five Theses*, making it the opening foray for his revolutionary rejection of the church's penitential system.

IMPORTANT EDITIONS OF THE BIBLE IN GREEK

1516   Erasmus's first edition of the New Testament in Greek

1518   Aldus Manutius of Venice prints the complete Bible in Greek. The text of the Old Testament is the Septuagint, the third-century B.C. translation, and it is the first edition of the Septuagint in print. The New Testament is from Erasmus's 1516 edition.

1518/19   Erasmus's corrected and expanded second edition. This was the basis for Martin Luther's translation of 1522.

c.1520   The Complutensian Polyglot Bible is published. The New Testament volume had been printed in 1514, that is before Erasmus's version. Nonetheless, the work was not released until *c.* 1520.

1522   The third edition of Erasmus New Testament in Greek. In this edition, Erasmus bowed to pressure from theologians and inserted the controversial *comma Johanneum*, a proof text for the Trinity that does not appear in the oldest manuscripts.

1550   Robert Estienne, the Royal Printer in France, produced a magnificent edition that would be declared the *textus receptus*, the 'received text'. This was a significant improvement over Erasmus. It includes readings from the Codex Bezae, an ancient Greek and Latin manuscript of the New Testament (probably 5th century). This is also the first edition to include a 'critical apparatus' that prints variant readings from manuscripts in the margins. Richard Bentley dubbed this edition the 'Protestant Pope'.

1551   Robert Estienne produced a tiny New Testament (in 16mo) that included the Greek text, the Latin Vulgate and Erasmus's Latin translation, all in parallel columns. This is the first Bible that divided chapters into verses. Estienne printed this work in Geneva, the city where he found refuge after fleeing from Paris in 1550.

1587   The Sixtine or Roman edition of the Septuagint based on the Vatican Codex B. The work was edited by Cardinal Antonio Carafa and became the authorised Catholic version.

Literary Attitude toward the Word of God

The first love of Erasmus's life was literature. While he would remain true to that first love, ultimately creating the greatest Latin literary work of the Renaissance – *Praise of Folly* – he would form new loves, most importantly, a love for scholarship and, in particular, a love for biblical scholarship.

One aspect of Erasmus's biblical research has not received adequate attention: his attitude toward the language, the literary quality of the holy word. In the introduction to the New Testament, Erasmus casually and repeatedly refers to the Bible as 'literature'. This was, daringly, the *bonae litterae*, the belles-lettres, that he would place at the entrance to the humanist library.

This was a departure, a profound one, from the traditional attitude toward the Bible. It was the utilitarian, artless, even rough, language of fishermen, if not fishmongers. The message, not the medium, was all that mattered.

Erasmus negotiates this shift by acknowledging the simplicity of biblical rhetoric, counting that as a virtue instead of a vice. But he does rewrite the Bible in his Latin versions. For his new Latin translation, he explicitly explains the degree to which he smooths over the roughness of the Greek original: 'I followed the rules of correct writing everywhere so far as it was possible to do so always provided that there was no loss of simplicity'.[4] Following 'the rules of correct writing' means, in his case, conforming to the highest standards of Latin rhetoric.

He went further in his *Paraphrases* of the books of the New Testament. Erasmus laboured long, hard and seriously on a most curious theological project: paraphrasing the words of the New Testament in diffusive Latin prose, modelled especially on the style of Cicero. The claim is that the *Paraphrases* are not translations but equivalents of the biblical message in a Roman literary style. In essence, the *Paraphrases* are stylistic exercises in finding classical equivalents and high-flying rhetorical amplifications for biblical words and phrases. The exercise of paraphrasing was known in the Renaissance from the handbook of Quintilian, the highly influential Roman rhetorician. After all, the New Testament does have a simple, sometimes even lapidary, manner. As we can see in the following extract, Erasmus's paraphrases certainly overcame that.

> Our father, which hast regenerated us to heaven, who were once unluckily born of Adam, and hast prepared for us (forsaking earthly things) a kingdom and inheritance everlasting: which art said to be in heaven because thou doeth replenish all and hast no manner of dross or earthly infirmity: grant that thy name be honourable and glorious among men through us, which by thy benefit, be perfect and pure.[5]

For better or worse, this is the paraphrase for the simple statement, 'Our father, who art in heaven, hallowed be thy name'.

What could something like this do to the history of the English Bible? The procedure frees the writer from the constraints of direct translation. More importantly, with its primary goal being the replication of the Bible in classical, Ciceronian style, this exercise compels the translator to explore the esthetics of the language of translation. In this case, the result is copiousness and clarity, even if that depends on a radical departure from the word-for-word rendition.

IMPORTANT EDITIONS OF THE BIBLE IN HEBREW

1477-87 Parts of the Hebrew Bible appear at Jewish presses in Italy. The first Hebrew printing of the Psalms is published in Bologna in 1477, followed by the editio princeps of the Pentateuch (Soncino, 1482) and the Hagiographa (Naples, 1486/87). The Pentateuch in Hebrew was also printed in Faro, Portugal in 1487.

1488 The first complete Hebrew Bible appears at the press of Joshua Solomon ben Israel Nathan Soncino in Soncino, Italy.

1491/93 The second complete Hebrew Bible is printed by Soncino, probably after his move to Naples.

1494 Third edition of the Hebrew, printed by Joshua Soncino's nephew Gershon ben Moses Soncino in Brescia. It became the *textus receptus* for some time. Martin Luther is known to have used this edition for his translation of the Old Testament into German.

1514/c.20 The first Christian production of Hebrew Bible occurs in Spain as part of the Complutensian Polyglot, a massive project undertaken by Cardinal Ximenes. Though printed 1514-17, the volumes were not published and released until c.1520. Four of the six volumes make up the Hebrew Old Testament.

1516/17 First Rabbinic Bible, Hebrew with full vowel points and accents. The text, edited by Felix Pratensis, includes important Jewish commentaries as well. The book was published by Daniel Bomberg, a Christian who specialised in printing Hebrew books for Jews.

1524/25 The second edition of the Rabbinic Bible, including the first edition of Massoretic texts. It was edited by Jacob ben Chayyim and printed by Daniel Bomberg. This edition of the Massora remains the standard today.

1535 Sebastian Münster's edition of the Hebrew Bible with his fairly literal Latin translation. A popular edition among reformers in Germany, Switzerland, England and France.

1575-79 Immanuel Tremellius, a converted Jew who soon left the Catholics and became Protestant, translated the Bible from Hebrew and Syriac, together with his son-in-law, Franciscus Junius. The fairly literal translation served as a useful aid to the translators of the King James Version.

THE SONCINO PRESS

The Soncino family of Italy produced over one hundred and thirty-five books in Hebrew from 1484 to 1547. Israel Nathan ben Samuel set up a printing press in the city of Soncino in 1483 and published the Berakot in early 1484. Though they kept the name Soncino, the press moved its location regularly after 1490, with works published in Casal Maggiore (1486), Naples (1490-2), Brescia (1491-4), Barco (1494-7), Fano (1503-6), Pesaro (1507-20), Ortono (1519), and Rimini (1521-6). They also printed in Salonica (1532-3) and Constantinople (1534-47). Joshua Solomon ben Israel Nathan Soncino succeeded his father and worked mainly in Naples. Joshua's nephew, Gershon ben Moses Soncino, was the most influential of the Soncino printers and printed books in Hebrew, Greek, and Latin. Gershon was the printer of the important 1494 Hebrew Bible.

Translating Erasmus into English

Erasmus's prestige was sufficient to guarantee a reception of this unusual procedure. He truly was the greatest European celebrity before Luther came onto the scene. More specifically for England, the Edwardian injunctions of 1547 conferred a special status on Erasmus's *Paraphrases*. Those injunctions renewed the 1538 mandate of Henry VIII that a printed English Bible of the largest size (i.e. in folio format) be set out on a lectern in every church in the realm, but with an additional requirement:

[Parsons, vicars and other curates] shall provide within three months next after this visitation, one book of the whole Bible, of the largest volume, in English. And within one twelve-months next after the said visitation, the Paraphrasis of Erasmus also in English upon the Gospels, and the same set up in some convenient place, within the said church that they have cure of, whereas their parishioners may most commodiously resort unto the same and read the same.[6]

As regards Erasmus's *Paraphrases*, this is an unusual policy and we need to pause to reflect on how it came about. The *Paraphrases*, though striking, were simply not one of Erasmus's most acclaimed works. Nonetheless, they do accord with the general English policy in place at the beginning of Edward's reign, of establishing the Bible as the icon of authority in the new church without a pope. Moreover, because the *Paraphrases* aim only to recast the biblical message, they disseminate a most moderate theology. Erasmus expands on the words of the New Testament with the sole intention of amplifying the philosophy of Christ. The paraphrases are daring in their literary flights but cautious in their strict adherence to the biblical text. They model a quite restrictive form of Bible-based evangelising – retelling the message of scripture. To use Shakespeare's words, we might say that Erasmus was 'retelling what is told' (Sonnet 76).

Moreover, Queen Catherine played a special role in the elevation of Erasmus's stature in England. Catherine Parr was Henry VIII's last wife, the fortunate survivor in the mnemonic device 'divorced, beheaded, died; divorced, beheaded, survived'. Her accomplishments were numerous. She was the force behind the reconciliation of the three children from Henry's previous marriages. Her gracious support of all the royal children proved highly influential as the Reformation unfolded in England, since each would become monarch. In part, her actions ensured, on the one hand, a Protestant education for Edward and, on the other hand, the rehabilitation of Mary, the Catholic daughter of Catherine of Aragon. In her enthusiasm for an Erasmian-style reform, Catherine Parr organised a group of scholars to translate into English the biblical paraphrases. The most notable participant in the project was Princess Mary, who would succeed her half-brother King Edward VI in 1553 and reconcile England with Rome. She translated the paraphrase of the Gospel according to John into a stately English version. Catherine, who recognised Mary's legitimacy, even used this project to reconnect Mary to the English church. Erasmus was the ideal figure for this delicate theological manoeuvring in the final years of Henry's reign. Indeed, in the mid-1540s, Erasmus was the only major figure who was admired by some people on all sides of the religious divides. The Edwardians and the future 'Bloody Mary' could share an enthusiasm for him. He was a reformer who had remained adamantly loyal to the Catholic faith. He could function as an icon of moderate reform, especially before the Council of Trent. Unfortunately, Trent ultimately articulated an official Roman Catholic scepticism toward Erasmus's career when it formally prohibited all of his books.

As it turns out, Mary was the only English monarch of the sixteenth century to compose an English version of a biblical text. All Henry's children were good scholars but only Mary put pen to paper to create an English biblical text, the translation of Erasmus's paraphrase of John. This is highly ironic, for, in the course of her re-Catholicisation, not a single English Bible would be printed in England.

Obviously, Erasmus did not himself produce a Bible in English or any European vernacular language. Nonetheless, an outstanding feature of Erasmus's Bible is its advocacy of universal access to scripture. This is all the more noteworthy because Erasmus's Greek edition and his new Latin translation formed a book that was obviously intended for scholars, and scholars such as Professor Martin Luther of the University of Wittenberg read it immediately. Yet, as the introduction makes abundantly clear, Erasmus looks beyond the scholarly Bible in the original language to the vernacular Bibles for the people:

> Christ wants his mysteries published as openly as possible. I would that even the lowliest women read the Gospels and the Pauline Epistles. I would that they were translated into all languages so that they could be read and understood not only by the Scots and the Irish but also by Turks and Saracens. . . . Would that . . . the farmer sing portions of them [i.e. scriptures] at the plough, the weaver hum some parts of them to the movement of the shuttle, the traveller lighten the weariness of the journey with stories of this kind. Let all the conversations of every Christian be drawn from this source.[7]

Sure enough, when Martin Luther and William Tyndale produced their revolutionary Bibles in German and English in less than a decade from then, they began by translating Erasmus's Greek.

ENDNOTES TO CHAPTER TWO

1. Olin 1975, 100.
2. Olin 1975, 101.
3. See De Jonge 1980.
4. *Collected Works of Erasmus* 1974-, 3:200 (letter 373).
5. Erasmus 1548, folio XXVII^v (modernised spelling and punctuation).
6. The Edwardian Injunctions of 1547, cited according to Bray 1994, 250.
7. Olin 1975, 97.

CHAPTER THREE
BREAKTHROUGH

Kindly permit me to have the Hebrew Bible, Hebrew grammar
and Hebrew dictionary, that I may pass the time in study.[1]
  – *William Tyndale, writing from prison (September 1535)*

Even if the formal charges were counts of heresy, it is not much of a stretch to say that William Tyndale died for the word of God in English. In the first phase of the English Reformation, Tyndale was by far the most notorious 'heretic', his renown, then and now, the result of his translation of the Bible.

The baleful execution occurred in the early days of October 1536 – we do not know the precise date, but tradition places it on the 6th. He was strangled and burned at the stake. He was not the first English martyr of the Protestant movement, but he has the distinction of being the father of the modern Bible in English. For the beauty of the Bible in English, we owe the largest single debt to him.

Scholar with a Cause
Many crucial aspects of Tyndale's life and work are shrouded in uncertainty. As so often in history, this has proven fertile ground for the growth of legends and abundant speculations, some of which sprang up in the sixteenth century and many of which are incautiously presented as facts in modern treatments of Tyndale. He was educated at Oxford University (BA 4 July 1512; MA 2 July 1515), although the particulars of his studies are unknown. Despite numerous assertions to the contrary, it is most doubtful that he later belonged to a group of important Protestant thinkers at Cambridge University.[2] At some point, he was ordained a priest and we know from his own writings that he worked as a tutor for the children of a certain John Walsh at Little Sodbury Manor in Gloucestershire; he may also have been a private chaplain at the manor. It was there that, *c.* 1522-3, he encountered, and began to accept, Luther's ideas. According to his own dramatic account (published later in the preface to his Pentateuch, 1530), he ran afoul of leading prelates in his provincial setting and formed the plan to go to London to translate the Bible. He also would have desired episcopal licence to undertake the translation because the Oxford Constitutions of

1407/09 were still in force. Those ecclesiastical statutes, brought in as a reaction to the Wycliffite movement, outlawed the unlicensed creation of a Bible in English.

The origin of Tyndale's Protestantism is significant. He did not set out to preach justification by faith alone; his primary goal was not the abolition of indulgences and he did not seek to foment antipapalism or anticlericalism, at least not initially. He wanted to translate the Bible into English. Moreover, the translation was to be of Erasmus's edition of the New Testament in Greek, not the medieval Latin Bible, and was to be distributed to ordinary people. According to John Foxe's *Acts and Monuments of the Martyrs*, Tyndale once said to a 'learned man': 'if God spare my life, ere many years I will cause a boy that driveth the plough shall know more scripture than thou dost'.[3]

It was a big dream. He went to London in order to petition Cuthbert Tunstall, then Bishop of London, for permission and support. He prepared for his audience by translating a speech by the ancient Greek rhetorician Isocrates into English. This work is lost but his manner of preparation is telling. It marks Tyndale as an Erasmian humanist and is even reminiscent of Erasmus's study of such classical texts as Euripides's plays as part of his preparation for the 'greater task,' the edition of the New Testament in Greek.[4] In later years, Tyndale would pour vitriol on the Dutch humanist for one simple reason – Erasmus disappointed Protestants deeply when, as of 1524-5, he became an outspoken critic of Luther. However, in 1523, Tyndale was still more of an Erasmian than a Lutheran.

Although celebrated by Erasmus in the introduction to the New Testament as one of the progressive forces in the English church, Bishop Tunstall rebuffed Tyndale with the announcement that 'his house was full',[5] meaning that he was either unable or unwilling to support the project. Thereupon, Tyndale found support among London cloth merchants and soon went to Germany to finish his undertaking. Our sources are inadequate for establishing much confidence about his doings in Germany. He may have gone to Wittenberg, where Luther was a professor. In some respects, the inability to be sure that he met Luther is the most unsatisfying element in Tyndale's biography. It is most probable, we believe, that he went to Wittenberg. In any event, it is certain that, by 1525, he completed a translation of the New Testament and tried to have it printed. This attempt, which failed, occurred in the city of Cologne in 1525. Johannes Cochlaeus, a priest and talented humanist scholar, got wind of the project and managed to have the work stopped in press. Older Protestant histories of the Reformation make Cochlaeus out to be an archfiend, but it should be noted that he was a most capable man and one of the first Catholics to respond vigorously and effectively to the Lutheran movement. As far as the Tyndale matter goes, what else could he have done?

Just one precious copy of this first attempt to print an English Bible survives and is held in the British Library. It includes an introduction which is based largely on Luther's preface to the *Septembertestament* (1522) and, most importantly, the text of Tyndale's translation of Matthew up to chapter 22. We do not know if Tyndale managed to flee Cologne with other copies of the beginning. Some have speculated that he did and could have used them in another imprint. No evidence of that has survived. What we do know, however, is that his flight took him down the Rhine River to the city

Fig. 3.1. William Tyndale (c. 1494-1536) was the first to translate the Bible from Hebrew and Greek into English, and the first to print an English Bible. He tried unsuccessfully to print his New Testament in Cologne in 1525, but succeeded in 1526 in Worms. He then laboured on revising the New Testament translation and also turned to the difficult task of translating Hebrew scripture. His first edition of the Pentateuch appeared in 1530.

Tyndale spent his career as scriptural translator in exile on the Continent, mostly in Antwerp. Just as England was entering into its first phase of reform, he was treacherously kidnapped in Antwerp through the connivance of Hapsburg officials and imprisoned in Vilvorde, near Brussels. He was executed as a heretic in October 1536. No authentic portraits of Tyndale are known. This engraved portrait from Henry Holland's Heroologia *of 1620, derived from earlier images of John Knox, became the basis for fanciful renderings.*

of Worms, where the first complete New Testament in English flew off Peter Schoeffer's presses in 1526. This momentous event in the history of the English language occurred on German soil for a number of reasons. Firstly, it was still illegal to produce an English Bible in England, and secondly, Henry VIII was, in the 1520s, one of the fiercest opponents of the Protestant movements.

Tyndale ended up finding refuge in Antwerp, where he enjoyed the support of English merchants, in particular a certain Thomas Poyntz. Antwerp was the ideal venue for his work because it was not only an extraordinarily wealthy free imperial city but also the most important home to the Protestant movement in the Low Countries. Tyndale thrived there. He produced new editions of the translation of the New Testament, the most significant of which was the thorough revision of 1534. He also turned to Hebrew scripture. He published the English Pentateuch (first five books of the Old Testament) in 1530 and the Book of Jonah in 1531. He wrote a few Protestant tracts that were heavily dependent on works by Luther and also engaged in a polemical exchange of pamphlets with no less a figure than Sir Thomas More. More – also a consummate scholar – conceded that Tyndale had translated scripture 'right well'. Nonetheless, More urged that both the translation and the translator be burned as perpetrators of heresy. This is one of the greatest blots on Thomas More's reputation, although he was not responsible in any way for Tyndale's eventual martyrdom. On 2 July 1535, More himself was executed on trumped-up charges of treason arising from his refusal to sign Henry VIII's Act of Succession (1534).

In the 1530s, Tyndale worked primarily on Hebrew scripture. It is even possible, but unlikely, that he continued his efforts during the long months he spent in prison (May 1535-October 1536). There is a consensus that a Bible published in 1537 (called the 'Matthew's Bible'; see below) contains much additional Tyndale material, specifically, Tyndale versions for the Old Testament from Genesis to 2 Chronicles. It is likely that these materials found their way into friendly hands at the time of Tyndale's arrest.

Tyndale's demise resulted from treachery. The story is often narrated in conscious analogy to Judas's betrayal of Christ. The sponsor of the vendetta is not known, although the agent is. A certain Henry Phillips, a disgruntled and disreputable gentleman, went to Antwerp to snare Tyndale. The task was easy. After luring Tyndale into his confidence, he was able to arrange for Hapsburg officials from Brussels to kidnap and arrest him. Treachery was necessary because Tyndale could not be arrested in Antwerp, a free imperial city, without the consent of the government there. Thus the archly anti-Protestant Hapsburgs were the main cause of the martyrdom. Nonetheless, considerable evidence indicates that an Englishman hired Phillips to hatch the plot. That Englishman would have been a powerful figure who was opposed to the Protestant turn in Henry's policies as of 1532-4. Tyndale's biographer J.F. Mozley has fingered the Bishop of Exeter as the culprit (a view also accepted by the more recent biographer David Daniell) but there is no smoking gun among the evidence. Probably at the instigation of Thomas Cromwell, the English government apparently did protest the incarceration, but to little effect except a possible slackening in the pace of the proceedings. After all,

Henry had put aside Catherine of Aragon, the aunt of the Hapsburg emperor, Charles V. We should also recall that in 1535 Catholic anxieties about Protestants spiked in the Low Countries. That was the year of the murderous Anabaptist debacle in the nearby city of Münster, an event that had terrified Catholics and Lutherans alike.

Tyndale spent the final year and a half of his life in the squalor of an abysmal cell in a castle keep at Vilvorde, a suburb of Brussels. The formal case against him was built up carefully. Among his accusers was James Latomus, a distinguished Professor of Theology at the University of Louvain. Latomus, also an Englishman, interviewed Tyndale several times and even published a carefully written account of those interviews and of Tyndale's heresy. The most precious document to survive from the lengthy imprisonment is an autographed letter (dated September 1535), requesting amelioration of the conditions in jail. It is not known to whom Tyndale addressed this petition, or if any of the requests were granted. After asking for some warmer clothing, Tyndale wrote: 'But most of all I beg and beseech your clemency to be urgent with the commissary, that he will kindly permit me to have the Hebrew Bible, Hebrew grammar, and Hebrew dictionary, that I may pass the time in that study.'[6] In his purest essence, Tyndale was a scholar with a single cause.

He was convicted of heresy in August 1536 and was immediately subjected to a public revocation of his consecration as a priest, as was the case for all notorious heretics under imperial law. Once that was accomplished, he was turned over to civil jurisdiction for execution. For unknown reasons, that was delayed until the beginning of October 1536. In his famous *Acts and Monuments of the Martyrs*, John Foxe recorded his last words as 'Lord, open the King of England's eyes,' a phrase which appears in the woodcut rendition of Tyndale's execution.

The New Testament

Like the Wycliffite Bible, Tyndale's translation was outlawed. It suffered confiscation and destruction; its owners were subject to criminal penalty. Consequently, even if Tyndale's words still sound forth amply in English versions today, precious few copies of the early editions have survived. The first burning of Tyndale's New Testament occurred at Paul's Cross (London) in either October or November of 1526.[7] There would be future burnings as well. The two earliest editions were so thoroughly suppressed that now only three copies of the Worms edition of 1526 survive, and only a single fragmentary exemplar of the interrupted Cologne printing of 1525. Thus, the early Tyndale imprints suffered a far more vigorous persecution than had the Wycliffite manuscripts.

Why? Because by 1525, the Lutheran movement posed a most credible threat. Several jurisdictions in Germany and in Switzerland had already taken the dire step of outlawing the Catholic Mass and initiating new church services. Against Thomas More's policy of destroying the English New Testaments, Tyndale responded: 'Saint Jerome . . . translated the Bible into his mother tongue. Why may not we also?'[8] This line of defence is perfectly valid but also patently disingenuous, for Tyndale openly advanced Protestant positions, to varying degrees, in all of his works.

Tyndale's New Testament is an English translation of the Greek text as it appeared in the second and third editions of

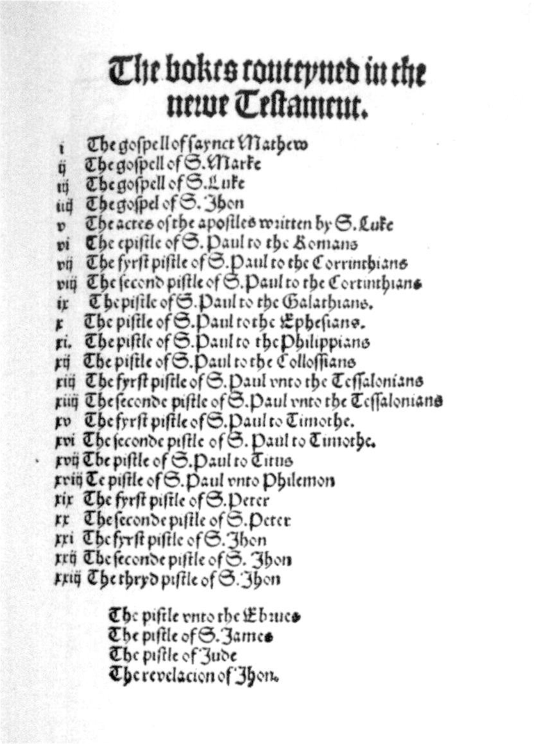

The bokes conteyned in the newe Testament.

i   The gospell of saynct Mathew
ij   The gospell of S. Marke
iij The gospell of S. Luke
iiij The gospel of S. Jhon
v   The actes of the apostles written by S. Luke
vi   The epistle of S. Paul to the Romans
vij The fyrst pistle of S. Paul to the Corrinthians
viij The seconde pistle of S. Paul to the Cortinthians
ix   The pistle of S. Paul to the Galathians.
x   The pistle of S. Paul to the Ephesians.
xi. The pistle of S. Paul to the Philippians
xij The pistle of S. Paul to the Collossians
xiij The fyrst pistle of S. Paul vnto the Tessalonians
xiiij The seconde pistle of S. Paul vnto the Tessalonians
xv   The fyrst pistle of S. Paul to Timothe.
xvi The seconde pistle of S. Paul to Timothe.
xvij The pistle of S. Paul to Titus
xviij Te pistle of S. Paul vnto Philemon
xix The fyrst pistle of S. Peter
xx   The seconde pistle of S. Peter
xxi The fyrst pistle of S. Jhon
xxij The seconde pistle of S. Jhon
xxiij The thryd pistle of S. Jhon

The pistle vnto the Ebrues
The pistle of S. James
The pistle of Jude
The revelacion of Jhon.

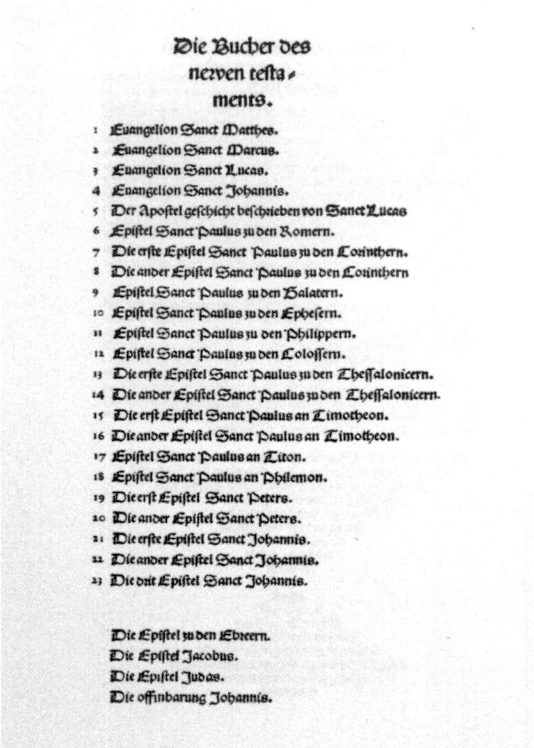

Die Bucher des newen testaments.

1   Euangelion Sanct Matthes.
2   Euangelion Sanct Marcus.
3   Euangelion Sanct Lucas.
4   Euangelion Sanct Johannis.
5   Der Apostel geschicht beschrieben von Sanct Lucas
6   Epistel Sanct Paulus zu den Romern.
7   Die erste Epistel Sanct Paulus zu den Corinthern.
8   Die ander Epistel Sanct Paulus zu den Corinthern
9   Epistel Sanct Paulus zu den Galatern.
10   Epistel Sanct Paulus zu den Ephesern.
11   Epistel Sanct Paulus zu den Philippern.
12   Epistel Sanct Paulus zu den Colossern.
13   Die erste Epistel Sanct Paulus zu den Thessalonicern.
14   Die ander Epistel Sanct Paulus zu den Thessalonicern.
15   Die erst Epistel Sanct Paulus an Timotheon.
16   Die ander Epistel Sanct Paulus an Timotheon.
17   Epistel Sanct Paulus an Titon.
18   Epistel Sanct Paulus an Philemon.
19   Die erst Epistel Sanct Peters.
20   Die ander Epistel Sanct Peters.
21   Die erste Epistel Sanct Johannis.
22   Die ander Epistel Sanct Johannis.
23   Die drit Epistel Sanct Johannis.

Die Epistel zu den Ebreern.
Die Epistel Jacobus.
Die Epistel Judas.
Die offinbarung Johannis.

Fig. 3.2. Tyndale's first attempted printing of the New Testament shows the strong influence of Martin Luther's 1522 New Testament in German. The preface is partially derived from Luther's work, as are many of the side notes. Tyndale's table of contents has the peculiarity of not 'counting' Hebrews, James, Jude and Revelation as fully canonical books, for these are placed in this order at the end of the table of contents and are not numbered. Tyndale adopted this unusual feature from Luther's first edition of the Testament in German, the Septembertestament *of 1522.*

The page on the right is Luther's table of contents from 1522; the page on the left is from the fragmentary printing of Tyndale's New Testament 1525.

Erasmus's Bible (1518-19; 1522). That does not mean that he faced the Greek text alone, without consulting other versions and aids. Tyndale clearly used Luther's German translation as well, eventually even rendering parts of Luther's German prefaces in English.[9] He also depended on Erasmus's Latin translations of the Greek and even consulted the Vulgate version, the biblical text that would have been the textbook for all of his formal education.

The hallmark of the designs for Tyndale's early editions is accessibility. From 1525 until 1536, all of Tyndale's Bibles appeared in small formats. These would have been cheaper than large folios and also potentially easier to smuggle. In 1536, a Tyndale New Testament finally appeared in a grand folio format, but this was after the crown abolished papal authority and began issuing Reformation legislation. Moreover, at the synod of Canterbury (December 1534), the bishops had petitioned the King to support the creation of an English Bible.[10]

1534 was a watershed year in the history of the English Bible. The Act of Supremacy rejected papal authority and, instead, declared the king 'supreme head' of the church in England. Tyndale does not explicitly state awareness of this profound change in English policy. According to his own account, he reissued a revised New Testament in 1534 because a certain George Joye, formerly one of his assistants, had pirated his translation. Ever the brash, colourful writer, Tyndale writes in the 1534 preface that, in stealing his work, Joye had 'pissed in another fox's hole'.[11] After this major revision, there is a Tyndale New Testament of 1535 with slight changes and a mysterious set of three slightly different quarto printings with more minor changes in 1536. The year 1536 also saw the printing of three or four octavos and even one 16mo version of Tyndale's New Testament. The Bible revolution had started.

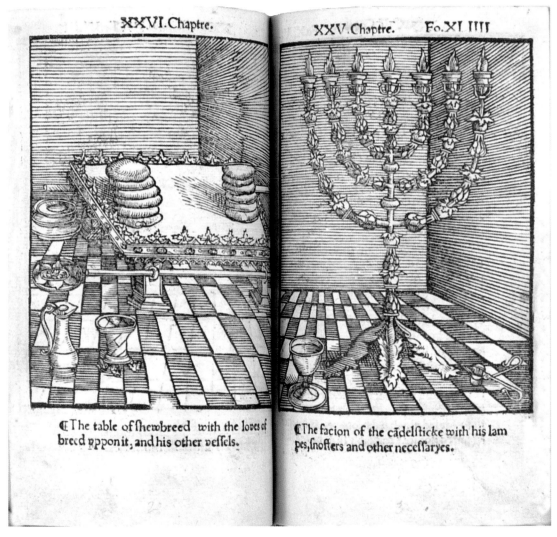

Fig. 3.3. *Tyndale published his Pentateuch in 1530. It is the first time that Hebrew scripture was translated directly into English and is consequently a milestone both in the history of the Bible and the history of the English language. The book has eleven full-page woodcut illustrations, all in Exodus. The images are based on woodcuts by Hans Holbein the Younger that first appeared in an Old Testament printed by Thomas Wolff (Basel, 1524).*

The Five Books of Moses: Tyndale's Pentateuch

Between 1526 and 1534, Tyndale did not reissue the New Testament.[12] He devoted his efforts to Hebrew scholarship, the first fruit of which was the appearance of the Pentateuch in 1530 (which he revised in 1534). The slender book of Jonah appeared separately in 1531, only one fragmentary copy of which has survived. By issuing the Pentateuch and Jonah separately Tyndale was following the precedent and even the chronology of Luther's biblical publications.

Tyndale was the first to translate the original Hebrew into English. It was a most successful beginning, for, as all scholars agree, his became the basis of all subsequent translations in English. While no one disputes that Tyndale sought to translate from the Hebrew as opposed to the Latin of the Vulgate, there is considerable uncertainty about his command of Hebrew. In all likelihood, we will never know how well he mastered Hebrew, no matter how unsatisfying that ignorance is to us.

Could a scholar have translated the Pentateuch, if his command of Hebrew was less than excellent? By 1530, the answer would be yes. The humanist movement had produced several significant aids to the study of the Hebrew Bible. Most important was Johannes Reuchlin's publication, in Latin, of a Hebrew grammar and lexicon (1506), which was followed by a valuable series of works on Hebrew and the Hebrew Bible by Sebastian Münster. Tyndale also may have used a translation of the Bible by Santi Pagnini (1528). This most unusual work puts the Hebrew Bible in Latin, but in such a way as to make the syntax of the Hebrew transparent in the Latin rendition. Renaissance scholars with excellent Latin and little Hebrew would repeatedly use Pagnini as a crib. Tyndale also worked directly from Luther's translation of the Pentateuch (first printed in 1523), the first Renaissance vernacular Bible based on the original Hebrew scripture. Luther's example certainly inspired him to bring out a separate edition of the Pentateuch before completing the Hebrew Bible, a goal that Tyndale's martyrdom would preclude.

Internal evidence indicates incontrovertibly that Tyndale was capable of making independent decisions about the meanings of words and phrases in Hebrew. Furthermore, Tyndale had enough confidence in his philology to boast of the compatibility of Hebrew with the English language (as opposed to Latin). In his *The Obedience of a Christian Man*, Tyndale claimed: 'the properties of the Hebrew tongue agreeth a thousand times more with the English than with the Latin. The manner of speaking is both one, so that in a thousand places thou needest not but to translate it into English word for word, when thou must seek a compass in the Latin.'[13]

The circumstances of the publication of the Pentateuch of 1530 are not clear. Most bibliographers hold to the view that the presswork was done by Johannes Hoochstraten in Antwerp and that the imprimatur of Hans Luft of Marburg is false. Hans Luft was a printer of great renown in Wittenberg who was, at that time, also manufacturing books in Marburg. It is also unusual that this imprimatur occurs only in the colophon to Genesis. Less unusual, but still noteworthy, is the fact that all five books have separate title pages and that the whole does not have a unifying title page but begins with the title page for Genesis.

The typography has similar irregularities, although its overall clarity has elicited a steady stream of praise from readers.

TYNDALE'S LORD'S PRAYER, 1534
THE FIRST PROTESTANT FORMULATION

O our father, which art in heaven, hallowed be thy name. Let thy kingdom come. Thy will be fulfilled, as well in earth as it is in heaven. Give us this day our daily bread. And forgive us our trespasses, even as we forgive our trespassers. And lead us not into temptation. But deliver us from evil. For thine is the kingdom and the power and the glory for ever. Amen.

In the first printing of 1525, Tyndale did not have the doxology (the final sentence). This was in keeping with the Vulgate version, which also lacked it. The presence of the doxology, which occurs in many Greek manuscripts of the New Testament, would differentiate Protestant from Catholic versions. Protestants thought they were being faithful to the original Greek, and Catholics thought the traditional Vulgate version was sufficient. Ironically, textual scholars now believe that the original Greek did not include the doxology; it was an interpolation (insertion) from the Greek liturgy into biblical manuscripts. In this case, the Vulgate helps us know what was in the most ancient Greek manuscripts.

Genesis and Numbers are set up in a bastarda font (a type of medieval black letter) that is notable for its simplicity and legibility. More significantly, the remaining three books are printed in a roman font, which represents a departure from the gothic style of the printed English book of the early Renaissance. The small octavo format also enhances the aura of scripture's accessibility. It is holy word, but one can carry this holy word quite conveniently – or even, as we might imagine, inconspicuously – in one's pocket.

Each book has a separate introduction, as had been the case with Luther's Pentateuch, except that the text of Genesis is preceded by two letters of introduction: 'W. T. To the Reader' and 'A prolog showing the use of the scripture'. Tyndale's prefaces depend upon Luther's, although these two are not direct translations. 'A prolog' expresses Luther's concepts of salvation and scripture, and he claims the 'pope's sect'

believes that 'heaven came by deeds and not by Christ, and that the outward deed justified them and made them holy and not the inward spirit received by faith'.[14] Tyndale echoes Luther's powerful formulation of the distinction in scripture between law and the promise of salvation (as set forth in the introduction to his *Septembertestament* of 1522), and does so with elegant lucidity:

So now the scripture is a light and showeth us the true way, both what to do, and what to hope. . . . Seek therefore in the scripture as thou readest it first the law, what god commandeth us to do. And secondarily the promises, which god promiseth us again, namely in Christ Jesus our lord.[15]

English Bible as Partisan Manifesto?
It is time to pause to reflect on the suppression of the English Bible. It is often easy

for Protestants to imagine a demonic plot to keep Bibles out of the hands of the people. In reality, the major problem in the history of the English Bible was the propaganda printed in the Bibles. In the eyes of authority, this tainted those Bibles with dangerous heresies.

The Tyndale Bibles were more than just Bibles. The English government and church did claim the danger of untutored lay access to scripture, but they especially sought to end dissemination of the Bible as a Lutheran pamphlet. Prior to his own fall, Thomas More used all his resources – law, propaganda and violence – to stop Protestantism from spreading. As long as Henry VIII remained a Catholic, this would be the policy.

The partisanship of the Tyndale imprints is a persistent problem in scholarship. Tyndale has repeatedly found apologists who plead his innocence on this score. Part of the problem is that the degree of partisanship varies in his books. The first attempted New Testament of 1525 begins with a Lutheran-based introduction and includes a few partisan side notes. The edition of 1526 eschews the Lutheran preface and side notes but includes a mildly Protestant afterword. The fierceness of future imprints may be a result of the hardening of the opposition in England. In 1530, English Protestants had their first martyr: Thomas Hitton, who was executed in Kent. Tyndale mentioned him in 1530 and linked him to Stephen, the first martyr, after Christ, in Christian history: 'That all the righteous blood may fall on their heads [i.e. the bishops, etc.] . . . from the blood of Stephen the first martyr to the blood of Thomas Hitton. . . .'[16]

The Pentateuch of 1530 is stridently militant. The fierceness of Tyndale's opposition to Catholicism has often been faulted on the grounds that it detracts from the dignity of holy scripture and it also offered justification to Catholic efforts to suppress the text. David Daniell attempted, with only limited persuasiveness, to argue that scholars have exaggerated the amount of polemic in the Pentateuch. After all, many of the side notes are explanations of Hebrew words as well as simple admonitions to the reader to attend to the meaning of passages. But even this is occasionally accomplished with a Protestant twist, as in Deuteronomy 8:18, 'God's power worketh and not we.' Tyndale encouraged Christians to read and ponder scripture directly, and he did express disdain for glosses that set forth allegorical meanings. At Deuteronomy 4:1, 'Ye shall put nothing unto the word,' he added the note, 'No: nor yet corrupt it with false glosses to confirm Aristotle: but rebuke Aristotle's false learning therewith.'

Unquestionably, anti-Catholic outbursts are sufficiently numerous to make a strong impression on any reader. Among the most notorious are some twenty attacks on the papacy. In the margin at Numbers 23 ('How shall I curse whom God curseth not and how shall I defy whom the Lord defieth not?'), Tyndale caustically noted: 'The pope can tell how.'

In the New Testaments of 1534-7, partisan notes appear and, more importantly, Tyndale included prefaces to the individual books of the Bible that he derived from Luther. He adapted several prefaces significantly, but they remain Luther's message, the most important of which is Luther's Preface to Romans (which runs to thirty-four pages in Tyndale's New Testament of 1534). This work is, in fact, one of Luther's most beloved tracts. It would be the work that inspired John Wesley's conversion at Aldersgate on 24 May 1738.

WILLIAM TYNDALE'S BIBLES

1525	Failed attempt to print the New Testament in Cologne. One copy of one fragment (which ends in the middle of Matthew 22) survives.
1526	New Testament successfully printed at Worms by Peter Schoeffer. Only three copies, two of which are imperfect, survive.
1530	Pentateuch. Probably printed in Antwerp. The first example of Biblical Hebrew being translated directly into English. Fewer than ten copies are known.
1531?	Book of Jonah. Probably printed in Antwerp. Only one fragmentary copy has survived.
1534	Tyndale publishes a thorough revision of his New Testament at Antwerp (printed by Martin de Keyser).
1537	'Matthew's Bible'. This includes Tyndale's translation of the New Testament, the Pentateuch, and the version of Joshua to 2 Chronicles that has been attributed to him. John Rogers edited this Bible under the pseudonym of 'Thomas Matthew'. Probably printed at Antwerp for the English publishers Richard Grafton and Edward Whitchurch. It became the basis for future English Bibles, initially for the Great Bible of 1539.

The 'Matthew's Bible'

In 1537, a grand, richly illustrated, complete Bible appeared in folio. It is a mystery, and a most important one. According to the title page, the editor was Thomas Matthew. But that is not so and it is all but absolutely certain that it was John Rogers. Why the pseudonym? Why no indication of printer or place of publication? Although the Bible was now legal, some people obviously felt caution was necessary. Moreover, the name 'William Tyndale' was still synonymous with 'notorious heretic'. Henry may have rejected papal authority, but Tyndale remained anathema to him. Indeed, Henry's policy would change again by 1539-40, and by 1541 the Bible revolution would stall in a doldrum.

The greatest mystery is the text of this Bible. The New Testament and the Pentateuch are Tyndale's. Ezra to the Apocrypha are from Miles Coverdale's version, except that John Rogers added his own translation of the Prayer of Manasseh (derived mainly from Olivétan's French translation). Whose is the text from Joshua to 2 Chronicles? The style points to Tyndale. There is a scholarly consensus – a rare case of unanimity for speculation on unsigned authorship – that this is Tyndale's work on the Hebrew scripture from the last five years or so of his life. John Rogers or another kindred spirit must have acquired this material from Tyndale's rooms when he was treacherously kidnapped.

The name Tyndale, which would always

be pestiferous to Henry VIII, does not appear explicitly in the book. Nonetheless, the initials W T are placed mysteriously at the end of the Old Testament. Moreover, the Lutheran Prefaces (in Tyndale's adaptations) are also printed in this book. Even the iconography advances Protestant principles. For example, the general title page (repeated as the title page for the New Testament) depicts the Lutheran concept of the Law and the Gospel, an issue that Luther discussed in many places, perhaps most prominently in the preface to his *Septembertestament* (1522). Lucas Cranach the Elder adapted this concept into a popular form of Lutheran iconography, which was used in both painting and, with remarkable frequency, in complex woodcuts. The doctrine holds that the laws of the Bible are replaced by the promise of redemption in Christ. Consequently, adherence to laws does not ensure salvation; salvation is attained through faith alone, a free gift from God. In this image, concepts of 'law' are associated with damnation, while belief in Christ, as conveyed by the Word of God, is depicted as the way to salvation. The iconographic scheme of the Law and the Gospel is also a major motif on the title page of the 1535 Coverdale Bible, although there it is annexed to the specifically English concept of royal supremacy over the church, and, as would be typical for the English tradition, the law receives a more positive treatment.

It is ironic, nonetheless, that the 'Matthew's Bible', mostly a Tyndale version, was probably the first Bible to appear with a 'royal licence'. Although the 'Matthew's Bible' was probably printed on the Continent, it was financed from England by Richard Grafton and Edward Whitchurch of London. In 1537 Grafton brought a copy to England to give to Archbishop Thomas Cranmer who in turn wrote to Thomas Cromwell, chief advisor to Henry VIII in all ecclesiastical affairs since 1535. Cranmer liked it 'better than any other translation heretofore made'[17] and urged Cromwell to seek the King's licence. In a week, approval was granted.[18] The 'Matthew's Bible' also formed the foundation for the Great Bible (1539, etc.) and is thus the major conduit for the survival of Tyndale's artistry in subsequent English versions to – and including – the Authorised Version of 1611.

The Translations

Tyndale was temperamentally well equipped to be a translator. He was a superb scholar who knew how to write forcefully and beautifully. Yet, like many Renaissance thinkers, he readily reformulated the ideas of others (often rather exactly and without giving credit). Very much in the manner of Martin Luther, Tyndale absorbed scripture and, having made the words of the Bible part of his being, he spoke them in the new language, as if those words were his own. His appropriation of scripture gave his renderings conviction and an individual stamp.

As he worked, he had Luther's German and Erasmus's Latin translations on his desk. We should not see these as cribs but rather as aids and, importantly, as models for style. Despite the language differences, Tyndale was exceedingly fortunate that these two versions were by translators who just happened to be among the greatest Continental writers of the Renaissance. He was also fortunate that their approaches were rather different. Luther was the master of a popular manner that could be both grandiloquent and colloquial. Erasmus was elegant, smooth, crisp and, like Luther, obsessed with clarity. Tyndale's

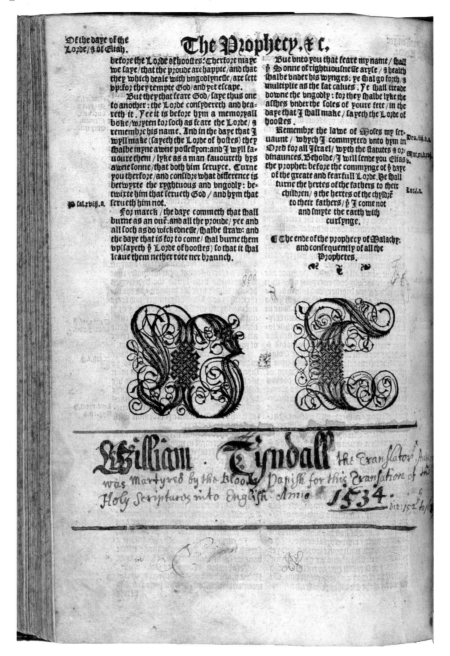

Fig. 3.4. In 1537, a beautiful English Bible appeared in folio. This Bible contains all of Tyndale's work as translator, roughly two-thirds of the entire Bible. It is the first edition of Tyndale's translation, published posthumously, of Joshua to 2 Chronicles. This volume was the basis for the Great Bible.

The editor was John Rogers, an associate of Tyndale and an important Protestant leader who would become the first victim of the persecutions under Mary I in 1555. Rogers himself exercised caution by using the pseudonym 'Thomas Matthew', the source of this Bible's name, 'Matthew's Bible'. Tyndale is not mentioned in the text but at the end of the Old Testament there is a conspicuous set of initials – W T – that must be intended as a tribute to Tyndale. A reader of this copy of the Matthew's Bible obviously recognised the initials, as we can see in the handwritten note.

masterpiece is all the brighter for the brilliance of his masters.

Of all the Renaissance English Bibles, Tyndale's are the most vernacular. After the sheer power of his fluency, the casual style may be his greatest contribution. This is not to say that his Bibles are the 'Good News for Renaissance Man'. Yet he aims for clarity, even simplicity, in English. One is reminded of Martin Luther's principle that one should translate the Bible in such a way that the reader feels it was written only yesterday. Like Luther, Tyndale makes charming descents to colloquial registers of language. In the prelude to the Lord's Prayer, he writes 'but when ye pray babble not much'. Here, he was certainly true to his inner voice but also consonant with Luther's approach, who even inspired the use of 'babble' with his equally colloquial 'plappern'. According to Luther, the biblical translator must capture the language of the man speaking in the market and the mother speaking to children.

The English of Tyndale's Bible is so joyful, so lucid, and so memorable that it has had an enormous impact. Despite the chasm between the culture of the Renaissance and now, readers are still remarkably moved by his literary talent and verve. His words and, equally importantly, his cadences echo in the King James versions and beyond. Many of the biblical aphorisms that spice our language are Tyndale coinages. The list is long and includes 'fruit of the vine', 'give up the ghost', and 'filthy lucre'.[19]

Tyndale certainly felt that a translation should not be anything less than accurate. However, he is routinely faulted for several lapses, most importantly, for ignoring the Greek connective particles in the New Testament. Quite often a 'for', 'and', 'then',

'thus', or 'therefore' is missing in his version, but Tyndale's point is obvious. Rendering all the particles would make the English stilted and the Bible sound like a translation. Naturally, English uses connecting particles but not as obsessively as Greek.

The following passage from Jesus' Sermon on the Mount gives a good sense of Tyndale's style. For a number of reasons, it is illuminating to compare these passages to the renderings of the King James Version.

Tyndale 1534

Judge not, that ye be not judged. For as ye judge so shall ye be judged. And with what measure ye mete, with the same shall it be measured to you again. Why seest thou a mote in thy brother's eye, and perceivest not the beam that is in thine own eye? . . . Give not that which is holy to dogs, neither cast ye your pearls before swine, lest they tread them under their feet and the other turn again and all to rent you. Ask and it shall be given you. Seek and ye shall find. Knock and it shall be opened.

King James Version, 1611

1 Judge not, that ye be not judged. 2 for with what judgment ye judge, ye shall be judged: and with what measure ye mete, it shall be measured to you again. 3 And why beholdest thou the mote that is in thy brother's eye, but considerest not the beam that is in thine own eye. . . . 6 Give not that which is holy unto dogs, neither cast ye your pearls before swine, lest they trample them under their feet, and turn again and rent you. 7 Ask and it shall be given you. Seek and ye shall find. Knock and it shall be opened unto you.

Fig. 3.5. The 'Matthew's Bible' of 1537 is illustrated throughout. In addition to woodcut title pages for the Old and New Testaments and a full-page woodcut of the expulsion from Eden, the imprint has one hundred and nineteen illustrations in the text (from forty-four blocks).

The title page for the New Testament (also used for the general title page) is a reprint of a woodcut title page used for a Lutheran Bible in 1533. The theme is the Lutheran contrast of the law with the promise of redemption in the gospel. The artist is the German Erhard Altdorfer.

Firstly, one cannot help noticing that the strong phrases in the KJV – the ones that cling to us – are taken from Tyndale. Obviously, the KJV shows some advance, too, in this extract by bringing order to the second half of Matthew 8:6, where Tyndale's colloquialism ('and *all* to rent you') became a little mushy. Overall, Tyndale's easy manner stands out in high relief. 'Seest thou' did not improve when it became the high-flying 'beholdest thou'. Similarly, the KJV observes a tight parallelism in 8:2 (which is also in the original Greek). Tyndale lightens the Greek rhetoric with his casual addition of 'with the same', which creates an oral, conversational feel. Perhaps Tyndale was wrong to do this, but the result is undeniably pleasant.

Similarly, Tyndale was unconcerned about translating the same Greek word with the same English word. He did this for no apparent reason other than delight in variety. Mozley conveys the feeling of this admirably: 'whatever the reader of his translation may suffer, he shall not suffer monotony. . . . Thus for the phrase *it came to pass* he gives us five renderings, adding also *happened*, *chanced*, *fortuned*, and *followed*. . . .'[20] This procedure occurs in many other cases as well, causing even Tyndale's admirers to concede 'waywardness'.[21]

Nonetheless, those translations which have aimed at a uniform English equivalent for the Greek words have largely failed. They are stilted and pedantic, the most important example of which is the Revised Version of 1881. The Authorised Version of 1611 comes down on this matter somewhere in between Tyndale and the Revised Version; it often uses different renderings for the same word but without Tyndale's exuberance. It is worth mentioning that variety of diction was a dominant spice in Erasmian rhetoric. In his *De copia*, Erasmus offered, for example, over two hundred ways to say 'I'll always remember you' (*semper dum vivam tui meminero*).

How much Tyndale survives in the King James Version? A standard high estimate is nine-tenths of the New Testament, a rough proportion that gained currency when Mozley used it.[22] Obviously, the figure is not grounded in a statistical analysis. It errs, perhaps tremendously, in favour of Tyndale's influence. Charles Butterworth estimated that only 18% of the final phrasings of the King James Version go back to Tyndale.[23] One should also reflect that a change of, say, twenty-five percent, is quite significant in a translation. And yet, Tyndale provided the basis for energetic, fluent, colourful translations. Tyndale was the first to write long passages of scripture in English that did not sound like a translation. This was compelling. Moreover, the tonal and temperamental filter of his mind was ebullient. As S.L. Greenslade put it, 'scripture made him happy, and there is something swift and gay in his rhythm which conveys his happiness'.[24] Readers will feel this when they encounter Tyndale.

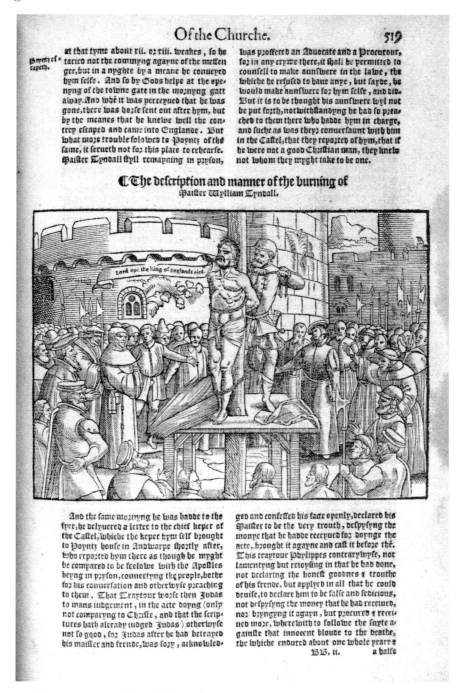

Fig. 3.6. Tyndale was strangled and burned at the stake in October 1536. The fullest Renaissance account of his life is in John Foxe's The Book of Martyrs, *a work begun in exile during Mary I's reign. This depiction is a portrayal of Tyndale as a powerful, heroic figure, defiantly facing death. Tyndale was in exile because of the harshly anti-Protestant policies of Henry VIII. Yet, with the annulment of Henry's marriage to Catherine of Aragon and his marriage to Anne Boleyn, policy turned 180 degrees. An injunction of 1538 would stipulate that a Bible be placed in every church. Thus, Tyndale's last words, 'Lord, open the King of England's eyes,' are supposed to sound prophetic.*

ENDNOTES TO CHAPTER THREE

1. Mozley 1937, 334. Quote is of Mozley's translation of the Latin letter.
2. Even the most recent study, Bobrick 2001, 81, places him in Cambridge as a matter of fact.
3. Mozley 1937, 37.
4. Hotchkiss and Price in Pelikan 1996, 82.
5. Pollard 1911, 97 (text of Tyndale's Preface to the Pentateuch 1530).
6. Mozley 1937, 334.
7. Mozley 1937, 117-18.
8. Daniell 1994, 229.
9. In his report on the interruption of the Cologne printing of the New Testament in 1525, Johannes Cochlaeus even says that Tyndale had translated 'the New Testament of Martin Luther' into English. See Pollard 1911, 104.
10. Pollard 1911, 175-7.
11. Bray 1994, 31 (Tyndale's Preface to the 1534 New Testament).
12. Mozley 1937, 347, uncompellingly speculates that there were a few editions of which no copies survive.
13. Daniell 1994, 290.
14. Tyndale 1530, Preface to the translation of the Pentateuch, 6^v.
15. Tyndale 1530, Preface to the translation of the Pentateuch, 5^v.
16. Mozley 1937, 347.
17. Pollard 1911, 215.
18. The records attesting the licensing of the 'Matthew's Bible' are reprinted in Pollard 1911, 214-22. They are two letters from Archbishop Cranmer and two from the publisher Richard Grafton to Thomas Cromwell.
19. See Daniell 1989, for a longer list.
20. Mozley 1937, 101-2.
21. E.g. Mozley 1937, 102.
22. Mozley 1937, 108; see also Bruce 1978, 44 (quoting J. Isaacs).
23. See Chapter Eight and Butterworth 1941, 231.
24. Greenslade in *Cambridge History of the Bible* [1963-70] 1978-80, 3:144.

CHAPTER FOUR
EDITOR-IN-CHIEF

Pray for us, that the word of God
May have free passage and be glorified.
– from the title page of the Coverdale Bible

If there be no heresies [in this Bible], then in God's name
let it go abroad among our people.
*– attributed to King Henry VIII, speaking
of the Coverdale Bible*

When William Tyndale cried, 'Lord, open the King of England's eyes,' as he was being martyred in 1536, his prayer had already been answered. As far as the English Bible was concerned, the answer had come in an unexpected way and through an unlikely person. The very year in which Tyndale was sent to prison (1535), the first English translation of the whole Bible began circulating in England with the approval of Henry VIII. It was the work of Miles Coverdale.

The Frequent Exile

Like Tyndale, Coverdale endured much hardship and danger in his determination to make the Bible available in English. Born in Yorkshire in 1488, educated at Cambridge, an Augustinian friar who left that order when he embraced the reform movement, in and out of royal favour all his life, Coverdale nevertheless lived to be eighty and died peacefully in his own bed.

In and out of favour and in and out of England is the story of Coverdale's life. In 1528, he was forced to seek safety on the Continent, initially in Germany. Some sources indicate that he met and assisted Tyndale during those years. In 1534, Jacob van Meteren, an Antwerp merchant sympathetic to the Reformation, encouraged Coverdale to undertake the momentous task. And it was probably with van Meteren's financial backing that the first complete printed English Bible appeared. The presswork was finished on 4 October 1535.

Returning to England in 1535, Coverdale enjoyed the favour of the new Queen, Anne Boleyn, and the new Chancellor, Thomas Cromwell. With the execution of Cromwell in 1540, he again fled to the Continent where he saw fit to remain until after Henry's death in 1547. This second exile quickened his Protestantism. He may have received a doctorate in theology from the University of Tübingen, a growing centre for Lutheran education. He certainly lived for three years in Strasbourg, overlapping with John Calvin's exile there from

Fig. 4.1. Miles Coverdale lived a long fruitful life from 1487 or 1488 until 1569. After William Tyndale, he is arguably the second most significant person in the history of the English Bible. He produced the first complete translation of the Bible in 1535.

Subsequently, he served as editor of the Great Bible, the project organised by Thomas Cromwell to produce an accurate and neutral translation. For that important work, he used as much of Tyndale's translation as possible. He may also have been involved in the creation of the Geneva Bible, which appeared in 1560. He concluded his life of ministry as part of the Puritan movement at the beginning of Elizabeth's reign.

Geneva. He knew and admired Calvin and expressed great appreciation for the hospitality of Calvin's wife, Odelette de Bure. Coverdale translated a number of tracts into English during this time, including several by Heinrich Bullinger, Zwingli's successor at Zürich. His German became so fluent that he was able to serve as an assistant minister and schoolteacher in Bergzabern, a small town north of Strasbourg.

With the accession of Edward VI (1547-53), Thomas Cranmer was able to coax him back to England, where he served from 1551 to 1553 as Bishop of Exeter. He was deprived, imprisoned and nearly executed under Mary I. He was saved only through the intervention of the Lutheran King of Denmark. When he went into his third exile, he again headed toward Switzerland and Southwest Germany, eventually spending most of his time as a leader of the famous exile community of

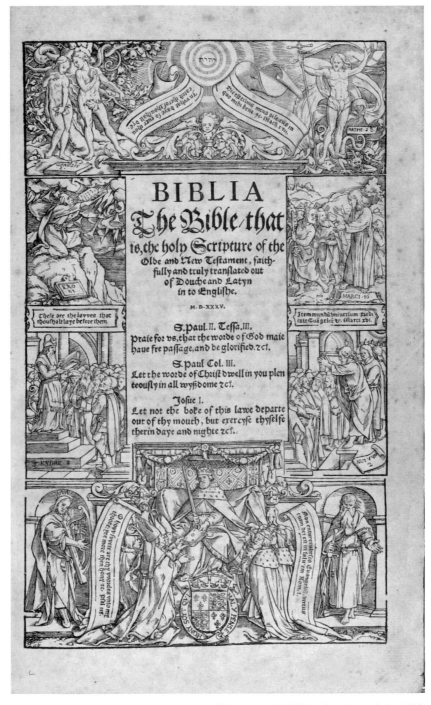

Fig. 4.2. The title page of the first complete English printed Bible, the Coverdale Bible of 1535. At the foot of the magnificent woodcut, attributed to Hans Holbein the Younger, King Henry VIII distributes the Bible to secular and ecclesiastical lords. This represents the Act of Supremacy of 1534, which made the king 'Supreme Head of the Church of England', ending papal authority.

At the top is the divine name in Hebrew (the tetragrammaton). The sides depict the Protestant concepts of the law (on left) and the gospel or promise of redemption in Christ (on right).

Geneva. There he was an elder of the English church and godfather to a child of John Knox, the Scottish reformer. He returned to England in 1559 and spent the last decade of his life in relative seclusion during the reign of Elizabeth I. He helped officiate at the installation of Matthew Parker as Archbishop of Canterbury on 17 December 1559, an occasion which marks the beginnings of the Elizabethan church. Coverdale wore a black gown to the service, a loud proclamation of his puritan inclinations.

The Translation of 1535: The Coverdale Bible

Unlike Tyndale, Coverdale's command of the biblical languages was minimal. In the prologue of the 1535 Bible, he wrote with candour about his qualifications: 'Considering how excellent knowledge and learning an interpreter of scripture ought to have in the tongues, and pondering also mine own insufficiency therein, and how weak I am to perform the office of a translator, I was the more loath to meddle with this work.... But to say the truth before God, it was neither my labour nor desire to have this work put in my hand: nevertheless it grieved me that other nations should be more plenteously provided for with the scripture in their mother tongue than we: therefore when I was instantly required, though I could not do so well as I would, I thought it yet my duty to do my best, and that with a good will.'[1]

If his linguistic abilities were limited, how did Coverdale accomplish the translation of the whole Bible and do so in such a short space of time? By being an editor as well as a translator. He frankly admitted on the title page that he translated 'out of Douche [German] and Latin', which means not from the Hebrew and the Greek. In his dedication

to the King, Coverdale says that his translation was 'out of five sundry interpreters' (i.e. translators).[2] So whose works did Coverdale use? He certainly used Tyndale as the basis for the New Testament, Pentateuch, and Jonah, and he consulted the translations of the Latin Vulgate and Martin Luther's complete German translation of 1534. He probably also depended on a German translation by Ulrich Zwingli and Leo Jud as well as a literal translation into Latin by Santi Pagnini. It is very hard to imagine that he did not also consult Erasmus's Latin translation of the New Testament. This boils down to the fact that Coverdale's Bible is a slightly edited reprint of Tyndale's renderings of the New Testament, the Pentateuch and Jonah, and Coverdale's own translation of the rest of the Old Testament and Apocrypha based on Latin and German sources, not the original languages.

Following the example of the German Protestant Bibles, Coverdale separated the apocryphal books from other Old Testament books and gathered them into an appendix (except for Baruch, which was not placed in the appendix until the second edition in 1537). In 'The Translator unto the Reader', which introduces the Apocrypha, Coverdale explains his reasoning: 'These books (good reader) which be called Apocrypha are not judged among the doctors to be of like reputation with the other scripture. . . . And the chief cause thereof is this: there be many places in them, that seem to be repugnant unto the open and manifest truth in other books of the Bible. Nevertheless I have not gathered them together to the intent that I would have them despised, or little set by, or that I should think them false, for I am not able to prove it.'[3]

Coverdale also introduced chapter summaries, which sometimes include explan-

Fig. 4.3. The Coverdale Bible of 1535 has both beautiful typography and captivating woodcut illustrations. This is an illustration of the six days of creation from Genesis 1. Altogether, the Coverdale Bible has one hundred and fifty-eight illustrations (made from sixty-eight woodblocks).

atory or hortatory notes. The summaries for each book of the Bible were printed together at the beginning of that book rather than at the head of separate chapters.

Publication of the First Complete Bible in English

To basic questions – who printed this Bible? and where was it printed? – there are no certain answers. Formerly, it was thought that Christopher Froschauer of Zürich was the printer. Current opinion favours Eucherius Cervicornus and Johannes Soter as the printers and either Marburg or Cologne as the place.

It most certainly could not have been printed in England.[4] Nonetheless, when the Bible was presented to Henry VIII and after the bishops who examined it could find no heresy in it, the king said, 'if there be no heresies, then in God's name let it go abroad among our people'.[5] That permission was only given verbally; no royal authorisation could, therefore, be printed on the title page. The first English Bible actually printed in England was the second edition of Coverdale's version, produced by James Nicholson, a London printer, in 1537. Other editions appeared in 1538, 1539, 1550 and 1553. The second edition of Coverdale and the first edition of the 'Matthew's Bible' (both published in 1537) have on their title pages 'Set forth with the king's most gracious licence'. This did not give authorisation for the Bible to be set up and publicly read in churches, but it did afford protection to those who read it privately – a freedom not enjoyed by the English people since the Constitutions of Oxford (1407/09) banned reading of the Bible in English.

Anne Boleyn probably lurked, in some mysterious way, behind the grant of limited permission from Henry VIII. She was well disposed toward the Reformation and keenly interested in the translation of the Bible into English. There is good evidence that she ordered that a copy of the Coverdale Bible be placed on the 'desk of her chamber' so that she and others could readily consult it.[6] Also, she may have extracted a promise from the King to have copies of the English Bible placed in all the churches. But this did not happen with the Coverdale Bible, for Anne fell out of favour and was executed in May 1536. The clergy probably thought it wise not to press the matter at the time. Such placement awaited the appearance of the Great Bibles in 1539-41. Boleyn's demise required a slight but dramatic change in Coverdale's second edition (1537). In the dedication to Henry, the name of 'dearest just wife and most virtuous Princess Queen Anne' had to be altered to say 'Queen Jane', referring to Henry's third wife, Jane Seymour. Indeed, this raises an intriguing question. If Queen Anne had not fallen from favour, would the Coverdale Bible have been placed in the churches of England several years before the Great Bible received that distinction?[7]

Not So Subtle Politicking

The most decorative feature of the Coverdale Bible is the title page, attributed to Hans Holbein the Younger. The border consists of four blocks. At the top is the sacred name of God in Hebrew with Christ on the right and Adam and Eve on the left. On the left side are scenes from the Old Testament (Moses giving the Law and Ezra reading it to the people). On the right side appear contrasting scenes from the New Testament (Christ commissioning the disciples and Peter preaching on Pentecost,

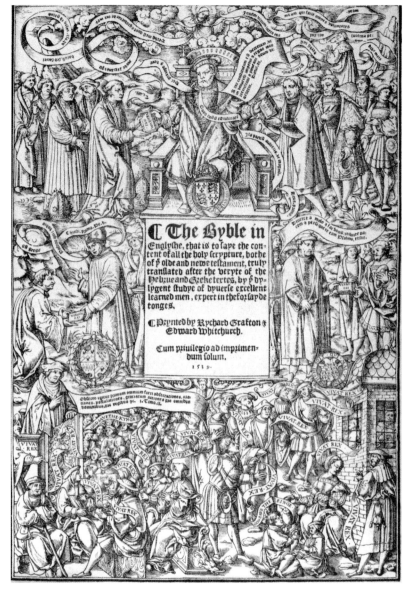

Fig. 4.4. The woodcut of the general title page of the first edition of the Great Bible, April 1539, is by an unknown artist (although in the past it was often ascribed to Hans Holbein the Younger, one of Henry VIII's favourite artists). At the top, Henry, on his throne, receives the Verbum Dei *(Word of God) from the translators; he hands a Bible to Thomas Cromwell on the right and to Archbishop Cranmer on the left. Actually Cranmer's only contribution to the project was the preface that appeared in the second and subsequent editions.*

Lower down on the left, Cranmer hands a Bible to a kneeling priest, and on the right side Cromwell presents one to a group of noblemen. At the bottom left stands a priest preaching to a group of people from whose mouths stream fifteen ribbons containing the words VIVAT REX *(Long live the King) and one ribbon that says it in English. On the bottom right is the outline of Newgate Prison from whose windows prisoners are watching the proceedings.*

God's head is at the very top (albeit much smaller than Henry's). Though both religious and patriotic, this title page also is intended to represent the royal authorisation of the Great Bible.

as recorded in Acts 2). The lower border depicts Henry VIII. In his right hand is a drawn sword. His left hand dispenses the Bible to the mitred bishops on his right and to kneeling nobles on his left. The message to Henry is that, while the Word of God comes from God (top panel), it must be dispersed to the people by the king (bottom panel). This is a visual proclamation of the king's authority as 'Supreme Head of the Church of England', a power Henry acquired in the Act of Supremacy (1534).

The flattery continued in the dedicatory 'Epistle unto the King's Highness'. There, Coverdale compares Caiaphas' unwitting prediction of the death of Christ (John 11:49-50) to Pope Leo X honouring Henry with the title 'Defender of the Faith', although the pope did not know that Henry would turn from defending the Catholic faith to embracing Protestantism. According to Coverdale, 'the blind bishop of Rome, (that blind Balaam, I say) not understanding what he did, gave unto your grace this title: *Defender of the faith*, . . . where in very deed the blind bishop (though he knew not what he did) prophesied, that by the righteous administration and continual diligence of your grace, the faith should so be defended, that God's word the mother of Faith with the fruits thereof, should have his free course throughout all Christendom, but specially in your realm'.[8] He goes on to condemn the pope, whom he calls, rather predictably, the Antichrist, 'and his false Apostles [who] have deceived all Christendom, specially your noble realm of England'. He then compares Henry to good King Josiah who 'commanded straightly (as your grace doth) that the law of God should be read and taught unto all the people'.[9]

The Great Bible

Coverdale's influence emerges decisively in the Great Bible of 1539, his revision of the Matthew Bible of 1537 (see Chapter Three). In September 1538, Thomas Cromwell ordered that 'one book of the whole Bible, in the largest volume, in English to be set up in some convenient place within the said church that you have cure of, whereas your parishioners may most commodiously resort to the same and read it'.[10] Four years earlier, Archbishop Thomas Cranmer had asked the king to nominate learned men to translate the Bible for the instruction of the people, but this never happened, for the bishops sat on their hands. This is one reason Cranmer promoted the Matthew Bible, since he felt there was little prospect of an improved translation appearing 'till a day after doomsday'.[11] But this time it did happen.

Recall that no English Bible had previously been authorised for public use in the church. Now the time had come for such a Bible, however distasteful this might be to the bishops. Coverdale and Cromwell had long been friends, so it was natural that Coverdale would be entrusted with this project. He was experienced in Bible translation and was a man of peaceable disposition. Although not so qualified as some, yet better qualified than when he undertook his 1535 Bible, he could be trusted.

Printing such a large volume (roughly 16 ½ by 11 inches) required adequate paper and skilled printers. Cromwell did not think such were available in England, so he sought permission to have the Bible printed in France where, he said, 'books are dispatched sooner than in any other country'.[12] However, printing English books, especially books that might support the reform movement, was an extremely risky business in Catholic France. Soon, the

BIBLE NICKNAMES AND CURIOSITIES

BREECHES BIBLE is the 1560 Geneva Bible. In Genesis 3:7, Adam and Eve put on 'breeches' instead of 'aprons'.

BUG BIBLE is the 1535 Coverdale. For Psalms 91:5, Coverdale translates: 'So yet thou shalt not need to be afraid for any bugs by night.'

CRANMER'S BIBLE is the 1540 edition of the Great Bible (as well as subsequent editions of this version). Archbishop Thomas Cranmer's introduction to the scriptures was first printed in the second edition of the Great Bible (1540). This preface was so powerful and influential that many named the Bible after Cranmer, even though he was not involved in the translation itself.

GREAT BIBLE is the 1539 version by Coverdale, so named because of its large size.

KING JAMES BIBLE. Americans tend to call the Bible of 1611 the King James Version; the British call it the Authorised Version. Both appellations are slightly problematic because King James did not translate it and because there is no surviving record of formal authorisation of the version when it appeared.

MURDERER'S BIBLE is a nickname for three different Bibles: a printing of the KJV from 1795 with the typographical error in Mark 7:27: 'Let the children be killed' (instead of 'filled'); an 1801 Bible that reads 'These are murderers' instead of 'These are murmurers' in Jude 16; and an 1804 edition where Numbers 35:18 renders 'the murderer shall surely be put to death' as 'the murderer shall surely be put together'.

THE PRINTERS' BIBLE is a 1702 edition of the King James Version, so named because of a printer's error in Psalm 119:16: instead of 'princes have persecuted me without a cause,' David complains, 'printers have persecuted me without a cause'.

REBECCA BIBLE is the version of 1823 in which, in Genesis 24:61, the matriarch arises with her 'camels' not her 'damsels'.

TREACLE BIBLE refers either to the Coverdale (1535) or to the Bishops' Bible (1568), both of which lament, in Jeremiah 8:22, that 'there is no more Triacle at Gilaad'. ('Balm' is the customary translation.)

UNRIGHTEOUS BIBLE is a 1653 King James Version printed in London by John Field, which renders 1 Corinthians 6:9 as 'the unrighteous shall inherit the kingdom of God'.

VINEGAR BIBLE. In a 1717 Oxford printing by J. Baskett, the heading of Luke 20 calls the parable of the vineyard 'The Parable of the Vinegar'.

WICKED BIBLE comes from a 1631 printing of the King James Version (London: Barker and Assigns of Bill), in which the sixth commandment is misprinted as 'Thou shalt commit adultery.' For this, Robert Barker, who also printed the 1611 King James, was fined and ruined, eventually ending up in debtor's prison.

WIFE BEATER'S BIBLE is a 1549 printing of the 'Mattthew's Bible' by the London printer John Daye. A note on 1 Peter 3 offers husbands some terrible advice: 'And if she be not obedient and helpful unto him [he] endeavoreth to beat the fear of God into her head, that thereby she may be compelled to learn her duty, and to do it.'

French printer Francis Regnault and his colleagues were being threatened by the authorities. They were charged with heresy on 17 December 1538. Grafton (the English publisher) and Coverdale managed to secrete some printed sheets out of France before fleeing. They left some 2,500 copies (likely incomplete) behind, all of which were promptly confiscated by the French authorities. It is possible, however, that Coverdale succeeded in quietly, probably secretly, moving the type and presses to London. Finally in April 1539 the first edition was published in London. Coverdale had succeeded once again.

Six further editions of the Great Bible appeared in the next two years. The second, published in April 1540, contains a considerable number of revisions from Coverdale's hand. It also bore a preface by Archbishop Thomas Cranmer. On the first title appear the words 'This is the Bible appointed to the use of the churches.' Thus, we could argue that the Great Bible was the first English Bible to be authorised and not merely licensed.

Shifting Winds

Miles Coverdale's great advantage of having an ally in Thomas Cromwell soon evaporated. Cromwell's arrangement of a marriage between Henry VIII and Anne of Cleves, which was to be the cornerstone of an alliance with German Protestantism, was an abysmal failure. This opened the door to intrigue by Cromwell's enemies. Before long, he was convicted of treason and beheaded on 28 July 1540. As a consequence, the original woodblock for the title page of the Great Bible had to be modified. In the fourth edition (November 1540), a blank circle of almost two inches diameter marks the place where Cromwell's coat of arms had been. This same edition also claims to have been overseen by Cuthbert Tunstall, who fourteen years before had bought and burned copies of Tyndale's New Testament. Now the bishop whose 'house was full' – too full to accommodate Tyndale's project – was promoting a Bible that contained much of that same New Testament.

As for Archbishop Cranmer, he continued to promote Reformation ideas. While moderate under Henry, he became decidedly progressive under Edward VI. It was then that he directed the composition of the reformed liturgy, the *Book of Common Prayer*. He is also responsible for the more Calvinist (or Swiss) sensibilities expressed in the second edition of the *Book of Common Prayer* (1552), including, most importantly, a memorialist interpretation of the Lord's Supper. His martyrdom was also a significant contribution to the cause, for his death (as well as the death of some 300 other Protestants) inspired the movement.[13] When Mary came to the throne, Cranmer was accused of high treason and sentenced. He signed several recantations of his views, but renounced the recantations and was burned at the stake on 21 March 1556. He put his hand into the flames first because 'this hand hath offended'.

Before politics shifted, the reception the Great Bible received was enthusiastic. Not only did churches have copies but ordinary people could also purchase a copy inexpensively. Those who could not read gathered eagerly to listen to the reading of the Bible by those who could. Now, at last, people had the entire Bible readily available to them.

Fig. 4.5. Detail from the title page of the fourth edition of the Great Bible, 1541. Thomas Cromwell, with the King's permission, played a crucial part in initiating, producing and promoting the Great Bible. He enlisted Miles Coverdale to revise the Matthew's Bible for the new translation. But on this title page, Cromwell's coat of arms was cut out since he was executed in July 1540.

Cranmer's Preface

Nowadays, the Great Bible is best remembered for its preface, written by Cranmer. This brief introduction has become a classic Reformation defence of universal access to scripture.

Thomas Cranmer played a crucial role in the first phases of the Reformation under Henry VIII. It was he who would prepare the nullification of Henry's marriage to Catherine of Aragon and who would officiate at the marriage to Anne Boleyn.[14]

But, under Henry, the pace of Reformation was slow, even slower, if not retrograde, in the final years of his reign, 1539-46. Consequently, it is not at all surprising that Cranmer's preface, which was first printed in the 1540 second edition, is both cautious and tentative. He adopts a brilliant rhetorical strategy of characterising the new governmental policy of distributing the English Bible as the moderate position between two opposing extremes. This is an early formulation of the policy of moderate reform. There is nothing in Cranmer's preface – except the endorsement of the Act of Royal Supremacy – that contradicts a Catholic position.

> For two sundry sorts of people, it seemeth much necessary that something be said in the entry of this book. . . . For truly some there are that be too slow, and need the spur;

some other seem too quick, and need more of the bridle. Some lose their game by short shooting, some by overshooting. Some walk too much on the left hand, and some too much on the right. In the former sort be all they that refuse to read, or to hear the scriptures in the vulgar tongues; much worse they that also let or discourage the other from the reading thereof. In the latter sort be they, which by their inordinate reading, undiscreet speaking, contentious disputing, or otherwise, by their licentious living, slander and hinder the Word of God most of all other, whereof they would seem to be greatest furtherers.[15]

Most of the remaining preface consists of passages quoted from the early Christian writers John Chrysostom (d. 407) and Gregory of Nazianzus (d. 389). The reliance on quotation is strategic. Clearly, Cranmer wants to avoid any charge of novelty in his position. Thus, he shows that the people's study of scripture in their native languages was characteristic of the early church.

The long passage from Chrysostom insists that people of all classes profit from frequent and private reading of scripture. Direct recourse to scripture will be the basis of morality: 'the reading of scripture is a great and strong bulwark against sin'. Cranmer summarises the message of Chrysostom in social terms: 'Herein may princes learn how to govern their subject; subjects obedience, love and dread to their princes.'[16] This political function was certain to please those in authority.

The passages from Gregory of Nazianzus,

on the other hand, warn of the danger of undisciplined or uncontrolled interpretation of scripture. It argues that an individual may not contradict the doctrine established by the church. Indeed, one must check the urge to speculate beyond the accepted norms of the faith. He cautions against 'tongue itch', 'exquisite judgments', 'sophistry or talking craft' and 'babblers'. Gregory even says 'I forbid to reason,' by which he means a condemnation on private opinions or speculations.[17]

'For speculation,' saith he [i.e. Gregory of Nazianzus], 'either high cunning or knowledge, if it be not stayed with the bridle of fear to offend God, is dangerous and enough to tumble a man headlong down a hill. Therefore,' saith he, 'the fear of God must be the first beginning, and as it were, an ABC, or an introduction to all them that shall enter to the very true and most fruitful knowledge of Holy Scriptures.'[18]

Coverdale's Legacy

It is difficult to characterise Coverdale's style because his versions depend so heavily on Tyndale and Luther. Sure enough, he sometimes introduces unidiomatic 'Germanisms', as in Genesis 25:16, where he uses 'land-princes' or in Romans 8:26, where he has 'unoutspeakable' (*Landesfürsten* and *unaussprechlich* are ordinary German words). Having learned from the master Tyndale, Coverdale sometimes adopts a colloquial style. One scholar even calls it 'racy'.[19] He uses 'good luck' in Psalm 45:5 and 'tush' for vividness (as in 1 Thess. 5:3). Several of his renderings produce unintentional humour, as in the phrases 'there is no more

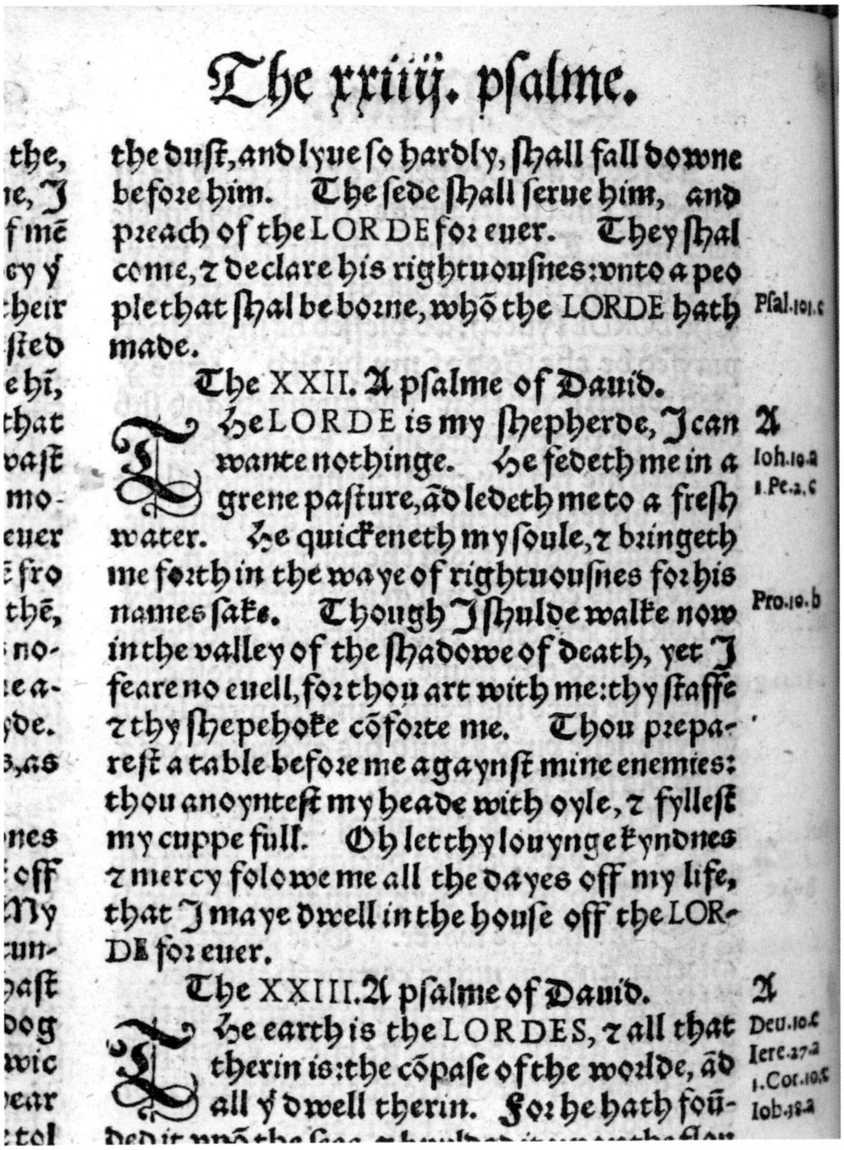

The xxiiij. psalme.

the duſt, and lyue ſo hardly, ſhall fall downe before him. The ſede ſhall ſerue him, and preach of the LORDE for euer. They ſhal come, z declare his rightuouſnes: vnto a peo ple that ſhal be borne, whō the LORDE hath made. *Pſal.101.c*

The XXII. A pſalme of Dauid.

THe LORDE is my ſhepherde, J can wante nothinge. He ſedeth me in a grene paſture, aō ledeth me to a freſh water. He quickeneth my ſoule, z bringeth me forth in the waye of rightuouſnes for his names ſake. Though J ſhulde walke now in the valley of the ſhadowe of death, yet J feare no euell, for thou art with me: thy ſtaffe z thy ſhepehoke cōforte me. Thou prepa- reſt a table before me agaynſt mine enemies: thou anoynteſt my heade with oyle, z fylleſt my cuppe full. Oh let thy louynge kyndnes z mercy folowe me all the dayes off my life, that J maye dwell in the houſe off the LOR- DE for euer. *Ioh.10.a / 1.Pe.2.c / Pro.10.b*

The XXIII. A pſalme of Dauid.

THe earth is the LORDES, z all that therin is: the cōpaſe of the worlde, aō all y dwell therin. For he hath fou- ded it vpō the ſee, ... *Deu.10.c / Iere.27.a / 1.Cor.10.c / Iob.38.a*

Fig. 4.6. *Coverdale's masterpiece was the translation of the Psalms. This was also his most influential contribution, for his Psalms remained the basis for the version in the Great Bible and, most importantly, for the* Book of Common Prayer. *The illustration is of Psalm 23, 'The Lord is my shepherd,' which is here labelled Psalm 22 because Coverdale is following the Vulgate text (according to the Septuagint).*

A transcription with modernised spelling would run as follows: 'The Lord is my shepherd. I can want nothing. He feedeth me in a green pasture, and leadeth me to a fresh water. He quickeneth my soul, & bringeth me forth in the way of righteousness for his name's sake. Though I should walk now in the valley of the shadow of death, yet I fear no evil, for thou art with me: thy staff & thy sheephook comfort me. Thou preparest a table before me against mine enemies: thou anointest my head with oil, & fillest my cup full. Oh let thy loving kindness & mercy follow me all the days of my life, that I may dwell in the house of the Lord forever.'

treacle at Galaad' (Jer. 8:22) and 'thou shalt not need to be afraid for any *bugs* by night' (Psalm 91:5). This last phrase has given the Coverdale Bible an unforgettable moniker – the 'Bug Bible'. Generally, however, he was as nimble at translating and editing the Bible as he was at reacting to the shifting winds of English policy.

Coverdale was conscious of his function as editor. Readers consistently note that his revisions are appreciably smoother than the Tyndale originals. For example, Coverdale retained over ninety-five percent of Tyndale's version of the Sermon of the Mount, but the few changes add elegant touches. With Coverdale, the first part of Tyndale's 'Happy art thou . . . upon this rock I will build my congregation' becomes the classic 'Blessed art thou'. Similarly, in Matthew 5, Coverdale improved 'maintainers of peace' (Tyndale) to 'peacemakers' and 'if the salt be once unsavoury' (Tyndale) to 'if the salt has lost its saltiness'.

Coverdale's most significant contributions were in the parts of the Bible Tyndale had not translated. His renderings of the Psalms, which had a greater impact than any other segment of his translation, possessed both an oratorical dignity and a poetic verve befitting the hymn-genre. Eventually, Coverdale's Psalms became the basis for the Psalms in the *Book of Common Prayer*, whence they entered the King James Version. Indeed, a major criticism of the first edition of the Bishops' Bible (1568) was the failure to use Coverdale's Psalms. Thus, many of the Psalm phrases so familiar to our ears, such as 'the valley of the shadow of death' (Psalm 23), originated with Coverdale. Comparison of the first edition of his Psalms (1535) with the new version he produced for the Great Bible (1539 etc.) shows that Coverdale was also successful

in revising his own translations. The 1535 version of the opening of Psalm 46 has a palpably wooden pedantry. Read the following verses aloud: 'In our troubles and adversity, we have found that God is our refuge, our strength and help. Therefore we will not fear, though the earth fell, and though the hills were carried into the midst of the sea.' The Great Bible revision combines a boldness and a melodic confidence: 'God is our hope and strength, a very present help in trouble. Therefore will we not fear though the earth be moved and the hills be carried in the midst of the sea.' The King James Version could do little to refine this formulation: 'God is our refuge and strength: a very present help in trouble. Therefore will not we fear, though the earth be removed: and though the mountains be carried into the midst of the sea.'

A special quality of Coverdale's career as translator of scripture is his caution. Although there is some doubt as to its reliability, a record indicates that his first biblical project was to translate the Vulgate into Latin in about 1527.[20] This would have been more palatable to conservatives who were not receptive to Erasmus's Bible. His 1535 Bible is grounded substantially in the Vulgate. He published a New Testament diglot of his English translation and the Latin Vulgate in 1537 in order to demonstrate conformity with the traditional Latin version. The 1535 Bible even uses the Catholic 'penance' instead of the Protestant 'repentance' in Matthew's Gospel. The Great Bible is less dependent on the Vulgate. Nonetheless, in this edition, Coverdale set an important precedent for the ideal of having 'no private or contentious opinion'. There is a sidenote at Romans 3:28 in the 1535 Bible, stating 'some read by faith alone', which is a cautious acknowledgement of Luther's blunt translation. The Great Bible excludes this and all such notes. This issue of theological notes would rankle the subsequent history of the English Bible until the King James Version decisively opted for the approach of Coverdale's Great Bible.

Coverdale's influence on the English Bible lives on. It began in his own translation and publication of the first complete printed English Bible that had royal permission to circulate. It continued in his second edition of 1537, which gained royal licence. The climax was his work on the Great Bible, which received royal authorisation. It is also possible that Coverdale played some part in the creation of the Geneva Bible, and we know that the Coverdale Bible was one of several that the King James translators were instructed to use in their work, especially his beautiful rendition of the Psalms, which has been enshrined in the *Book of Common Prayer*.

ENDNOTES TO CHAPTER FOUR

1. *Coverdale Bible 1535* 1975, fol. + 4ᵛ ('A Prologe: Myles Coverdale unto the Christian Reader').
2. *Coverdale Bible 1535* 1975, fol. +4ʳ ('An Epistle unto the Kinges Highnesse').
3. *Coverdale Bible 1535* 1975, fol. A1ᵛ of Apocrypha section ('The Translatoure unto the reader').
4. Except that the title page and preliminaries are thought to have been printed in London (Southwark), by James Nicholson.
5. Mozley 1953, 112-14. The statement is attributed to Henry VIII in William Fulke's attack against the Catholic Rheims New Testament, *Defence of the Translation of the Holy Scriptures into English*, first published in 1583.
6. MacGregor 1968, 123.
7. See Mozley 1953, 121.
8. *Coverdale Bible 1535* 1975, fol. +2ʳ ('An Epistle unto the Kinges Highnesse').
9. *Coverdale Bible 1535* 1975, fol. +3ᵛ ('An Epistle unto the Kinges Highnesse').
10. Pollard 1911, 261-2 (footnote) and Bray 1994, 179.
11. MacGregor 1968, 132.
12. MacGregor 1968, 137.
13. Chadwick [1964] 1990, 123.
14. See MacCulloch 1996 for detailed information.
15. Bray 1994, 234 (Cranmer's Preface to the Great Bible, 1540), punctuation modified.
16. Bray 1994, 238.
17. Bray 1994, 240-1.
18. Bray 1994, 242.
19. Bruce 1978, 61.
20. See Bobrick 2001, 143.

CHAPTER FIVE
EXILE

I see the wolves coming towards the flock; as at this
point I warn you the wolves be coming out of Geneva and
other places of Germany; they have sent their books
before them full of pestilent doctrine, blasphemy and
heresy to infect the people.[1]
— *Bishop John White at the funeral of Queen Mary*

There are good reasons for arguing that the English Reformation begins in earnest with the reign of Edward VI. The Edwardian Reformation brought in the first English liturgy and a rigorously Protestant creed; the churches were whitewashed in a legislated action of iconoclasm; and in the place of images the Bible in English appeared in unprecedented numbers. The primacy of Rome may have ended in 1534, but it was only under Edward that English Christianity started to look and sound different. These events had little continuity with Henry's policies. The government's programme of reform had no momentum whatsoever in the final years of Henry's rule. As early as 1539, the Act of Six Articles declared such Protestant positions as opposition to clerical celibacy and transubstantiation capital offences. Perhaps all Henry had ever wanted was Catholicism without the pope. Thomas Cromwell, who was the architect of the Henrician Reformation, had dramatically expanded the authority of the state when he made the king supreme head of the church. With the dissolution of English monasteries, he also redistributed much of the church's vast wealth into the coffers of the crown and gentry. But as he proceeded toward reform in practice and doctrine, the movement ended. Cromwell himself was executed on 28 July 1540 on trumped-up charges of treason and heresy.

Before that, Cromwell had legalised and promoted the English Bible. That was a major success. The Bible became the authorising principle for religious change; the basis of a new religious sensibility; and, very broadly, a new foundation for English culture. Yet in the aftermath of Cromwell's execution, the Bible revolution stalled. The last five years of Henry's reign would witness the reprinting of only one partial Bible, a New Testament in the version of the Great Bible (10 November 1546). In the Convocation of 1542, Bishop Stephen Gardiner urged the creation of a new translation that would be based more on the Latin Vulgate and would use a latinate (technical) vocabulary. This conservative ploy to redirect the Bible revolution prefigures some elements of the Douai-Rheims version, the first English version for Catholics. Some have thought that Archbishop Cranmer played this difficult hand brilliantly. He referred the matter to the universities for review, knowing that nothing would be likely to come of that. More ominously, new injunctions in 1543 expressly forbid any 'unlicensed' person, explicitly including women under that category, to read the Bible. They also outlaw Bibles with notes. A result of this last stipulation is that many pre-Edwardian Bibles survive with their notes defaced.

Edward VI

Whether one calls his reign the beginning of the real thing or its resumption, it is certainly true that the English Reformation reached its most advanced progression under Edward.

Edward, however, became King of England at the age of nine. Naturally, much care was expended on his education. And he turned out to be a star pupil, perhaps even more so than his several gifted relatives. By the time he died at the age of 15, he had mastered a rigorous Christian-humanist curriculum, a sign of the great triumph of both humanism in general and biblical studies in particular. Roger Ascham (1515/16-68), better known as the tutor and then advisor of his half-sister Elizabeth, and John Cheke, Regius Professor of Greek at Cambridge University, were his most distinguished teachers. Cheke, who would go to exile in Strasbourg upon Mary's accession, was then working on a fresh translation of the New Testament, although the fragments of it (Matthew and the beginning of Mark) would not be printed until the

mid-nineteenth century.[2] Under their tutelage, the boy became fluent in Greek. He also regularly attended sermons by the leading reformers, all of them supported by the government. Among those were Hugh Latimer, Nicholas Ridley, Martin Bucer and John Knox. He is said to have taken careful notes, all of which have disappeared. Others of his school exercises have survived, including some Greek compositions.

Regency was necessary. Edward was precocious, but still only nine. His father's will established that sixteen trustees would form the regency to be headed by Edward's uncle, Edward Seymour, the Duke of Somerset. The Protestant dominance in the council of regency was partially an accident of events. After her marriage to Henry in July 1543, Catherine Parr, his sixth wife, became increasingly Protestant in her convictions. She, who had been the childhood confidante of Princess Mary, was the force behind Henry's reconciliation with both of his daughters. Edward called her 'mother', and, until her death in 1548, she attended to his upbringing, including the supervision of his education and the appointment of humanist tutors with Protestant leanings. She also organised the project to translate Erasmus's *Paraphrases of the New Testament*. Moreover, the major conservative power in England, the Howard family, suffered a crushing blow in autumn 1546. Its heir, Henry, Earl of Surrey, was executed on charge that he had plotted to become king. According to Diarmid Mac-Culloch's account, the disablement of this conservative (essentially Catholic) family was an unforeseen boon to the Protestants, as they took over the government upon Henry's death in January 1547.[3]

There would be two phases in the regency. The first, under Edward Seymour,

The burning of Tharchbishop of Cant. D. Tho. Cranmer, in the town dich at Oxford, with his hand first thrust into the fyre, wherwith he subscribed before.

L. Receiue my spirit.

Frier Iohn.

Thus haue you the full scorpe concernynge the lyfe and death of this reuerend Arche- partes yet be ertant, and peraduenture (if God geue time and life) may hereafter be published:

Fig. 5.1. Thomas Cranmer's Martyrdom from Foxe's Book of Martyrs. *While exiled in Frankfurt and Basel, John Foxe began writing church history from the perspective of martyrdom. His 1563* Acts and Monuments of these Later and Perilous Days, *commonly called* The Book of Martyrs, *was a sensation. It is an important source of information, not always reliable, for the English Reformation. Archbishop Cranmer was imprisoned from September 1553 till his death in Oxford on 21 March 1555. In the weeks before his execution, he signed six abjurations of his faith, but on the day of his execution, to the dismay of the government, he openly confessed his Protestant faith. At the stake, he showed his remorse over the recantations, putting his right hand into the flames.*

lasted until October 1549; the second under John Dudley, Duke of Northumberland, lasted until Edward's death on 6 July 1553. Just months after Edward's accession, on 31 July 1547, Edward Seymour issued new injunctions for governing the church. They provided for a massive promotion of the English Bible. More radically, they also outlawed images, processions and the cult of the saints. The iconoclasm was mostly orderly. Within two years, medieval art had largely vanished from English churches. Endowments (called chantries in English parlance of the time) were dissolved as well. Archbishop Thomas Cranmer intended the chantries to be converted to charity funds. In December 1547, however, Parliament assigned those considerable proceeds to the crown, most of which was wasted in a war against Scotland. This war was a major reason for Seymour's fall from power. Yet before that happened, he also secured approval for the *Book of Common Prayer* in 1549, the first English-language liturgy. The 1549 version still uses Catholic language and concepts. This was intended in part to appease Charles V, who was still riding the crest of his complete victory over German Protestants in the Schmalkaldic War. For example, the words describing the Eucharist would not offend a traditional Catholic: 'The body of our Lord Jesus Christ which was given for thee, preserve thy body and soul unto ever lasting life.'

Upon his rise to dominance in the regency council, John Dudley was even more aggressive in his religious policy, and, as some would say, less circumspect, than Seymour had been. He did not feel a need to make concessions to Catholic sensibilities for fear of Charles V. After all, the emperor's fortunes, which reached a peak in his 1547 triumph over the Protestant princes of Germany, slumped after 1551. So powerful had the Catholic emperor been at the time of Edward's accession that, for Protestants, England was one of the few hopeful spots on the map. All of that would flip. Mary's accession ended Protestantism in England. The Revolt of the Princes in 1552, with the assistance of France, completely reversed Charles's triumph over the Protestants; the Holy Roman Empire returned to the pre-1547 state of having a rough parity of Catholic and Lutheran territories. Nonetheless, Edwardian England had profited from Charles's temporary hegemony after 1547. With the eclipse of Protestant fortunes in the Holy Roman Empire, some important reformers sought refuge in England. Among them were the theologian Martin Bucer and the Hebrew specialist Immanuel Tremellius.

During Dudley's regime, Cranmer produced the second edition of the *Book of Common Prayer* in November 1552. This liturgy left little room for Catholic consciences. Now, there is no real presence in the Eucharist: 'Take and eat this in remembrance that Christ died for thee and feed on him in thy heart by faith.' The Elizabethan church, although it was formally based on the 1552 edition, would return to the formulation of 1549: 'The Body of our Lord Jesus Christ which was given for thee, preserve thy body and soul unto ever lasting life.' On 12 June 1553, only three weeks before Edward's death, Dudley introduced the *Forty-Two Articles*, an uncompromisingly Protestant creed for England. It was also a creed that mandated several Calvinist positions. Article 17 endorsed a Calvinist or Zwinglian sounding doctrine of predestination and Article 30 defined the Eucharist in memorialist terms, as first endorsed in the Swiss Reformation. Others, such as Article 11 on justification by faith alone, had a more generically Protestant cast.[4]

Edwardian Bibles

The Injunctions of 31 July 1547, which technically renewed the royal injunctions of 1538, also expanded the mandate to disseminate scripture. The government removed virtually all constraints and conditions for printing the English Bible. The Bible inundated the country as a result – some forty imprints appeared during Edward's brief reign. Indeed, this may have set a precedent for a policy of not regulating the distribution of the Bible (implicitly observed by Elizabeth as well). Several Bibles reprint authorising statements used during the Henrician phase of the Bible revolution (1535-41), making slight alterations to reflect the new circumstances of government. Some declare the translation to be the one 'appointed to be read in the churches';[5] others assure readers that they had been 'perused by the commandment of the King's majesty and his honourable counsel,

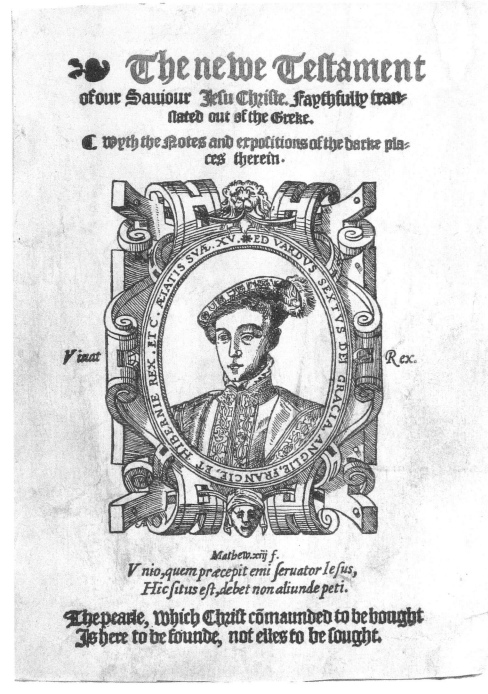

Fig. 5.2. *Edward VI was only nine years old when he succeeded his father, Henry VIII, in 1547. He died only six years later of tuberculosis. His government promoted far-reaching Protestant reforms, including the dissemination of the Bible in English. Injunctions of 1547 renewed the requirement, as expressed in the Injunctions of 1538, that a folio Bible be made accessible to all in every church in the realm. Altogether, some forty Bibles would be printed during his reign. Many of them displayed the crown's explicit endorsement, as in this example, a 1552 edition printed by Richard Jugge.*

and by them authorised'.[6] Several even appeared with portraits of Edward on the title page (see fig. 5.2).

The pace of publication was furious. The diverse array of versions was dazzling. Among the imprints were various versions by William Tyndale; the title pages of these now proudly credit the translator by name. Great Bibles reappeared, as did John Taverner's Bible (which was a 1539 revision of the Matthew's Bible). Even the old Coverdale New Testament was reissued. There were no projects to create a genuinely fresh translation, but several new formattings of the older versions were produced. The great publisher Richard Jugge created a revision of Tyndale in 1552. Edmund Becke undertook a revision and alteration of the notes to the Matthew's Bible. John Daye also produced a revision of the notes to the Matthew's Bible in 1548. Reinold Wolf published a Coverdale version that was revised according to Tyndale's renderings.[7] The first edition of the English translation of Erasmus's *Paraphrases of the New Testament* appeared in 1549, answering the new requirement of the injunction of 1547 that this work, too, be set up in every church in the realm. From distant, but keenly interested, Geneva, Sebastian Castellio dedicated his new Latin translation to Edward VI in 1551.[8] The English Bible was in ferment.

The lack of uniformity – however delightful the biblical chaos may appear in retrospect – may have been a reason why some of the Marian exiles decided to launch a new project to translate the Bible. The Great Bible was influential in Edward's reign but it obviously had not set a standard. Lack of uniformity suggests instability – a problem that would have been felt ever more keenly with each new imprint.

Mary I

The prime cause of the creation of the Geneva Bible was Queen Mary. Mary I has elicited singularly unsympathetic treatment in historical assessments of Tudor England. Nonetheless, she had many distinctions. One is that she was the first woman crowned ruler of England. No one would deny that she was a person of culture, who had enjoyed an excellent education. She was able to appreciate the scholarly developments of the Renaissance. Educational works by major humanist authors were dedicated to her in her youth. At the request of Queen Catherine and with the assistance of Nicholas Udall, Princess Mary had translated Erasmus's paraphrase of the Gospel of John into English. This is the translation that Protestants under Edward VI would promote.

She was devoutly Catholic. Some say fanatically so. A woman of conviction, she was prepared to die for her faith when Edward, in March 1551, denied her the right to have the Catholic Mass celebrated in England. She, however, prevailed, in part through Charles V's intervention.

Mary succeeded Edward to the throne in accord with the terms of the Act of Succession of 1544. Edward, however, had overturned this act by declaring that Lady Jane Grey, the great-granddaughter of Henry VII (and great-niece of Henry VIII) was the rightful heir. Jane Grey's father-in-law just happened to be John Dudley, and it was he who machinated this plot. Dudley and Grey paid for this with their lives, even though it was reported that Grey was initially unwilling to lay claim to the throne. The challenge was well organised and well executed. Grey was declared Queen but her claim fell flat.

Mary's succession – which because of

Edward's action was technically a revolution – went relatively smoothly, in large part because the vast majority of the English felt she was the rightful heir. People of London proclaimed her Queen on 19 July 1553, and they did so even though she did not conceal her intention of restoring Catholicism.

Certainly many people worried about this and perhaps even more worried about her matrimonial status. She was thirty-seven and single when she became Queen. Whom would she marry? Would she be able to produce an heir?

Unquestionably, her least popular move was the marriage to Philip II of Spain, the son of Charles V. This was a daring initiative, and its success, the union of England and Spain, depended on the couple's fertility – the procreation of an heir. It was, in fact, the announcement of the marriage – and not the executions of Protestants – that provoked the only major rising against her, the revolt by Thomas Wyatt in February 1554. Princess Elizabeth was not implicated directly in this revolt but she was put in prison (essentially placed under house arrest) and held in suspicion thereafter. It is important that Elizabeth had not been a part of the challenge to Mary's accession.

England and Spain married on 25 July 1554. The result was disastrous for Mary and for the history of Catholicism in England.

As bad luck would have it, the marriage even complicated Mary's restoration of Catholicism. The volcanic (and reckless) Gian Pietro Carafa became Pope Paul IV in 1555. He was an earnest reformer, one eager to stamp out Protestantism. He was also an inveterate foe of the Hapsburgs. His policy was resolutely anti-Spanish. He even waged war against Philipp II and Charles V in 1556-7. Mary must have had little joy in her sincere effort to reconcile England with Rome, only to have Rome embark on a policy against half of the royal couple.

On 30 April 1555, the bells of London tolled in thanksgiving for the child that was never born. Mary's pregnancy proved to be a phantom. In September 1555, Philipp left England. The Hapsburg marriage alliance had failed. He only returned once thereafter. In March 1557, he came, not with the hope of producing a child, but rather to persuade Mary to enter war with him against France. The result of that debacle was England's loss of its last continental possession, Calais, a city it had held for over two hundred years (since 1347). Mary was ill, dying almost certainly of cancer. On her deathbed, she had comforting images of angelic children welcoming her to heaven. Her end came on 17 November 1558.

She did, however, reconcile England with Rome. Cardinal Reginald Pole, who became Archbishop of Canterbury upon the degrading of Cranmer, formally brought England back into communion with Rome on 30 November 1554.

On the issue of religion, she exercised leniency at first. She was not a cruel person and did not intend initially to send heretics to the stake,[9] even if historians blame her for prolonging the failed policy throughout her reign. On one basic level, Catholicism had principles that now needed to be reinstated. In early 1554 she began reforming the clergy. All told, perhaps as many as two thousand clerics (roughly 20%) had to be removed. This was undertaken by Bishop Stephen Gardiner, and apparently with enthusiasm. (He had been imprisonment during Edward's regime.) The major reason for dismissal was marriage.

Some stone altars were restored; some

endowments re-established. But Mary lacked the means to buy back the monastic lands. The crown could afford to revive only a few monasteries, most importantly, Westminster. Thomas Cromwell's dissolution of the monasteries had permanently weakened the church.

Some prominent Protestants, beginning with Cranmer, Latimer and Ridley, were incarcerated as early as spring 1554. Almost a year later, executions began. The first victim was John Rogers, the compiler of the Matthew's Bible (1537). He went to the stake on 4 February 1555. Latimer and Ridley followed, bound together, on 16 October 1555. Latimer said, 'we shall this day light such a candle, by God's grace, in England as I trust shall never be put out'. On 21 March 1556, Cranmer made his famous retraction, placing his hand in the flames, as he said: 'This hath offended. Oh this unworthy hand' (see fig. 5.1). Some three hundred Protestants, altogether, would be executed for their faith under Mary. This persecution has ruined her historical reputation, in part because it became the focus of Protestant propaganda, including a masterpiece in the genre, John Foxe's *Acts and Monuments of these Latter and Perilous Days* (1563; preliminary version 1559). Essentially, the gruesome persecution backfired badly, for the public executions horrified people and gave fervour to the Protestant movement. According to Owen Chadwick, her reign made England 'more nearly Protestant'.[10]

Genevan Exiles

Many Protestant leaders escaped. During her five-year reign, some seven hundred to one thousand English Protestants fled to the Continent, mainly to Switzerland and

Germany. They were small in number, but large in influence. The group published an astonishing ninety-eight books and pamphlets supporting their faith.[11] Many of the political and religious leaders of Queen Elizabeth's reign would come from the ranks of the exiles. Altogether, seventeen of twenty-five bishops would be former Continental exiles, although none would come from the Geneva contingent.[12]

The English established expatriate churches in Aarau, Basel, Emden, Frankfurt, Strasbourg, Wesel, Zürich and Geneva.[13] The Genevan expatriates were mostly a break-off group from the English at Frankfurt. A dispute arose there over the use of the 1552 Book of Common Prayer. This liturgy has a strong Calvinist tinge, but many of the Frankfurt English wanted to be uncompromisingly, radically Calvinist. This segment went to Geneva, where Calvin was directing the local reform and was, after many struggles, finally in ascendance. As of the 1550s, Geneva was replacing Zürich as the centre of the universe for Reformed theology.

Geneva was also a centre for biblical philology. The Geneva Academy would be founded in 1559 as the crowning event in the city's distinguished efforts to expand its educational system. The Academy immediately became an international centre for advanced theological study. Its first rector, Theodore de Bèze was arguably the preeminent authority on the Greek New Testament of his generation. He was there, and apparently gave assistance, during the work on the English Bible. Robert Estienne also lived there from 1551 until his death in 1559. While still in Paris and holding the position of 'Printer to the King', he had produced a series of Greek editions of the

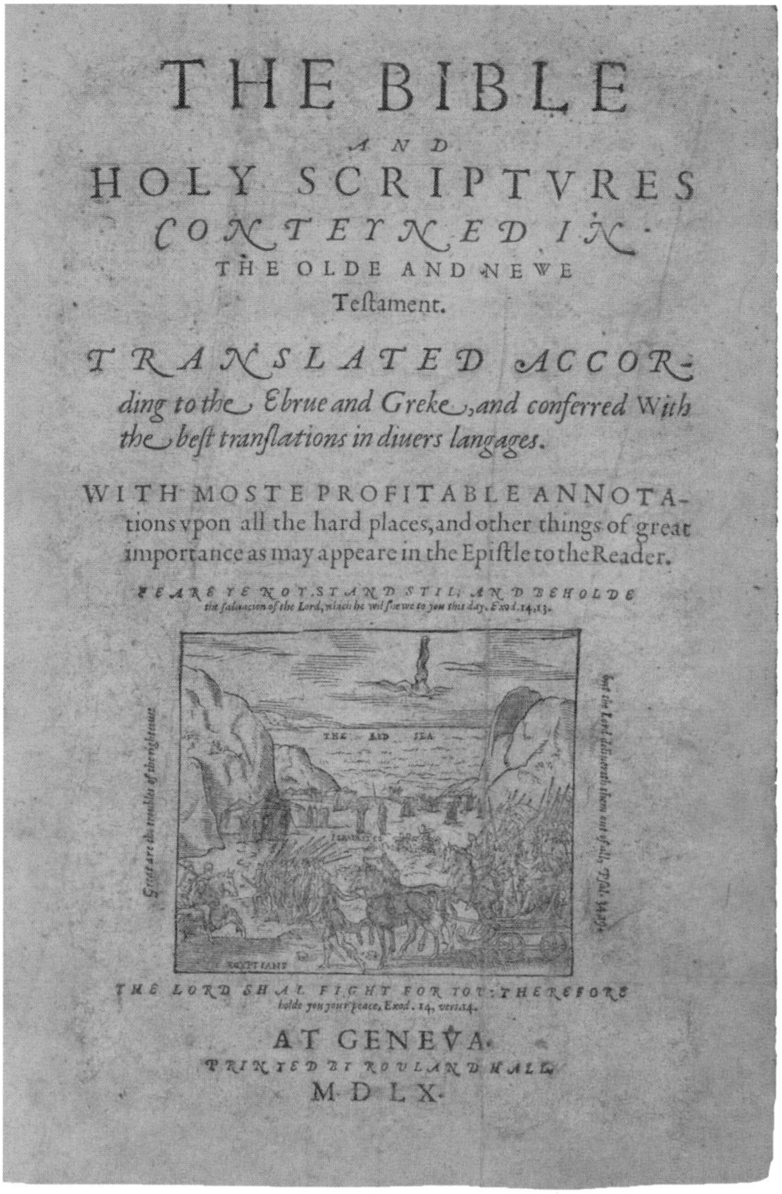

THE BIBLE
AND
HOLY SCRIPTVRES
CONTEYNED IN
THE OLDE AND NEWE
Teſtament.

TRANSLATED ACCOR:
ding to the Ebrue and Greke, and conferred With
the beſt tranſlations in diuers langages.

WITH MOSTE PROFITABLE ANNOTA-
tions vpon all the hard places, and other things of great
importance as may appeare in the Epiſtle to the Reader.

FEARE YE NOT, STAND STIL, AND BEHOLDE
the ſaluacion of the Lord, which he wil ſhewe to you this day. Exod.14.13.

THE LORD SHAL FIGHT FOR YOU: THEREFORE
holde you your peace, Exod. 14. ver.14.

AT GENEVA.
PRINTED BY ROVLAND HALL.
M.D.LX.

Fig. 5.3. Title page of the first edition of the Geneva Bible, 1560. Published by English exiles who fled to the Continent in the reign of Mary, the Geneva Bible was the most popular English translation until the King James Version. The translators, chief among whom was William Whittingham, worked from the Hebrew and Greek, relying also on the Great Bible and Tyndale. The size and presentation of the Geneva Bible contributed to its success: it was a quarto, small and easy to carry; and it included useful, if often polemical notes. It is sprinkled with maps and woodcuts, and has a clear, well spaced, layout.

The title page woodcut shows the Israelites crossing the Red Sea, a fitting image for an exiled people about to return to their homeland. The scriptural quotations bordering the woodcut also seem to speak to their plight, consoling them with the idea that they will prevail through God's aid. Indeed, by the time the Geneva Bible appeared in 1560, the English Protestant movement had prevailed, as it were, for Elizabeth I had succeeded her half-sister Mary to the throne in 1558.

WILLIAM WHITTINGHAM

William Whittingham is a lesser-known but significant contributor to the Reformation. Educated at Brasenose College, Oxford, he also studied in France and Germany. He left England in 1553, when Mary ascended the throne, to become a pastor of English exiles at Frankfurt. In 1559 he succeeded John Knox as the leader of the English congregation in Geneva. While in Geneva, he translated the New Testament into English in 1557. When many returned to England in 1558 (after Mary's death), Whittingham did not leave Geneva until the entire English Bible was published in 1560. He served in France until 1562, and then he returned to England as the Dean of Durham Cathedral. There he suffered some criticism, perhaps because of his strong Puritan sensibilities, and was even charged with not having been properly ordained. He died in 1579, before the case was decided. In addition to his work on the Bible, Whittingham also composed metrical translations of some of the Psalms in the English and Scottish Psalters.

he also directed the on-going revisions of the French Olivétan Bible.[14] The definitive version would appear in 1588, well after Calvin's death in 1564, but with a heavy debt to his revisions.

There is considerable uncertainty about the work of the Geneva translators. The Preface credits 'many godly and learned men', who laboured somewhat more than two years. Who were they? For sentimental reasons, it is common to argue that such luminaries as Miles Coverdale and John Knox may have been on the team. But there is no evidence for Knox's involvement and no indication that Coverdale's role was significant. An anonymous, sixteenth-century biography of William Whittingham, *The Life of Mr. William Whittingham*, indicates that William Cole, Miles Coverdale, Anthony Gilby, Christopher Goodman and Thomas Sampson were Whittingham's colleagues as he worked on the project. James F. Mozley produced a letter by Coverdale to William Cole in Geneva (22 February 1560) that gives evidence that John Baron, Cole, Gilby and William Williams had remained in Geneva in part to help Whittingham get the Bible through press.[15] It is plausible that Sampson and Gilby were major contributors. Sampson (1517?-89) had been a rising star in the Edwardian clergy. He was to have continued success under Elizabeth, even though he was prominent among the non-conforming clergy. It is not known that he took any degrees, but he did study theology at Oxford. Archbishop Parker was later to deprive him of his deanery at Christ Church Cathedral in Oxford during the Vestiarian Controversy. Gilby (d. 1585) was a graduate of Christ's College, Cambridge (BA 1531-2; MA 1535), where he became expert in the three biblical languages. He

New Testament that culminated, in 1550, in the so-called 'received text', the version that became the standard for centuries. After he fled France and settled in Geneva in 1551, he continued his biblical research and publishing, as did his successors at the press. John Calvin himself was a phenomenal biblical scholar, best known for his set of commentaries on all books of the Bible, with only two exceptions: the Song of Songs and Revelation. Since at least 1546,

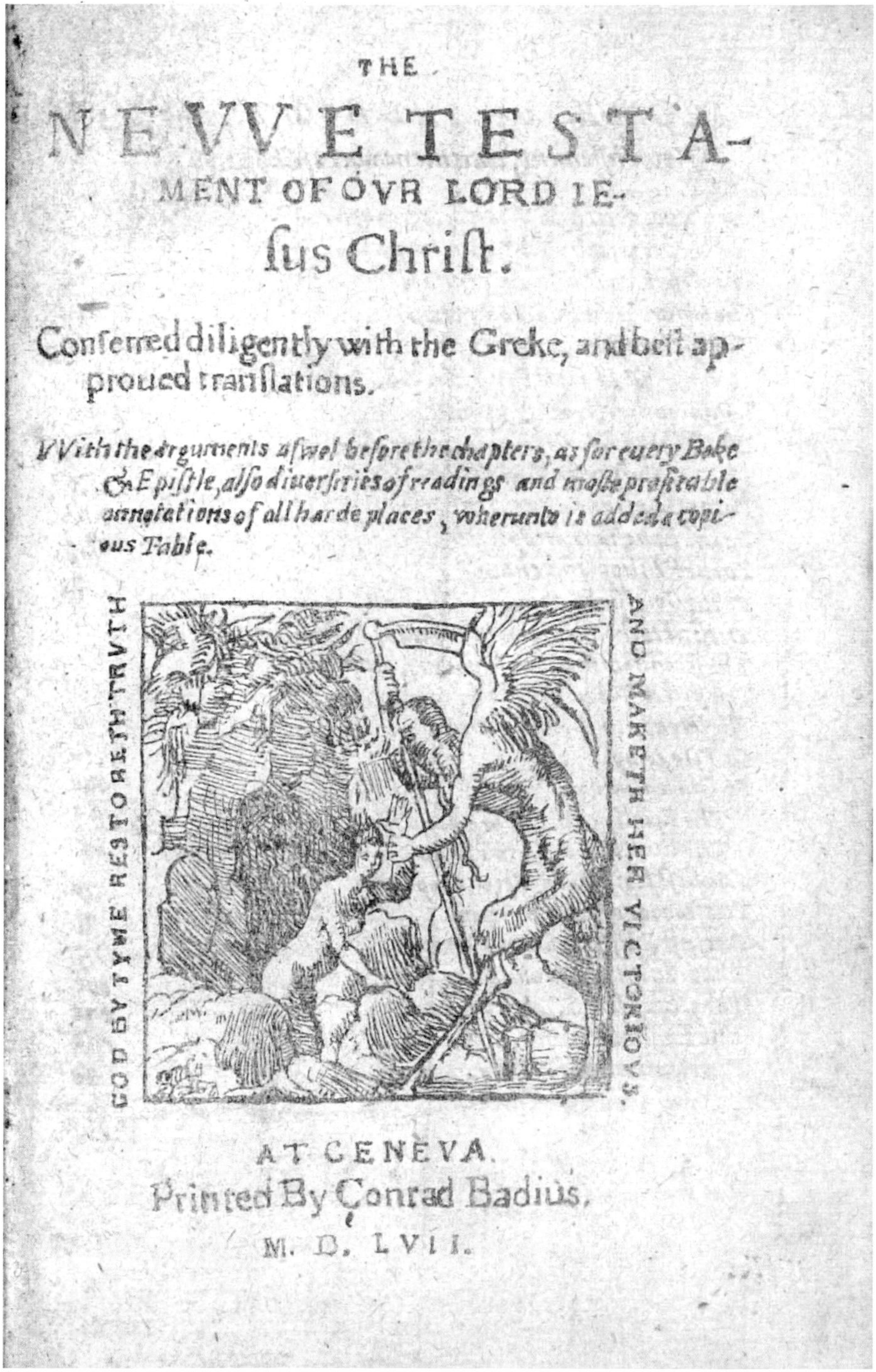

THE

NEVVE TESTA-

MENT OF OVR LORD IE-

ſus Chriſt.

Conferred diligently with the Greke, and beſt ap-
proued tranſlations.

VVith the arguments aſwel before the chapters, as for euery Boke
& Epiſtle, alſo diuerſities of readings and moſte profitable
annotations of all harde places, wherunto is added a copious Table.

GOD BY TYME RESTORETH TRVTH

AND MAKETH HER VICTORIOVS

AT GENEVA.

Printed By Conrad Badius.

M. D. LVII.

Fig. 5.4. *Three years before the Geneva Bible appeared, an English New Testament was published in Geneva. Though the New Testament texts were different, both were the work of William Whittingham. Here, for the first time in an English Bible, verse divisions are used. The title page woodcut of 'Time' freeing 'Truth' from an abyss is bordered by an apt motto for the English exiles in the year of Mary I's death: 'God by time restoreth Truth and maketh her victorious.'*

wrote several pamphlets in favour of Puritan principles, as well as a partisan commentary on Micah. As a Marian exile, he went to Frankfurt, where he became one of the leaders in the dispute over the prayer book. He was a co-author of the *Form of Common Order*, the liturgy used by the Genevan splinter group. He, too, became a prominent non-conformist upon his return to England. It is supposed that he was an active contributor to the Old Testament revisions.[16] The leader of the project was certainly William Whittingham (1524?-79), who was also responsible for a preliminary New Testament version, published in Geneva in 1557. Whittingham was steeped in biblical philology and also fluent in French, for his wife was a Frenchwoman (who is thought by some to have been the sister of John Calvin's wife). He had enjoyed affiliations with Brasenose, All Souls and Christ Church and had become expert in Greek and Hebrew. He succeeded Knox as the minister of the Genevan congregation in 1559. After returning to England, he would become an active opponent of the Elizabethan Settlement. In addition to these Englishmen, it is imperative to note that John Calvin, Theodore de Bèze and other locals were among the 'godly men'. It is altogether appropriate that this version has always been known as the Geneva Bible.

The Bible finally appeared on 10 April 1560, by which time many of the exiles had already returned to Elizabeth's England. But prior to that landmark event, three other English translations had appeared in exile. The first, on June 10, 1557, was a New Testament in English, prepared by William Whittingham as a revision of the Tyndale New Testament. It is the most important precursor for the 1560 Geneva. The second was a translation of the Psalms in 1557,

which was also printed in roman type with verse divisions. The third was a 1559 edition of the Psalms, printed in honour of Queen Elizabeth upon her accession to the throne. An English translation of a work by Calvin, 'Christ is the End of the Law', served as the introduction to the 1557 New Testament.

The Translation of 1560

As far as the Old Testament is concerned, the Geneva version represents a thorough revision of the Great Bible that made it conform more precisely to the Hebrew text. Where close translation was not possible, the literal sense is given scrupulously in the notes. The New Testament was based on Richard Jugge's 1552 revision of Tyndale and the 1557 revision by Whittingham. The translators used a tremendous body of scholarship, all of which was conveniently available in Geneva: the Complutensian Polyglot (1514-17), Robert Estienne's Greek New Testament of 1550, Theodore de Bèze's 1556 Latin translation of the New Testament with notes,[17] the literal Latin translation of Santi Pagnini (1528), Sebastian Münster's edition and Latin translation of the Hebrew Bible (1534-5) and the Zürich Latin translation of the Bible (1543, etc.).[18] By far the greatest impact came from the French Geneva Bibles. Even the most distinctive elements of the format are derived from the French: roman font, copious notes – historical, philological and theological – chapter summaries (called 'arguments'), not to mention explanations of names. Like the French models, the English Geneva uses italics for words interpolated into the translation for the sake of clarity or felicity. Even the five maps and twenty-six woodcut illustrations are taken from French Bibles.[19] Some of these woodcuts even had French inscriptions.

In some passages, it is possible to see that the vast improvements to the English

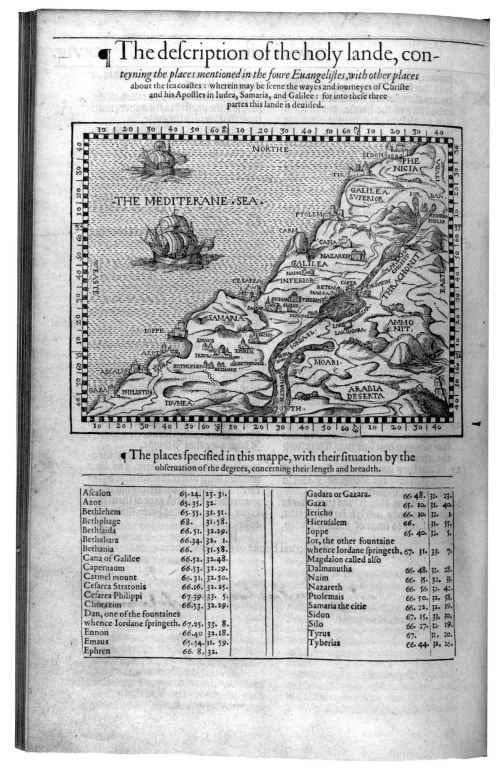

Fig. 5.5. The use of maps lends the Geneva Bible a scientific and authoritative character. Here a map depicts the places mentioned by the four evangelists with a key to important sites in the Holy Land.

translation – often new phrases that would also flow into the KJV – were either inspired by comparison with the French version or borrowed directly from it.

Tyndale 1526	Geneva 1560	French Geneva 1554
Though that prophesying fails, other tongues shall cease, or knowledge vanishes away, yet love falls never away. For our knowledge is imperfect and our prophesying is imperfect. But when that which is perfect, is come, then that which is imperfect, shall be done away. When I was a child, I spoke as a child, I understood as a child, I imagined as a child. But as soon as I was a man, I put away childishness. Now we see in a glass, even in a dark speaking: but then shall we see face to face. Now I know imperfectly: but then shall I know even as I am known. Now abides faith, hope, and love, even these three: but the chief of these is love.	8 Love does never fall away, though that prophesyings be abolished, or the tongues cease or knowledge vanish away. 9 For we know in part, and we prophesy in part. 10 But when that which is perfect, is come, then that which is in part, shall be abolished. 11 When I was a child, I spoke as a childe, I understood as a child, I thought as a child: but when I became a man, I put away childish things. 12 For now we see through a glass darkly: but then *shall we see* face to face. Now I know in part: but then shall I know even as I am known. 13 And now abides faith, hope *and* love, *even* these three: but the chiefest of these *is* love.	8 Charité jamais ne dechet, encore que les Propheties soyent abolies, & que les langues cessent, & que science destruicte. 9 Car nous cognoissons en partie, & prophetizons en partie. 10 Mais quand la perfection sera venue, lors ce qui est en partie, sera aboly. 11 Quand j'estoye enfant, je parloye comme enfant, je jugeoye comme enfant, je pensoye comme enfant: mais quand je suis deuenu homme, j'ay mis hors les choses qui estoyent d'enfans. 12 Car nous voyons maintenant par un miroir en obscurité: mais alors *nous verrons* face à face. je cognoy maintenant en partie: mais a donc je cognoistray comme aussi j'ay esté cognu. 13 Maintenant demourent ces trois choses, foy, esperance, charité: mais la plus grande d'icelles, c'est charité.

Virtually all the significant changes in this passage can be explained in terms of the encounter with the French. In verse 8, the new (and effective) word order and the replacement of 'fails' with 'be abolished' originate in the French. Verse 9 of the Geneva is a major achievement in making the English correspond more literally to the Greek. Tyndale (and most after him) uses the noun phrase 'our knowledge', whereas

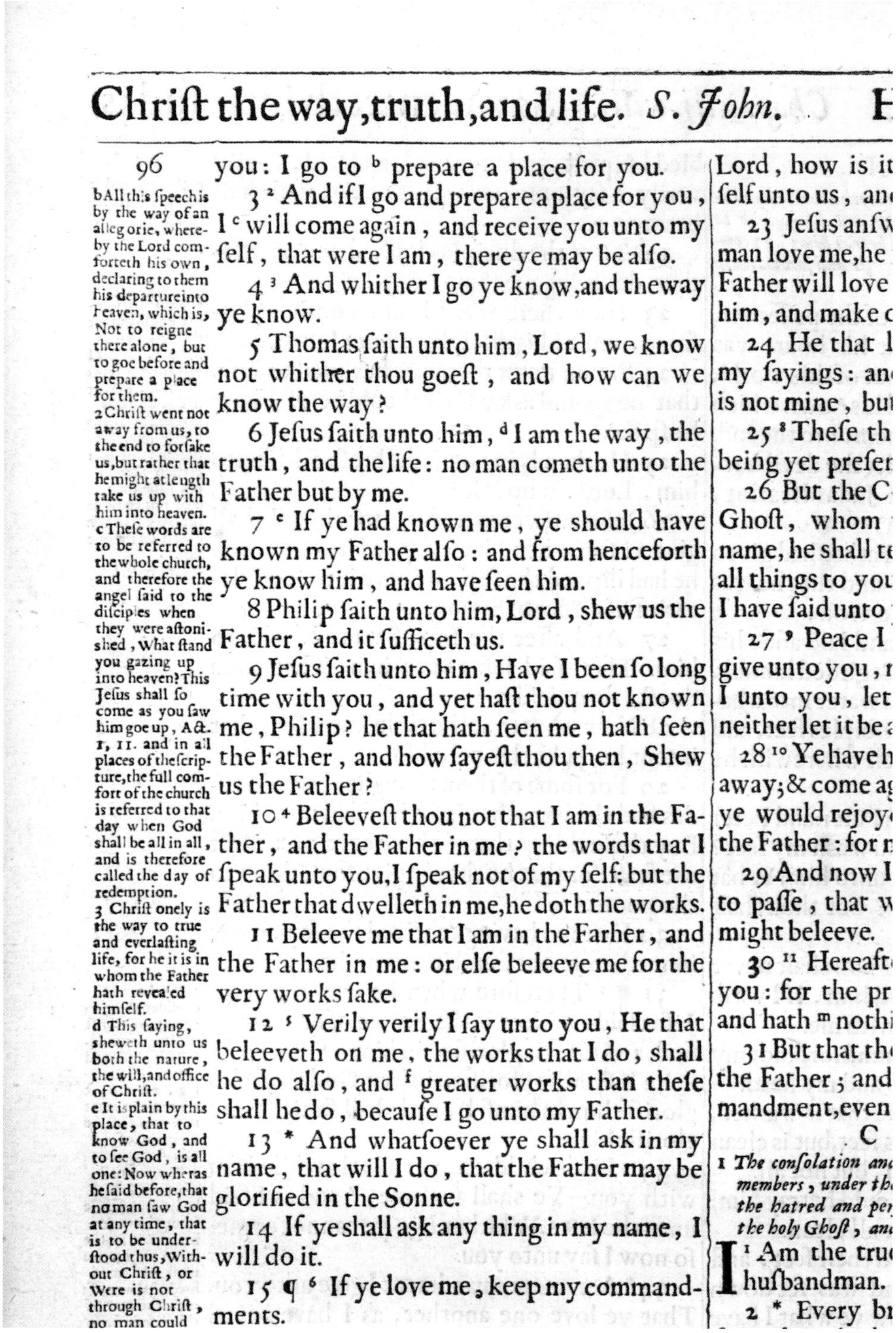

96

b All this fpeech is by the way of an allegorie, whereby the Lord comforteth his own, declaring to them his departure into Feaven, which is, Not to reigne there alone, but to goe before and prepare a place for them.

2 Chrift went not away from us, to the end to forfake us, but rather that he might at length take us up with him into heaven.

c Thefe words are to be referred to the whole church, and therefore the angel faid to the difciples when they were aftonifhed, What ftand you gazing up into heaven? This Jefus fhall fo come as you faw him goe up, Act. 1, 11. and in all places of the fcripture, the full comfort of the church is referred to that day when God fhall be all in all, and is therefore called the day of redemption.

3 Chrift onely is the way to true and everlafting life, for he it is in whom the Father hath revealed himfelf.

d This faying, fheweth unto us both the nature, the will, and office of Chrift.

e It is plain by this place, that to know God, and to fee God, is all one: Now wheras he faid before, that no man faw God at any time, that is to be underftood thus, Without Chrift, or Were is not through Chrift, no man could

you: I go to b prepare a place for you.

3 2 And if I go and prepare a place for you, I c will come again, and receive you unto my felf, that were I am, there ye may be alfo.

4 3 And whither I go ye know, and the way ye know.

5 Thomas faith unto him, Lord, we know not whither thou goeft, and how can we know the way?

6 Jefus faith unto him, d I am the way, the truth, and the life: no man cometh unto the Father but by me.

7 e If ye had known me, ye fhould have known my Father alfo: and from henceforth ye know him, and have feen him.

8 Philip faith unto him, Lord, fhew us the Father, and it fufficeth us.

9 Jefus faith unto him, Have I been fo long time with you, and yet haft thou not known me, Philip? he that hath feen me, hath feen the Father, and how fayeft thou then, Shew us the Father?

10 4 Beleeveft thou not that I am in the Father, and the Father in me? the words that I fpeak unto you, I fpeak not of my felf: but the Father that dwelleth in me, he doth the works.

11 Beleeve me that I am in the Father, and the Father in me: or elfe beleeve me for the very works fake.

12 5 Verily verily I fay unto you, He that beleeveth on me, the works that I do, fhall he do alfo, and f greater works than thefe fhall he do, becaufe I go unto my Father.

13 * And whatfoever ye fhall ask in my name, that will I do, that the Father may be glorified in the Sonne.

14 If ye fhall ask any thing in my name, I will do it.

15 q 6 If ye love me, keep my commandments.

Lord, how is it felf unto us, an

23 Jefus anfw man love me, he Father will love him, and make c

24 He that l my fayings: an is not mine, bu

25 8 Thefe th being yet prefer

26 But the C Ghoft, whom name, he fhall t all things to you I have faid unto

27 9 Peace I give unto you, r I unto you, let neither let it be z

28 10 Ye have h away; & come ag ye would rejoy the Father: for r

29 And now I to paffe, that w might beleeve.

30 11 Hereaft you: for the pr and hath m nothi

31 But that th the Father; and mandment, even

C

1 *The confolation an members, under th the hatred and per the holy Ghoft, an*

I 1 Am the tru hufbandman.

2 * Every bi

Fig. 5.6. *After the Geneva Bible ceased publication, printers occasionally produced a King James Version with Geneva marginal notes. Here is a section of John 14 from a King James Bible printed in Amsterdam in 1672. The 1611 King James has no notes on this section, but clearly there was still a public for the confessional – and copious – notes of the Geneva.*

the Greek has the verb 'we know'. The elegant Geneva phrase 'we know in part' matches the Greek, yet it is probably derived from the French 'nous cognoissons *en partie*'. The use of 'en partie' is the basis of the further changes in verses 10 and 12, too. Verse 11 has the brilliant correction of 'childish things' instead of Tyndale's slightly wrong 'childishness' for the Greek 'tà toû nepíou'. It is almost certain that the French use of 'choses' inspired this, even though we should grant that the English improves on the French 'les choses qui estoyent d'enfans'. Similarly, the classic rendering of 'through a glass darkly', which is a Geneva invention, may have been prompted by the comparison with the French. The traditional rendering in Tyndale of 'in a dark speaking' for the Greek 'en ainígmati' is nearly opaque, a rendering of the phrase that suggests it means the rhetorical trope of enigma. But the alternative French interpretation of the phrase as 'en obscurité' may have helped the translators achieve the stylistic breakthrough.

The division of the Bible into verses was a Genevan innovation. Legend says that Robert Estienne began the task of dividing the text into numbered verses on horseback as he fled from Paris to Geneva. The result was incorporated into his 1551 Greek New Testament. French Bibles began using the divisions in an imprint of 1553 from Robert Estienne.[20] Whittingham introduced them to the English Bible in the 1557 New Testament and the 1560 complete Bible. The beginning of each verse is numbered and indented, making it easy to find and read the text. Today the New American Standard text follows the same format, while the New Revised Standard Version and the New International Version group verses (and their respective numbers) into paragraphs.

The Notes

Notes overwhelm many a page of the Geneva Bible. In some ways, this contradicts the general trend toward doctrinal neutrality in the English Bible. Unquestionably, the notes are the most controversial aspect of the work. The intention is clarification of difficult words and passages, explanation of literal sense or even, occasionally, alternative readings from manuscripts.[21] But theological dogma appears as well, especially in the chapter summaries, which, like the notes, are largely drawn from the French Bible. In the preface, the authors offer a broad justification for their apparatus of notes:

> And considering how hard a thing it is to understand the holy Scriptures, and what errors, sects and heresies grow daily for lack of the true knowledge thereof, and how many are discouraged (as they pretend) because they cannot attain to the true and simple meaning of the same, we have also endeavoured both by the diligent reading of the best commentaries, and also by the conference with the godly and learned brethren, to gather brief annotations upon all the hard places, as well for the understanding of such words as are obscure, and for the declaration of the text, as for the application of the same as may most appertain to God's glory and the edification of his church.[22]

Some of the notes would become notorious for their political implications. When he charged the translators of a new version to avoid marginal notes, James I complained that the Geneva version had notes that were 'very partial, untrue, seditious, and savouring too much of dangerous, and

CHAP. I.

a He sheweth that through the abundant mercie of God we are elect and regenerate to a liuelie hope, 7 And how faith must be tried, 10 That the saluation in Christ is no newes, but a thing prophecied of olde. 23 He exhorteth them to a godlie conuersation, forasmuche as they are now borne a newe by the worde of God.

a Which were Iewes to whome he was appointed to be an Apostle.
b The free election of God is the efficient cause of our saluation, the material cause is Chrißts obedience, our effectual calling is the formal cause, and the final cause is our sanctification.
2.Cor.1.3.
ephe.1.3.
*Or, vnto obedience.
c To wit, of Christ.
d For it is but dead & vaine hope which is without Christ
e Therefore they oght to loke for no earthlie kingdome of the Messias.
f At the day of iudgemens

ETER an Apostle of IESVS CHRIST, to ᵃ the strangers that dwell here and there throughout Pontus, Galacia, Cappadocia, Asia and Bithynia,

2 Elect according to the ᵇ foreknowledge of God the Father vnto sanctification of the spirit, "through ᶜ obedience and sprinkling of the blood of Iesus Christ: Grace and peace be multiplied vnto you.

3 * Blessed *be* God euen the Father of our Lord Iesus Christ, which according to his abundant mercie hathe begoten vs againe vnto a ᵈ liuelie hope by the resurrectió of Iesus Christ from the dead,

4 To an inheritance immortal and vndefiled, and that fadeth not away, reserued in ᵉ heauen for you,

5 Which are kept by the power of God through faith vnto saluation, which is prepared to be shewed in the ᶠ last time:

Fig. 5.7. The confessional bias of the marginal notes of the Geneva Bible is clear in this explanation of 1 Peter 1:2 on the elect. As Calvinists, the English exiles in Geneva believed in a predestined elect. The marginal notes draw attention to proof texts for this and other beliefs. The 1560 Geneva is the first complete English Bible with verse divisions.

traitorous conceits'. These are significant, and will be discussed in Chapter Eight, but the main source of wariness was Calvinism. Calvin's theology informs the apparatus of glosses, even if the vast majority of the notes is exegetical rather than argumentative. As one would expect, several anti-Roman notes appear, especially in Revelation. The anti-Catholic fury increases tremendously in Bibles published in the context of the Wars of Religion in France (especially in the aftermath of such atrocities as the St Bartholomew Day's Massacre of 1572).

Many notes express Calvinist doctrine on election and reprobation. The following are a sample.

> Proverbs 16:4: 'The Lord hath made all things for his own sake: yea even the wicked for the day of evil.' The note says, 'So that the justice of God shall appear to his glory, even in the destruction of the wicked.'

> John 6:37: 'All that the Father giveth me, shall come to me . . . .' The note states, 'God doeth regenerate his elect, and causeth them to obey the Gospel.'

> John 10:26: 'But ye believe not: for ye are not of my sheep, as I said unto you.' The note reads, 'The cause whereof the reprobate cannot believe [because they are not of Christ's sheep].'

> Acts 13:48: '. . . as many as were ordained unto eternal life, believed'. The note explains, 'None can believe, but they whom God doth appoint before all beginnings to be saved.'

> Romans 11:29: 'For the gifts and calling of GOD are without repentance'. The note declares, 'To whom God giveth his spirit of adoption,

and whom he calleth effectually, he cannot perish: for Gods eternal counsel never changeth.'

> Titus 1:2: 'under the hope of eternal life, which God, that can not lie, hath promised before the world began.' The note says, 'Hath willingly, and of his mere liberality promised without foreseeing our faith or works as a cause to move him to this free mercy.'

> 1 Peter 1:2: 'Elect according to the foreknowledge of God . . . .' The note declares, 'The free election of God is the efficient cause of our salvation, the material cause is Christ's obedience, our effectual calling is the formal cause, and the final cause is our sanctification.'

How did the editors explain the non-Calvinist words of Christ in the parable of the Good Samaritan when Jesus said that the priest came down 'by chance'? Here's their best effort: 'For so it seemed to man's judgment, although this was so appointed by God's counsel and providence.' Many of the notes in Whittingham's 1557 New Testament reappear in the 1560 New Testament. Some were lightly edited. The main difference between the 1557 and 1560 editions is the vast augmentation of the notes in the latter.

The Evolution of the Geneva Translation and Notes

A revised edition of the Geneva New Testament appeared in 1576, the work of Laurence Tomson. Skilled in twelve languages, he based his version on de Bèze's new 1565 Latin translation. The title pages of these Bibles goes so far as to give most credit for the work to de Bèze: *The New*

Testament of Our Lord Jesus Christ Translated Out of the Greek by Theod. Beza.[23] The Tomson version, which perhaps should be called the De Bèze-Tomson Version, immediately gained considerable popularity and, from 1587 onward, was regularly substituted for the 1560 New Testament (but still called the Geneva version). Tomson was a Member of Parliament and also a protégé of Sir William Walsingham, a powerful force in Elizabethan England. (Walsingham promoted both the Geneva Bible and Archbishop Grindal, who, as a liberal, fell afoul of the Queen.) In 1578 and 1579 two Calvinist catechisms were appended to the Geneva Bible, thus adding to the Calvinist emphasis of the notes.

Some imprints of the Geneva Bible have a different version of Revelation. It is based on a Latin translation with notes by Franciscus Junius (François de Jon; 1545-1602). A learned French Huguenot divine, he was the son-in-law and collaborator of Immanuel Tremellius, the great Hebrew scholar. It is not known who put this work into English. The English version of Junius first appeared in *c.* 1592[24] and was first incorporated into a Geneva Bible in 1599.[25]

The publication history of the Geneva Bible attests to its popularity and durability. At least 140 editions were issued between 1560 and 1644. From 1560 to 1611 over 120 editions were published, and from 1575 to 1618 at least one new edition appeared each year in various sizes. In those decades, it dominated English culture. Even Shakespeare used the Geneva Bible.[26] After the release of the King James Bible in 1611 the Geneva retained some popularity for a while, coming out in nearly twenty editions (including New Testaments) until 1644. Curiously enough, a biblical quotation used in 'The Translators to the Reader' section of the King James Bible is from the Geneva version.[27] After 1616, the Geneva was published in Amsterdam, and Archbishop William Laud managed to suppress it almost entirely. In 1644, an Amsterdam edition of the King James was issued with the notes of the Geneva Bible and Junius's notes on Revelation.

In 1643 'The Soldiers' Pocket Bible' containing selected passages from the Geneva Bible was published for the use of Oliver Cromwell's troops 'in this miserable time of War'. More than two hundred years later, during the American Civil War, about fifty thousand copies of this book were reissued to help boost the morale of the Union soldiers.

Though never authorised by Queen Elizabeth, the Geneva Bible won the hearts of English readers and played a major part in strengthening the Puritan movement. Indeed, when the Pilgrims went to North America, it was the Geneva Bible they brought along. (A copy actually used on the Mayflower has survived.[28]) It also became the official version of the Church of Scotland. Despite his subsequent rejection of the version, several editions were dedicated to 'the richt excellent richt heich and michtie prince James the Sext King of Scottis',[29] who was also the future James I of England. The Church of Scotland was determined to see that the people of Scotland became well acquainted with the Geneva Bible. Not only was every parish to have a copy but also every householder with an income over a certain sum had to purchase a copy.

Furthermore, 'searchers' were appointed to make sure that householders possessed their own copy, and if they could not produce one, then they were fined a sum that was greater than the price of a Bible.[30]

ENDNOTES TO CHAPTER FIVE

1. Quoted from King 1989, 221.
2. Herbert 1968, no. 1847.
3. MacCulloch 2001, 7.
4. Bray 1994, 284-311.
5. Herbert 1968, no. 85 (published in 1550).
6. Herbert 1968, no. 89; there are other examples as well.
7. Herbert 1968, no. 80.
8. Darlow and Moule [1903] 1963, no. 6131.
9. See Dickens [1964] 1989, 293-5, for a harsher view of Mary's character.
10. Chadwick [1964] 1990, 123: 'In 1553 England was by no means a Protestant country. It was made more nearly Protestant by the reign of Queen Mary.'
11. Bartlett 1996, 9.
12. MacCulloch 1990, 31.
13. See Garrett 1938.
14. Darlow and Moule [1903] 1963, no. 3716 (the first French Bible Calvin definitely revised).
15. Mozley 1953, 316. See also Lloyd Berry in *Geneva Bible* 1969, 8.
16. Hall 1995, 132, etc., offers a plausible assessment of his role.
17. Darlow and Moule [1903] 1963, no. 6140. The New Testament title page is dated 1556, while the general title page is dated 1557. See Backus 1980, 13-18, on the impact of de Bèze's notes.
18. Darlow and Moule [1903] 1963, no. 6124. This is often referred to as Leo Jud's Latin Bible because he did most of the work on the Old Testament, although he died in 1542 before it was complete. Theodore Bibliander completed the Old Testament and Apocrypha, and Rudolf Gwalter, who would be Bullinger's successor as head of the Zürich church, prepared the New Testament. As of 1564, the Zürich Latin Bible would have a new text, this one based on Pagnini and de Bèze. See Darlow and Moule [1903] 1963, no. 6145.
19. See Darlow and Moule [1903] 1963, no. 3721, the note on Rebul's 1560 Geneva Bible.
20. Darlow and Moule [1903] 1963, no. 3719.
21. In particular, the Geneva Bible offers translations of a few alternative readings from the Codex Bezae, a fifth- or sixth-century manuscript of the Gospels and Acts. See Metzger 1961 and Hall 1995, 131.
22. Geneva Bible 1560, fol. ***4^v.
23. Herbert 1968, no. 146. This is based on an edition of de Bèze's New Testament by Pierre L'Oiseleur de Villers (London, 1574). See Backus 1980, 22-8.
24. Herbert 1968, no. 214.
25. Herbert 1968, no. 248.
26. Noble [1935] 1970 is the classic study of Shakespeare and the Geneva Bible.
27. This is clear in the quotation of 1 Corinthians 14:11.
28. Martin 1961, 51.
29. Herbert 1968, no. 158 (the first version printed in Scotland).
30. See note to Herbert 1968, no. 158.

CHAPTER SIX
QUEEN ELIZABETH VERSION

This is the Jewel that we still love best,
This was our solace when we were distressed.
This book that hath so long concealed itself,
So long shut up, so long hid; but now Lords see,
We here unclasp, forever it is free!
— *Elizabeth I speaking in Thomas Heywood's drama*
If You Know Not Me, *lines 1582-6*

When Mary died on 17 November 1558, Henry VIII's surviving child was proclaimed Queen. In some ways, her accession occasioned more uncertainty than had Mary's. What would happen next? One change became apparent on her coronation day, 15 January 1559. During the elaborate progress from the Tower to Westminster, Elizabeth was presented with an English Bible. She kissed it, elevated it over her head, pressed it to her breast, and thanked the city for it.[1]

The first Parliament of her long reign nullified Mary's repeal of Edward's An Act for the Uniformity of Common Prayer and Administration of the Sacraments. This returned the church to the foundations of the Edwardian prayer book of 1552, though with some important changes. The words of administration of the Eucharist returned farther back to the formulation of 1549, which allowed for understanding an endorsement of the true presence. Moreover, the 'Ornaments Rubric' of 1552 was struck. It had forbidden ministers to wear elaborate garb – in particular, the despised surplice. Now, the clergy was to

revert to the vestments of the 'second year of the reign of Edward VI'. That apparel may have been stately and dignified, but it also dressed the Catholic priesthood. This would touch off the Vestiarian Controversy, and it signals the real differences between the Queen and those with Genevan convictions. Those differences, or the awareness of those differences, would grow, but, for the moment, Protestants were delighted with the general thrust of using the policies in place at the end of Edward's reign as the point of departure for building a new church. No doubt, the more aggressive Protestants, surmising that Elizabeth could not install a Genevan system where a Catholic polity was still functioning, without taking intermediate steps, were hopeful that with time the church might embrace such things as a presbyterian form of government, a simplification of the liturgy and an uncompromisingly Calvinist stance on the sacraments (in particular, a memorialist doctrine of the Eucharist). They were wrong. As her motto indicated, she would remain 'Ever the Same' (*Semper*

Eadem). But the disaffected would grow steadily in number and fervour. The non-conforming Protestants, and not the Catholics, would ultimately be the charge that exploded into civil war in the seventeenth century, but that lay in the distant future. On the whole, Elizabeth would enjoy extraordinary success in charting a middle way, a religious path between Rome and Geneva, albeit far closer to the latter. The policy held for some eighty years. And its launch in 1559 was smooth. As A.G. Dickens wrote, 'few religious revolutions have been more dramatic and momentous than that of 1558-9, yet none have encountered such feeble opposition'.[2]

The Elizabethan Injunctions of 1559 also have a retro-look. Most of the items are verbatim restatements of the Edwardian Injunctions of 1547. As before, the government lays down that the clergy of the realm 'shall provide within three months next after this visitation, one book of the whole Bible, of the largest volume, in English. And within one twelve-months next after said visitation, the Paraphrasis of Erasmus also in English upon the Gospels, and the same set up in some convenient place, within the said church that they have cure of, whereas their parishioners may most commodiously resort to the same and read the same.'[3] This touched off a modest revival of the Great Bible. Between 1559 and 1568 four editions of the Great Bible were produced, as well as two imprints of Jugge's revision of Tyndale's New Testament. Perhaps the days of Edward really were here again.

Yet, that first Elizabethan decade fell far short of the Bible production of Edward's six years. Not even the new Geneva Bible added much output. It was printed only four times between 1560 and 1574 (1560,

twice in 1562, and 1570). Production was modest in large part because of the expectation of a new standard, a new Bible that the Bishops of the realm were preparing. It would be the new official, authorised version.

When the Bishops' Bible finally appeared in 1568, it unleashed a torrent of Bible printing. Between then and 1580, England would produce five editions of the Great Bible, eighteen of the Bishops' Bible and thirteen of the Geneva Bible. In 1575, the Geneva version was finally printed for the first time in England, the presswork of Thomas Vautroullier for Christopher Barker. Thereafter until 1644, it was printed nearly one hundred and fifty times.

The statistics show that in the 1570s the Bishops' Bible successfully replaced the Great Bible as the authorised version. That was, indeed, the principal goal of Archbishop Matthew Parker, the initiator and editor of the project. The Bishops' Bible resulted from the recognition by the government, in particular by Matthew Parker and William Cecil, that the Great Bible was not up to scholarly standards. It could not remain credible for much longer as the Bible 'authorised' for reading in the churches. Indeed, the appearance of the Geneva Bible in 1560, with all of its textual and historical notes, made that patently clear. Why not promote the Geneva Bible? Parker rebuffed it as the Bible that originated in that Continental stem-cell of the growing movement of nonconformity. In a letter sent to Elizabeth, Parker articulated a fear about the translation that was 'not laboured in your realm' (i.e. written in Geneva) and that was beginning to be used even in the churches ('in certain places be publicly used'). As would soon become commonplace, Parker singled out the issue of the 'diverse prejudicial notes which

Fig. 6.1. The Bishops' Bible is a revision of the Great Bible carried out by more than a dozen bishops and other church officials under the direction of Matthew Parker, Archbishop of Canterbury. In 1571 the order went out from Canterbury that every church in the realm had to set up a copy of the Bishops' Bible for the use of the laity, thereby replacing the Great Bible version with this revision. The title page depicts Queen Elizabeth, surrounded by symbolic figures and the royal arms of Ireland and Wales. A tablet below reads, in Latin, 'I am not ashamed of the gospel of Christ, because it is the power of God for the salvation of every believer, Rom 1.'

might have been also well spared'.[4] After all, most of the known translators and many of the Continental exiles, especially those from Geneva, were fast becoming the recognisable leaders of nonconformity. Miles Coverdale himself had worn a black gown – and not his episcopal vestments – at Parker's ordination in 1559. It is, however, difficult to assess the degree of Parker's opposition to the Geneva Bible. It was never subjected to legal suppression. Parker did not object to a petition to grant a licence for the printing of the Geneva Bible.[5] Yet, on the other hand, the fact is that the Geneva Bible was not printed in England until after Parker's death in 1575.

Matthew Parker

John Calvin has been called a 'God-frustrated scholar'. The same could be said of Matthew Parker. In many respects, he was a natural choice to be Elizabeth's first Archbishop of

Canterbury. He had been chaplain to Queen Anne Boleyn, Elizabeth's mother. Even long after Anne's fall, Henry VIII recommended that Parker, 'our well-beloved chaplain', be appointed master of Corpus Christi College, Cambridge, in 1544.[6] Moreover, Parker had not gone into exile under Mary, thus having avoided the tendency of the Marian exiles toward radicalisation. Still, he was very reluctant to accept Elizabeth's appointment. He preferred the life of study at Cambridge, where he had spent most of his career. He was a devoted alumnus of Corpus Christi College and it is largely through his munificence that his college now has a spectacular collection of medieval manuscripts. But, acceding to the royal will, he did accept the appointment and, as Archbishop of Canterbury, he proved, on the whole, to be skilful in overseeing the affairs of the church. After all, he had had considerable experience in administration during his Cambridge years. He also managed to continue his scholarly research as archbishop, evoking the memory of Thomas Cranmer. His greatest scholarly enterprise was the Bishops' Bible. In addition to overseeing the entire project, Parker did much of the work. He translated Genesis, Exodus, Matthew, Mark and 2 Corinthians to Hebrews. He also produced the first edition of the Anglo-Saxon Gospels in 1571.[7]

It was on the heels of the publication of the Geneva Bible that Parker, in 1561, first announced his desire to undertake the project.[8] His plan was to enlist the collaboration of the bishops of the realm. In 1711, John Strype, Parker's first biographer, described the scope of the project:

> The Archbishop took upon him the labour to contrive and set the whole work a going in a proper method, by sorting out the whole Bible into parcels . . . and distributing those

---

MATTHEW PARKER, 1504-75

During his studies at Cambridge, Parker became identified with a group of moderate reformers. He came under the patronage of Anne Boleyn, Henry VIII and Edward VI. But when Mary came to the throne he was stripped of his offices. Nonetheless, he did not go into exile, but chose to live in Catholic England, albeit in obscurity. On 17 December 1559, under Queen Elizabeth, he was consecrated Archbishop of Canterbury. A wise and tolerant man, he preferred scholarship to controversy, maintaining a middle way between the traditions of the past and the demands for more reform.

---

parcels to able bishops and other learned men to peruse and collate, each the book or books allotted to them; sending withal his instructions for the method they should observe; and they to add some short marginal notes for the illustration or correction of the text. And all these portions of the Bible being finished and sent back to the Archbishop, he was to add the last hand to them, and so to take care for printing and publishing the whole.[9]

The exact number of supervisory bishops is not known. Perhaps fifteen. The matter is even more confusing because Parker's list of participants does not match the signatory initials that appear in the Bishops' Bible itself.

A scrap that survives among his papers indicates that he formulated a set of guidelines for the participants in their disparate settings. In a modest way, this approach prefigures the KJV project, even if the specific guidelines, except item one, do not.

Fig. 6.2. The first edition of the Bishops' Bible is a typographical master-piece. It is also the most lavishly illustrated English Bible of the Renaissance. The famous page designs for the King James Version actually derive from the Bishops' Bible. This woodcut, created by the German designer Virgil Solis, depicts chapter three of Genesis. An older Bible from which this illustration is taken had a pictorial image of God that the printer removed (substituting the Hebrew letters for Yahweh) lest using an image would seem too Catholic.

(1) To follow the common English translation, used in the churches and not to recede from it but where it varieth manifestly from the Hebrew or Greek original.

(2) To use such sections and divisions in the texts as Pagnini in his translation useth, and for the verity of the Hebrew to follow the said Pagnini and Münster specially. And generally others learned in the tongues.

(3) To note such chapters and places as containeth matter of genealogies or other such places not edifying, with some strike or note that the reader may eschew them in his public reading.

(4) That all such words as soundeth in the Old Translation to any offence of lightness or obscenity be expressed with more convenient terms and phrases.[10]

Items three and four account for some striking peculiarities of the Bishops' Bible. Many passages deemed 'non-edifying' are indicated by single quotation marks in the margin (e.g. Genesis 10-11; Numbers 2-20; Leviticus 1-8; see fig. 6.5). Apparently, these technical and legal passages, and others like them, promise little of interest to laypeople. Moreover, potentially offensive words were changed, as in 1 Corinthians 6:9, where the Great Bible's 'wantons nor buggers' becomes 'weaklings, nor abusers of selves with mankind'.

The Bishops' Version

All in all, the translation is uneven. Parker ordered a revision of the Great Bible according to the original Hebrew and Greek versions, which was indeed done, but with several compromises. The brief instructions themselves urge the use of Santi Pagnini's literal Latin translation from 1528. That work did not offer a text in the original languages. The use of Münster's edition of 1534-5 is more defensible since it also gives the Hebrew original, but the translators leaned heavily on Münster's parallel translation into Latin. (Of course, Münster's Latin also influenced the KJV translators, but they always – and rigorously – consulted the original Hebrew.) Not all the bishops were linguists. And, indeed, the various sections came out looking rather different despite Parker's chore of revising the whole.

There are several places where the KJV owes more to the Bishops' Bible than to the Geneva or to Tyndale's formulations. It is from the Bishops' Bible that the KJV acquired such expressions as 'fruits meet for repentance' (Matthew 3:8), 'middle wall' (Ephesians 2:14), 'fellow-citizens' (Ephesians 2:19), and 'less than the least' (Ephesians 3:8). One can readily see, from a sample in Ephesians 1, that occasionally the Bishops' Bible exerted more influence on the King James Version than did the Geneva.

Geneva

to be adopted (v.5)
rich grace (v.7)
glorious inheritance (v.18)
made all things subject (v.22)
filleth all in all things (v.23)

Bishops' and King James

adoption of children
riches of His grace
glory of his inheritance
put all things under
filleth all in all

Psalm 23 is perhaps one of the most glaring examples of the shortcomings in the new version. Certainly, the translator tried to follow the Hebrew more exactly, but the result was awkward pedantry.

God is my shepherd, therefore I can lack nothing: he will cause me to repose my self in pasture full of grass, and he will lead me unto calm waters. He will convert my soul: he will bring me forth into the paths of righteousness for his name sake.

Yea though I walk through the valley of the shadow of death, I will fear no evil: for thou art with me, thy rod and thy staff be the things that do comfort me.

Thou wilt prepare a table before me in the presence of mine adversaries: thou hast anointed my head with oil, and my cup shall be brim full.

Truly felicity and mercy shall follow me all the days of my life: and I will dwell in the house of God for a long time.

The Psalmes of Dauid.

ing prayer.

¶ The argument of the first psalme.

¶ The first psalme seemeth to be a preface vnto the residue. It declareth th only hath the true felicitie in this worlde, whose delight is wholly in practi of God. As for the vngodly man, although he seeme for a tyme to prosper a yet his ende is very miserable and wretched.

Fig. 6.3. One hundred and forty-three woodcuts, engravings and maps decorate the Bishops' Bible. Most of the woodcuts are taken from a 1560 German Bible designed by Virgil Solis. Some images, such as this intricate engraved portrait initial, were created for this edition. The initial 'B' of the first Psalm ('Beatus vir' or, as here, 'Blessed is the man') was a major illumination in many medieval manuscripts. This image is a tribute to (and portrait of) William Cecil, soon to be Lord Burghley, the most powerful advisor in Elizabeth's privy council.

The Psalms, by far the least successful segment of the work, are thought to have been the work of Thomas Bickley, Bishop of Chichester. In the preface to the Bible, Parker expressed particular concern about the reception of the new Psalms: 'Let the gentle reader have this Christian consideration within himself that though he findeth the psalms of this translation following, not so to sound agreeable to his ears in his wonted words and phrases, as he is accustomed with, yet let him not be much offended with the work, which was wrought for his own commodity and comfort.' Apparently, the gentle reader was, nonetheless, much offended. In the revision of 1572, the old translation (principally the work of Miles Coverdale), which presum-ably 'sounded agreeable', was printed alongside the new version. As of 1577, the new translation disappeared entirely with one exception (a printing of 1585).

Queen Elizabeth Version

Parker sent the new Bible to the Queen and her Principal Secretary, William Cecil, on 15 October, 1568.[11] The imprint was a monumental panegyric to the Queen.

The royal presence in the Bishops' Bible is reminiscent of the glorification of the royal supremacy in the Coverdale Bible of 1535 and in the title pages of the Great Bibles (1539-41). Moreover, the Lutheran concept of the law versus the gospel, which was so prominent in the Coverdale and the Matthew's Bible, and which would reappear

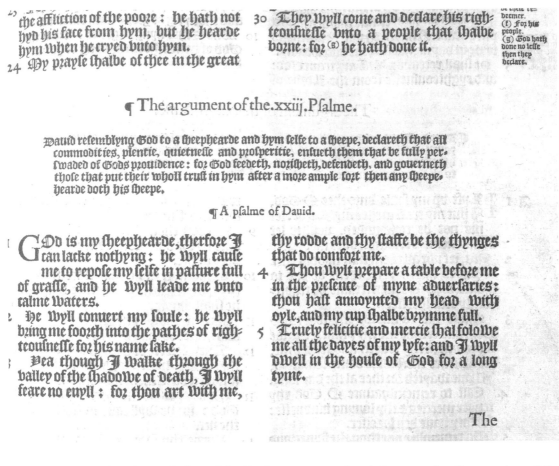

Fig. 6.4. *The Bishops' translation of the Psalms never replaced the more familiar version of the Great Bible (1539). In the 1572 Bishops' Bible, the translations of the Psalms were printed side by side, but by 1577 the Great Bible translation had triumphed. This illustration is of Psalm 23 from the first edition of 1568.*

God is my sheephearde, therfore I can lacke nothyng: he wyll cause me to repose my selfe in pasture full of grasse, and he wyll leade me unto calme waters.

He wyll convert my soule: he wyll bring me foorth into the pathes of righteousnesse for his name sake.

Yea though I walke through the valley of the shadowe of death, I wylll feare no evyll: for thou art with me, thy rodde and thy staffe be the thynges that do comfort me.

Thou wylt prepare a table before me in the presence of myne adversaries: thou hast annoynted my head with oyle, and my cup shalbe brymme full.

Truely felicitie and mercie shal folowe me all the dayes of my lyfe: and I wyll dwell in the house of God for a long tyme.

on the title page of the KJV, has vanished. Nothing detracts from the glorification of Elizabeth as supreme governor of the Church of England (see fig. 6.1).[12] As 'Queen of England, France and Ireland', as well as 'Defender of the Faith' (translations of the Latin titles framing her portrait), and holding the orb and sceptre as symbols of her authority, she dominates the general title page and the woodcut title page of the New Testament. If anything, her presence is even more powerful than had been Henry's in the earlier Bibles. Apart from the allegorical figures, she is the only person represented on the title page. Moreover, she, too, is an allegory of Christian virtue. The two allegorical women are Charity (woman nursing children on the left) and Faith (woman holding an open Bible and the cross on the right). This combination clearly indicates that Elizabeth is Hope, the completion of the triad of Paul's Christian virtues (1 Corinthians 13:13).[13] The Latin passage in the cartouche is translated into English on the New Testament title page: 'I am not ashamed of the Gospel of Christ, because it is the power of God unto salvation to all that believe.'[14] This passage from Romans 1 also appeared most prominently in the representation of Henry on the Coverdale title page (see fig. 4.2; it is in the banderole on the right of the enthroned king in the lower register of the page). The Coverdale and the Great Bible title pages depict the two leading architects of the government's reform programme – Thomas Cranmer and Thomas Cromwell. In the Bishops' Bible version, the title page shows only the Queen. Nonetheless, two splendid copper plate engravings within the book lionise her two weightiest courtiers. Robert Dudley, the Earl of Leicester, appears at the beginning of Joshua. He was the most influential minister at Elizabeth's court in the 1560s and 1570s with strong Puritan sympathies. William Cecil, soon to be Lord Burghley, is in the illuminated B that begins the Psalms ('Blessed is the man'). Cecil was Elizabeth's Principal Secretary and advisor in all affairs of state, especially in the formulation and promulgation of the religious settlement (see fig. 6.3). Although the three engraved

portraits bear no signature, they have been plausibly attributed to the Continental artist Franciscus Hogenberg.[15] The Bible contains no portrait of Parker and he did not sign the two prefaces he contributed. Nonetheless, the table of the genealogy of Christ has a large initial T in which Parker's paternal arms are impaled with those of Christ Church, Canterbury. The reprint of Thomas Cranmer's prologue, which will become a standard feature of the Bishops' Bible, has a large initial C containing the arms of the See of Canterbury side by side with those of Cranmer.

Sumptuous, rich, luxuriant, and handsome aptly describe the 1568 Bishops' Bible. It is the grandest of the sixteenth-century folio Bibles. The first edition also has several maps (all of which, except one, were copied from those in the 1560 Geneva) and, most significantly, 124 elegant woodcut illustrations of biblical scenes. These were the designs of Virgil Solis, an internationally successful graphic designer from Nuremberg. They first appeared in a Lutheran Bible printed in 1560 at Frankfurt. Thereafter, they were closely copied for a 1564 Catholic German Bible and a 1566 Catholic Dutch Bible, both published in Cologne.[16] From there, they went to England, where several of the blocks were modified for the Bishops' Bible. Curiously enough, the blocks next appear in 1570-1 in Antwerp, where they were used in a Catholic Latin Bible. Thus the same illustrations were used in a German Lutheran Bible, a Dutch Catholic Bible, an English Episcopalian Bible and a Roman Catholic Latin Vulgate. Is this ecumenicity or economy?

However, Richard Jugge, the printer, or Matthew Parker himself did modify the blocks before they were used in the Bishops' Bible. Someone carefully removed the pictorial representation of God in the first two woodcuts of Genesis which illustrate creation and the birth of Eve. Now, the tetragrammaton, the four Hebrew characters for Yahweh, appears. This was done in deference to the idea that any pictorial representation of God was looked on in England as 'papist' or 'idolatrous'. Nevertheless, the expurgator was inconsistent, for smaller images of God remain in other places such as the illustration for Genesis 9. They were not removed and they did elicit a fierce attack from Puritans. Just before stating that the 'order of bishops is unscriptural', the *Puritan Second Admonition to Parliament* (1572) condemns the images of the Bishops' Bible: 'in their last great Bible [meaning the Bishops' Bible] in the first edition of it, such a sight of blasphemous pictures of God the Father, as what they deserve for it, I will refer them to none other than their own note upon the 15 verse of the fourth of Deuteronomy'.[17] That note states that 'plagues hang over them that would make any image to represent God by'. The elegant woodcuts were not used in subsequent editions of the Bishops' Bible. The revision of 1572, however, has a new set of woodcuts, none of which represent God the Father figurally (as an old man).

The Notes

The total number of notes in the Bishops' Bible is far fewer than in the Geneva. Surprisingly, a few Geneva notes were taken over without change (or with very minor changes). For instance, in Romans 6 the Geneva Bible has nineteen notes while the Bishops' has only four, and one of the four is taken over from the Geneva. Moreover, all the Genevan notes for Galatians are reproduced in the Bishops' Bible except

two that concern alternate readings. Some of the changes do not de-emphasise Calvinism at all. For example, in Romans 9, a predestination chapter, the note at verse 15 in the Geneva reads: 'As the only will and purpose of God is the chief cause of election and reprobation: so his free mercy in Christ is an inferior cause of damnation.' The Bishops' Bible, which places the note at verse 11, changed it this way: 'The will and purpose of God, is the cause of the election and reprobation. For his mercy and calling, through Christ, are the means of salvation: and the withdrawing of his mercy, is the cause of damnation.' Furthermore, in Romans 11:35 ('who has first given to him?') the Bishops' Bible states the doctrine of election unequivocally, explaining that 'the Apostle declareth that God by his free will and election, doth give salvation unto men, without any deserts of their own'.

The reason for this harmony between the competing versions is, quite simply, that the hierarchy of the Elizabethan church basically accepted Calvin's doctrine of salvation, even in Theodore de Bèze's harsher formulations on double predestination. Disagreements with Calvinist nonconformists lay elsewhere. The groups and individuals we now tend to label as 'Puritan' objected to church polity (episcopal instead of presbyterian structure) and to the conservative elements in the liturgy. After all, the English rites, as laid down in the prayer book of 1559, were the most conservative in Protestant Europe. Despite that, the Church of England and Puritans did not disagree on the doctrine of salvation. So strong was the Calvinist orientation that Diarmid MacCulloch was able to describe the dominance of Calvinism in Elizabethan theology.[18] By 1600, no fewer than ninety works by Calvin and fifty-six by de Bèze had been published in English.[19]

Fig. 6.5. This page shows the beginning of Leviticus in the Bishops' Bible. Its layout prefigures that of the early folio editions of the King James Version, with one major exception: the single quotation marks standing at the beginning of each line (and running down both outside margins) are a peculiarity of this version. Archbishop Matthew Parker placed them in the text to mark the passages that he deemed unedifying and that could be omitted in public reading. All of Leviticus is so marked except chapters 10, 19 and 25:14–26.

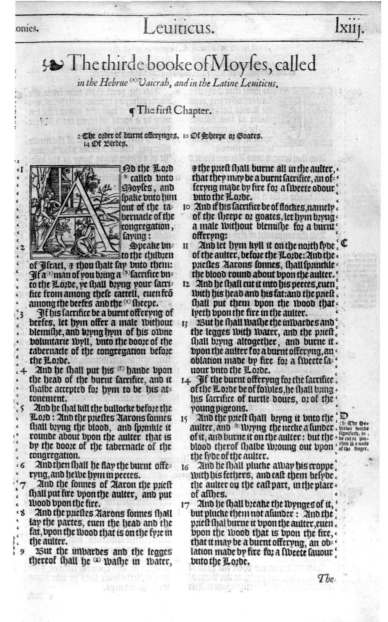

Despite its shortcomings, the Bishops' Bible appeared in a respectable number of editions. In sixty-five years of being in print, there were thirty-eight different editions. Of these, fifteen were folio, ten quarto, and thirteen octavo. Eighteen included both Old and New Testaments, nineteen were New Testament only, and one was Gospels only. Yet, when measured against the popularity of its competitor, the new translation was a failure. The Convocation of Canterbury sanctioned the version and decreed in 1571 that every bishop and cathedral and church should have a copy. The bishop's own copy was to be placed in his home 'in the hall or large dining room, that it might be useful or to servants or to strangers'.[20] Its words resonated in the churches and the Bishops' palaces, but nowhere else, it seems. And this was the case despite the wise effort to produce the Bishops' Bible in small formats. No decree would have been able to secure its place in the households of England. Nonetheless, it would serve as the official basis for the new version, even if the other versions were to be consulted directly as well.[21] Its failure was a major reason for the government's sponsorship of a new project.

ENDNOTES TO CHAPTER SIX

1. Westcott 1905, 96; see also King 1989, 229.
2. Dickens [1964] 1989, 349.
3. Bray 1994, 336-7.
4. Pollard 1911, 295.
5. Pollard 1911, 285-6. The letter, signed by Parker and by Edmund Grindal (then Bishop of London), even states that it would 'do much good to have diversity of translations and readings' (p. 286).
6. Parker 1853, 16-17.
7. See Herbert 1968, no. 131. Parker was also the very first to print Anglo-Saxon in an Anglo-Saxon font, a feat accomplished in his edition of a homily by Aelfric printed in 1567.
8. The list given by Parker includes the following: W. Alley (Bishop of Exeter); R. Davies (Bishop of St David's); E. Sandys (Bishop of Worcester); A. Pierson (Prebendary of Canterbury); A. Perne (Dean of Ely); R. Horne (Bishop of Winchester); T. Bentham (B. of Litchfield and Coventry); E. Grindal (Bishop of London and to be Parker's successor as Archbishop of Canterbury); J. Parkhurst (Bishop of Norwich); R. Cox (Bishop of Ely); E. Guest (Bishop of Rochester) who was replaced by Thomas Bickley (Bishop of Chichester), E. Scambler (Bishop of Peterborough); N. Bullingham (Bishop of Lincoln), and perhaps Hugh Jones (Bishop of Llandaff). The list is in Parker 1853, 335-6 (letter from Parker to Sir William Cecil), and in Herbert 1968, no. 125.
9. Strype 1711, 3:208.
10. Pollard 1911, 297-8.
11. As he was ill, Parker had to send the Bible to Cecil for presentation to the Queen. See Pollard 1911, 292-5.
12. With the Elizabethan religious settlement, the monarch receives the title 'supreme governor' instead of the former 'supreme head'.
13. King 1989, 105.
14. The Latin version on the engraved general title page reads: 'Non me pudet Evangelii Christi. Virtus enim Dei est ad salutem Omni credenti. Rom. 1.'
15. From 1574 on, the engravings no longer appear in Bishops' Bibles.
16. Several older studies mistakenly state that the Cologne woodcuts (and those thereafter) are from the original Frankfurt woodblocks.
17. Frere and Douglas 1954, 118. See also Aston 1992, 271-2.
18. MacCulloch 1990, 70.
19. MacCulloch 1990, 72.
20. Westcott 1905, 101.
21. It is generally thought that a folio imprint of 1602 was the basis for the KJV.

CHAPTER SEVEN
PERSECUTION AND THE CATHOLIC BIBLE

> And now O Lord Christ, most just and merciful, we thy poor creatures that are so afflicted for confession and defence of the Holy, Catholic, and Apostolic truth, contained in this thy sacred book . . . we cry also unto thy Majesty with tenderness of our hearts unspeakable, Come Lord Jesus quickly, and judge between us and our adversaries, and in the meantime give patience, comfort, and constancy to all that suffer for thy name and trust in thee. O Lord God, our only helper and protector, tarry not long. Amen.
>
> *– the final note in the Rheims New Testament (1582),*
> *a gloss on Revelation 22:20: 'Come Lord Jesus.'*

In 1582, a completely new, utterly independent translation appeared. Nonetheless, like so many of its English precursors, the Douai-Rheims version could not be printed in England. It was a new version of scripture for an outlawed and persecuted movement – the Roman Catholic Church.

The origin of the Douai-Rheims Bible even recalls that of the archly Protestant Geneva Bible. The Geneva version was created by a group of English scholars and churchmen in exile on the Continent, fleeing persecution but determined to keep their movement alive despite the chilling toll of martyrdoms in England. That was under Queen Mary. Now, during the reign of Queen Elizabeth, Catholic exiles on the Continent, mindful of martyrs in England, published a Bible to support the illegal missions to England to keep their outlawed faith alive. Both were noble efforts. By the time the Geneva Bible was published in 1560, fortune had turned nearly 180 degrees for English Protestants. Consequently, there is a triumphant tone in that version, and often unbecomingly so. With the passage of time, however, matters only worsened for Roman Catholics. Thus, the tone of the Douai-Rheims can be both bellicose and mournful.

Background

Two historical factors are significant for an appreciation of the Douai-Rheims Bible: the Council of Trent (1545-63) and the religious policy under Elizabeth I, especially the growing suppression of Roman Catholicism.

The Catholic Bible in English conforms to policies decided at the Council of Trent, the Church's response to the challenges posed by the successes of the reform movements throughout Europe. The council addressed many issues of discipline and doctrine, including fundamental questions about the Bible. This was necessary because the subject of the Bible, its status and its availability, had become a phenomenally effective issue for Protestant propaganda. The Council of Trent responded to this avenue of attack in part by endorsing the sufficiency of the Vulgate version, an affirmation that came in the first phase of the council, in Session 4 (8 April 1546).

> [The holy council] decides and declares that the old well known Latin Vulgate edition which has been tested in the church by long use over so many centuries should be kept as the authentic text in public readings, debates, sermons and explanations; and no one is to dare or presume on any pretext to reject it.[1]

For the specific question of a Roman Catholic Bible in English, this meant that the translation would have to be based on the Vulgate, the Latin translation of St Jerome, and not on the Greek and Hebrew originals. In large measure, this decision amounted to a repudiation of the thrust of Renaissance biblical scholarship.

It also looked rigid and authoritarian. Even so, the council did have some good reasons for the action. One was that the Vulgate was an ancient and valuable version of the Bible. Indeed in some instances the Vulgate preserves an authentic text where the Greek manuscripts for the New Testament do not. The preface to the Rheims New Testament rightly stresses that even the Protestant heretic Theodore de Bèze had begun championing the critical importance of the Latin Vulgate in biblical philology.[2] Furthermore, the council held that the Vulgate was a valid part of the traditions of the church. The Holy Spirit had worked through it without apparent detriment for over a millennium.

Protestants gleefully assailed the Roman Catholic church for this decision. This is also the primary issue in the scorching Protestant criticisms of the Douai-Rheims Bible. Humanists – both Protestant and

Catholic – had returned to the scriptures in the original languages for their theological studies. That was a major innovation in the Renaissance church.

The return to scriptures in Hebrew and Greek did cast doubt on some of the dogma and practices of the medieval church, even in a matter as central to Christian life as the sacrament of penance. Yet, there was no need to fear that new biblical philology would provide a fatal blow to medieval doctrine, even if the church would obviously have been compelled to face questions raised by the comparison of scriptures in Greek and Hebrew with St Jerome's ancient Latin translation.

The other issue was Elizabeth I and her religious policies. She was circumspect and even laconic on the subject of religion. She would encourage the English bishops to produce a new translation of the Bible (Bishops' Bible of 1568, etc.), publish it with her portrait on the title page, but would not mandate the exclusive use of this version in her realm. Moreover, as far as liturgy and even the understanding of the Eucharist go, most evidence indicates that she stood closer to traditional Catholic practices than to Puritan doctrine. It seems that her policy aimed to limit unnecessary offence to people with Catholic sensibilities, even though Roman Catholicism was outlawed.

There is also the vexing matter of political instability. Elizabeth succeeded her half-sister Mary I, who had reconciled England with Rome, and had begun a policy of executing those who rejected her faith. Some three hundred people died, many of them prominent figures, such as Archbishop Thomas Cranmer and John Rogers. Elizabeth's accession immediately ended the persecutions and also marked the

Fig. 7.1. Title page of the first edition of the first English translation of the Bible for Roman Catholics. Its source text is the Vulgate, although its chief translator, Gregory Martin († 1582), also consulted the Greek, as well as earlier Protestant English translations, and particularly Coverdale's Bible. Many English Roman Catholics had to flee persecution under the reign of Queen Elizabeth. Some refugees established a school in Douai in 1568, which from 1578-93 was relocated to Rheims. Martin was assisted by three other exiles: William Allen (1532-94), Richard Bristow (1538-81) and William Reynolds (1544-94). Although they had completed the entire Bible by 1582, they could only afford to publish the New Testament, and that in a very modest edition intended for the dangerous task of missionary work in England. The Old Testament would come later, in 1609-10 at Douai, so this translation is often called the Douai-Rheims Bible. In their preface to the New Testament, the translators expressed misgivings at the notion of putting the Bible into English, but overcame their doubts when confronted with the need to keep the faith alive in England.

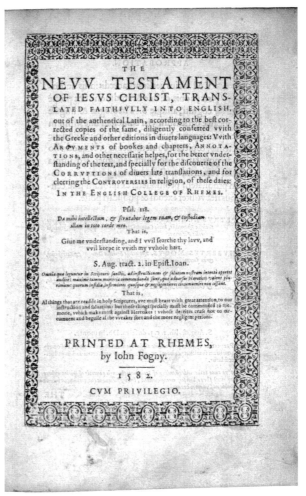

resumption of a reforming policy that rejected the primacy of the Bishop of Rome.

Generally speaking, it remained very difficult throughout the sixteenth century for a ruler to imagine that people could be both religious dissenters and loyal subjects.

Moreover, Catholic opposition to Elizabeth from the Continent, especially Spain, was at times brutal and at times supported by English recusant exiles. Attempts to overthrow her were coupled with the goal of restoring Roman Catholicism. There were plots, risings, and even the Spanish Armada. The Spanish problem was serious, although mitigated by the complete victory over the Spanish Armada in 1588.

Prior to that, a major threat was Mary Queen of Scots, who had resided in England since 1568 and had a claim to the throne. The Scottish queen was a patently dangerous figure. She fled Scotland in 1567 after she had had her husband, Henry Stuart, Lord Darnley, murdered and, moreover, married the perpetrator. Elizabeth had her executed for treason in 1587.

Catholic Recusancy

These were some of the political issues of the time. There were, obviously, ordinary Roman Catholics in England who had no thoughts of treason but who did wish to practise their faith. The Act of Uniformity of 1571 and other legislation, however, required all to accept the same faith and practices, as defined by the Church of England. Those who 'refused' were now known as Recusants, and several of those, especially those determined to remain Roman Catholic clerics, left England or went underground.

A major figure in the history of recusancy was William Allen. He settled in Flanders and in 1568 he founded the English College of Douai. In an attempt to increase its financial support, the college moved to Rheims in 1578-93, whence it finally returned to Douai. Allen established the college in order to educate priests for illegal and dangerous missions to England. The first seminary priests slipped back into England at the end of the 1570s, and almost immediately, some became martyrs for the cause. The best-known case was that of Edmund Campion. He was executed in 1582, after having studied at Douai and having initiated, in 1580, the Jesuit mission to England.

The Catholic Bible was created at the college for such missions. Despite mis-givings about vernacular Bibles, it became apparent that priests and laity in England needed a Bible in English in order to sustain their faith under these trying circumstances.

Professor Gregory Martin translated the entire Bible with only minimal assistance, it seems, from a few colleagues. He had an excellent education at Oxford, where he held his first teaching appointment as an instructor of Greek. Eventually, he became professor of Greek and Hebrew at the English College at Douai (and then at Rheims).

Martin was an early publicist in the

Catholic recusant movement and a close friend of Edmund Campion. Given his excellent linguistic preparation, it is not surprising that, while the Vulgate is the base text for the translation, Martin also consulted the Greek and Hebrew versions and added notes on important variances between them and the Vulgate text. The title page of the New Testament states: 'diligently conferred with the Greek and other editions in diverse languages'.

The project began on 16 October, 1578, and he put the 'final touches' to the work in March 1582, just before his death.[3] However, the college's poverty prevented the immediate publication of the entire Bible. Only the New Testament appeared in 1582. The Old Testament finally came out in 1609-1610, after the college had returned to Douai – hence the designation 'Douai-Rheims Version' for the complete Bible in English. After Martin's death, the Old Testament also required a light revision in order to ensure conformity to the Sixto-Clementine edition of the Vulgate, which appeared in 1592 (thus, after Martin's death) and which had become the official Roman Catholic version.

The Text

In the preface to the New Testament, Martin concedes that the English of the translation 'at the first may seem strange'.[4] The reason for this was his decision to hew as close as possible to the phrasing and even the vocabulary of the Vulgate. Interestingly, he also cites Jerome's stylistic orientation to Hebrew and Greek originals to justify his word-for-word procedure. According to him, the point is that the Vulgate is a close translation of original scriptures as they existed in the late fourth and early fifth century. Thus, a literal rendering of the

WILLIAM ALLEN, FOUNDER OF THE ENGLISH COLLEGE AT DOUAI, ON THE NEED FOR A ROMAN CATHOLIC BIBLE IN ENGLISH

'Catholics educated in the academies and schools have hardly any knowledge of the scriptures except in Latin. When they are preaching to the unlearned and are obliged on the spur of the moment to translate some passage into the vernacular, they often do it inaccurately and with unpleasant hesitation because either there is no vernacular version of the words, or it does not occur to them at the moment. Our adversaries, however, have at their finger tips from some heretical version all those passages of scripture which seem to make for them, and by a certain deceptive adaptation and alteration of the sacred words produce the effect of appearing to say nothing but what comes from the Bible. This evil might be remedied if we too had some Catholic version of the Bible, for all the English versions are most corrupt. . . . If his Holiness shall judge it expedient, we ourselves will endeavor to have the Bible faithfully, purely and genuinely translated according to the edition approved by the Church, for we already have men most fitted for the work.'

From a letter to Joannes Vendeville, 16 September 1578. *Letters and Memorials of Cardinal Allen* [1882] 1965, 64-65; translated by Pope 1952, 250.

Vulgate should yield a close rendering of the originals, an argument that might look good on the surface, but experience would rapidly disprove it. Moreover, Martin pleads the sanctity of scripture as justification for the style: we acknowledge 'with St Jerome that in other writings it is enough to give in translation sense for sense, but that, in scriptures, lest we miss the sense, we must keep the very words'.[5] Obviously, this contradicts the stylistic history of the English Bible ever since the second Wycliffite version. Indeed, the preface acknowledges this and even includes an attack on the aesthetics of Protestant Bibles.

Thus, in style and, to a degree, in methodology, the Douai-Rheims is a retrograde version. Its text nonetheless has many virtues and its rendering of the New Testament did exert some influence on the King James Version. Indeed, Martin's renderings of the direct articles are the most correct of the sixteenth century. A reason for the systematic focus on articles was that the Vulgate does not have articles (since the Latin language lacks them generally). Thus Martin was compelled to study the direct articles in the original Greek New Testament. Moreover, the enrichment of the English scriptural vocabulary with Latinate words also had an impact on the translators of the KJV.

Martin was aware that the diction of his translation had its oddities. He even felt the need to include a glossary of some 58 unusual terms. Some of the neologisms are truly strange, such as 'exinanited' in the phrase Christ 'exinanited himself' (Philippians 2:7), which is the rendering of the Latin 'semet ipsum exinanivit' and means 'emptied himself'. The use of 'Dominical day' (literal rendering of the Latin *dies dominica*) for 'Sabbath' is stylistically beyond the pale. Nonetheless, several of the Latinisms would become ordinary English words, very much analogous to the adoption

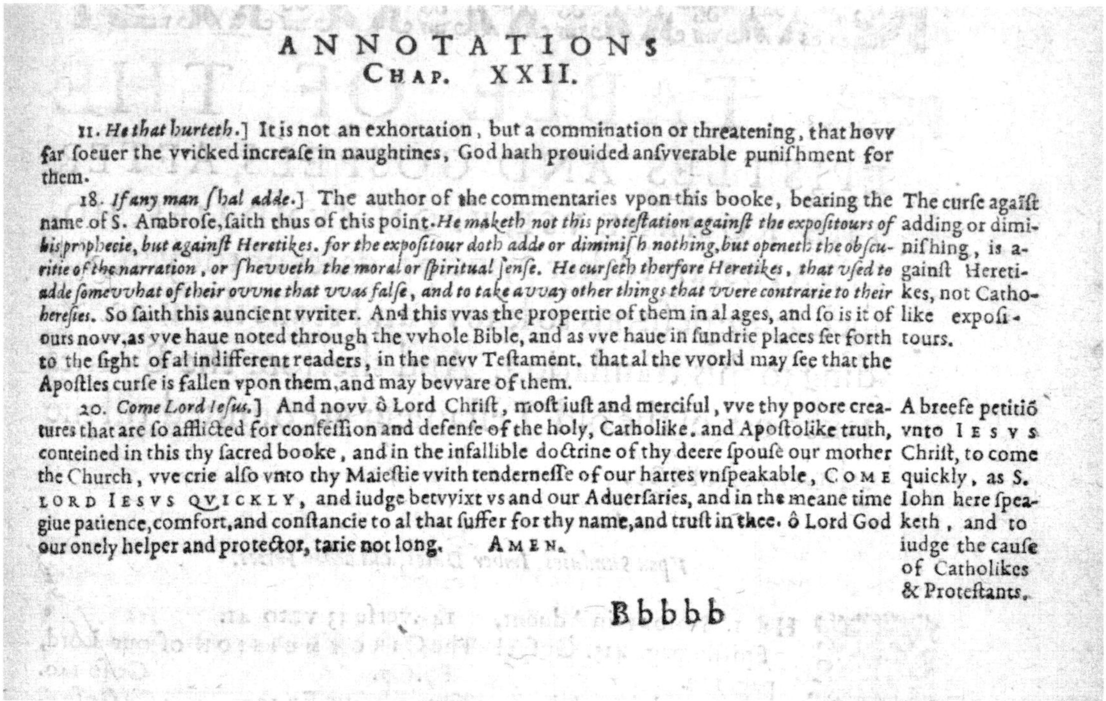

ANNOTATIONS
CHAP. XXII.

11. *He that hurteth.*] It is not an exhortation, but a commination or threatening, that hovv far foeuer the vvicked increafe in naughtines, God hath prouided anfvverable punifhment for them.

18. *If any man fhal adde.*] The author of the commentaries vpon this booke, bearing the name of S. Ambrofe, faith thus of this point. *He maketh not this proteftation againft the expofitours of his prophecie, but againft Heretikes. for the expofitour doth adde or diminifh nothing, but openeth the obfcuritie of the narration, or fheweth the moral or fpiritual fenfe. He curfeth therfore Heretikes, that vfed to adde fomevuhat of their ovune that vuas falfe, and to take avuay other things that vuere contrarie to their herefies.* So faith this auncient vvriter. And this vvas the propertie of them in al ages, and fo is it of ours novv, as vve haue noted through the vvhole Bible, and as vve haue in fundrie places fet forth to the fight of al indifferent readers, in the nevv Teftament, that al the vvorld may fee that the Apoftles curfe is fallen vpon them, and may bevvare of them.

The curfe againft adding or diminifhing, is againft Heretikes, not Catholike expofitours.

20. *Come Lord Iefus.*] And novv ô Lord Chrift, moft iuft and merciful, vve thy poore creatures that are fo afflicted for confeffion and defenfe of the holy, Catholike, and Apoftolike truth, conteined in this thy facred booke, and in the infallible doctrine of thy deere fpoufe our mother the Church, vve crie alfo vnto thy Maieftie vvith tendernelle of our hartes vnfpeakable, COME LORD IESVS QVICKLY, and iudge betvvixt vs and our Aduerfaries, and in the meane time giue patience, comfort, and conftancie to al that fuffer for thy name, and truft in thee. ô Lord God our onely helper and protector, tarie not long. AMEN.

A breefe petitiõ vnto IESVS Chrift, to come quickly, as S. Iohn here fpeaketh, and to iudge the caufe of Catholikes & Proteftants.

Bbbbb

Fig. 7.2. The Rheims New Testament of 1582 includes annotations on the text at the end of each chapter. Here are reproduced the notes for Revelation 22 (called Apocalypse in this edition). The annotations often introduce anti-Protestant polemic, as in the second note above that condemns commentaries by 'heretics' but condones Catholic expositors. The final note, however, strikes a sympathetic chord even in its partisanship, as these exiled and persecuted Catholics pray that Jesus might come quickly to give them comfort and end their suffering.

of Hebraisms in Protestant Bibles in the aftermath of Tyndale; among them: 'acquisition', 'advent', 'cooperate', and 'holocaust'.

The Lord's Prayer displays elements of the Latinate style. It follows here in modernised spelling and punctuation.

> Our Father, which art in heaven,
> sanctified be thy name. Let thy
> kingdom come. Thy will be done,
> as in heaven, in earth also. Give
> us today our supersubstantial bread.
> And forgive us our debts, as we also
> forgive our debtors. And lead us not
> into temptation. But deliver us from
> evil. Amen.

Naturally, one cannot quite understand this text as normal English, especially the 'supersubstantial bread' and the Latinate syntax of 'as in heaven, in earth also'. The use of 'sanctified' is an excellent example of the preference for Latinate vocabulary, derived directly from the Vulgate. The 'supersubstantial bread' is the 'supersubstantialis panis' of the Vulgate. The obvious point of this translation is that the adjective might designate something more significant than 'daily', a secondary sense of the Greek original and the sense used in the Vulgate's rendering of the parallel version of the Lord's Prayer in Luke 11:2. Martin includes a marginal note for 'supersubstantial', indicating that it renders the Greek 'epiousios' and that the Luke version of the Lord's

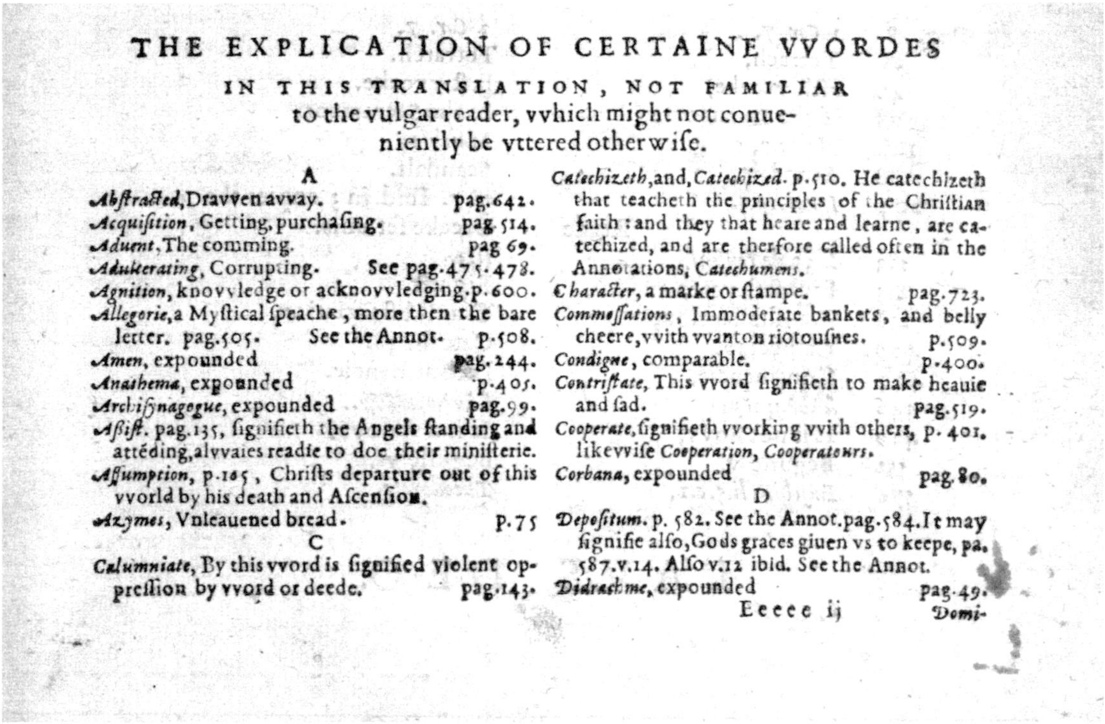

THE EXPLICATION OF CERTAINE VVORDES

IN THIS TRANSLATION, NOT FAMILIAR
to the vulgar reader, vvhich might not conue-
niently be vttered otherwise.

A

Abstracted, Dravven avvay.   pag.642.
Acquisition, Getting, purchasing.   pag.514.
Aduent, The comming.   pag 69.
Adulterating, Corrupting.   See pag.475.478.
Agnition, knovvledge or acknovvledging. p.600.
Allegorie, a Mystical speache, more then the bare
    letter. pag.505.   See the Annot.   p.508.
Amen, expounded   pag.244.
Anathema, expounded   p.405.
Archisynagogue, expounded   pag.99.
Assist. pag.135, signifieth the Angels standing and
    attending, alvvaies readie to doe their ministerie.
Assumption, p.165, Christs departure out of this
    vvorld by his death and Ascension.
Azymes, Vnleauened bread.   p.75

C

Calumniate, By this vvord is signified violent op-
    pression by vvord or deede.   pag.143.

B

Catechizeth, and, *Catechized*. p.510. He catechizeth
    that teacheth the principles of the Christian
    faith : and they that heare and learne, are ca-
    techized, and are therfore called often in the
    Annotations, *Catechumens*.
Character, a marke or stampe.   pag.723.
Commessations, Immoderate bankets, and belly
    cheere, vvith vvanton riotousnes.   p.509.
Condigne, comparable.   p.400.
Contristate, This vvord signifieth to make heauie
    and sad.   pag.519.
Cooperate, signifieth vvorking vvith others, p. 401.
    likevvise *Cooperation, Cooperatours*.
Corbana, expounded   pag.80.

D

Depositum. p. 582. See the Annot.pag.584.It may
    signifie also, Gods graces giuen vs to keepe, pa.
    587.v.14. Also v.12 ibid. See the Annot.
Didrachme, expounded   pag.49.

E e e e e ij   *Domi-*

Fig. 7.3. The translators of the Rheims New Testament went to great lengths to keep as close to the original Vulgate text as possible. This compunction led them to create a number of Latinate neologisms. For this reason, they included a glossary at the end of the book. Protestant opponents ridiculed such tortured expressions as commessation (rowdy dinner parties), donaries (gifts to the church), Dominical Day (Sunday, i.e. the Lord's Day), exinanite (abase oneself exceedingly) and repropitiate (make reconciliation for sins). But it should be noted that many of the new words were taken up into English and even used in later Protestant translations. To the Rheims translation we owe the words calumniate, Advent, acquisition, resuscitate, Pentecost and many other now common terms. Indeed, not only the words, but also complete phrases from the Rheims New Testament turn up in the King James Version itself, for example: 'to publish and blaze abroad'; 'she rejoiced with exceeding great joy'; 'behold a multitude'; and 'the only begotten of the Father'.

Prayer in the Vulgate has 'daily bread'. The gloss at least clarifies the text. We should also note that the doxology – 'For thine is the kingdom . . .' – is missing, distinguishing Roman Catholic from Protestant Bibles to this very day. It is worth noting that most scholars now firmly believe that the Vulgate's omission of the doxology is the correct version. The Greek manuscripts, none of which predates St Jerome's lifetime, record an interpolation (an insertion) into the text of the Bible from the liturgy.

The canon, which basically means the approved books of scripture, is also different from that of Protestant Bibles. The Psalms, for example, are based on St Jerome's Gallican Psalter. This means they are grounded ultimately in the Septuagint version instead of the Hebrew Old Testament (the difference also affects the numbering of Psalms). Many of the Apocryphal books were accepted at the Council of Trent as being 'deutero-canonical'. Sixteenth-century Protestant

Bibles typically group apocryphal books in a separate segment, but the Douai-Rheims does not. It mixes Apocryphal books with books of the Hebrew canon, a feature that had been typical of the medieval and early printed Vulgates.

The Bible as Partisan Manifesto

The issue of partisan notes has bedevilled the history of the Bible in English. It has also bedevilled the historiography of English Bibles, for many partisan historians have defended the presence of weighty apparatuses of commentary. The typical apologetic strategy is to argue that most notes are explanatory and, indeed, would have been helpful to people unable to attend services freely. This approach, which has been taken variously for Tyndale, Geneva, and Douai-Rheims versions, misses the mark, for the question is indoctrination not elucidation.

There are many neutral explanatory notes in the Rheims New Testament. There are also many notes explaining Roman Catholic doctrine, a feature that might well be understandable for a Bible that tried to support the survival of an underground church. Unquestionably, the notes would have been useful to people deprived of priests.

Nonetheless, the Rheims New Testament launches barb after barb against the Protestants, especially against Puritan tendencies as expressed in the Geneva Bible (we should recall that the Geneva Bible was strident in its anti-Catholicism). In 2 Corinthians 1:18, for example, there is the following note on the issue of vacillating:

> We have notorious examples in the Protestants, who being destitute of the spirit of peace, concord, constancy, unity, and verity, as they vary from their own writings which

they retract, reform, or deform continually, so both in their preachings and form of Service, they are restless, changeable, and repugnant to themselves, that if they were not kept in awe with much ado, by temporal laws or by the shame and rebuke of the world, they would coin us every year or every Parliament, new communions, new faiths, and new Christs, as you see by the manifold endeavours of the Puritans.[6]

In Matthew 24:15, we read that the Mass has been abolished by 'Antichrist and his precursors'.[7] In Acts 11:26, Martin says 'This name, Christian, ought to be common to all the faithful and other names of schismatics and sectaries must be abhorred' and then singles out the appellations 'Lutherans, Calvinists, Protestants' as designating, ipso facto, heretics.[8]

Protestant Criticism

English Protestants persecuted not only Roman Catholics but also their Bible. The fiercest polemicist against the Rheims New Testament was a theologian named William Fulke, who, in 1589, published *The Text of the New Testament of Iesus Christ . . . with a Confutation*. This is a point-by-point refutation of the Rheims New Testament. Fulke reprinted the text of Martin's translation and the text of the Bishops' Bible in parallel columns. He also composed rebuttals – often exceedingly long ones – to the Roman Catholic notes.

The result is incandescent, even if often tedious, as in the six-page rejection of the papal interpretation of Matthew 16:18 ('Thou art Peter and upon this rock. . .'). Nonetheless, Fulke's work became popular. After the first edition, it was reprinted four times: 1601 (twice), 1617, and 1633. The

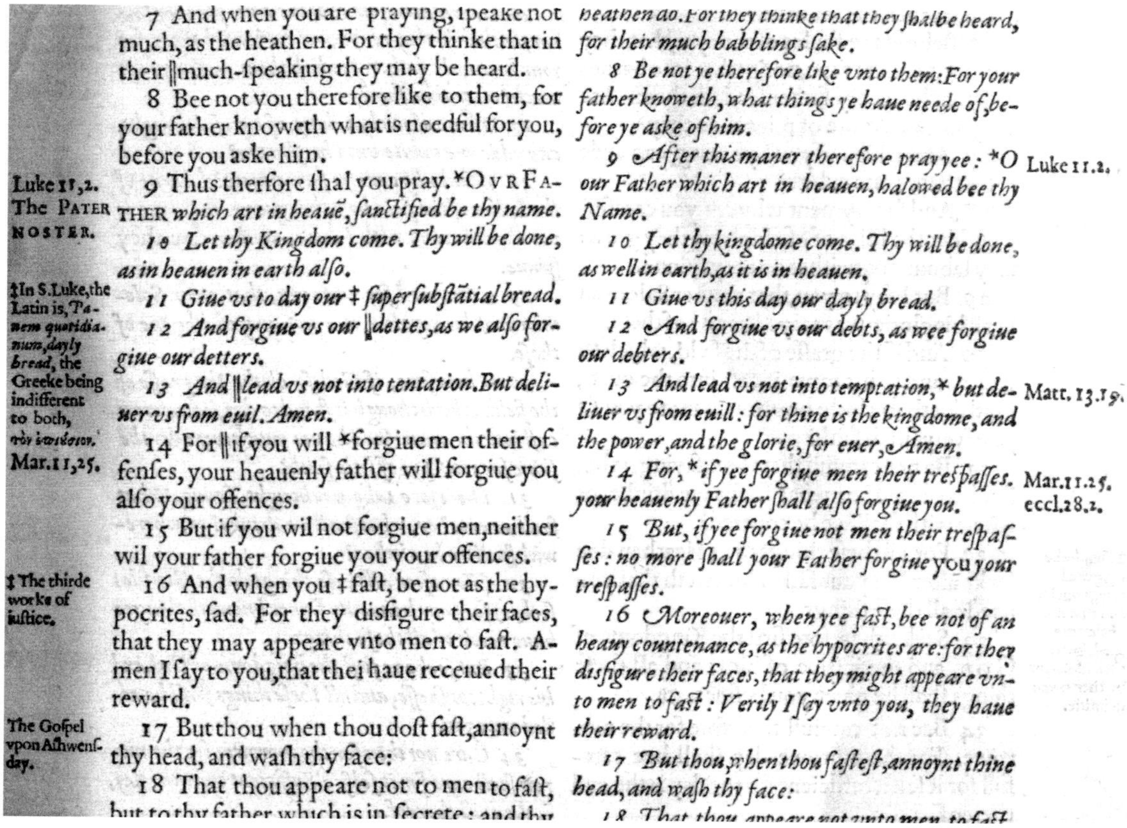

[Luke 11,2. The PATER NOSTER.] 7 And when you are praying, speake not much, as the heathen. For they thinke that in their ‖much-speaking they may be heard.

8 Bee not you therefore like to them, for your father knoweth what is needful for you, before you aske him.

9 Thus therfore shal you pray.*OVR FA-THER which art in heaue, sanctified be thy name.

10 Let thy Kingdom come. Thy will be done, as in heauen in earth also.

[‡In S.Luke, the Latin is, Panem quotidianum, dayly bread, the Greeke being indifferent to both, τὸν ἐπιούσιον. Mar.11,25.] 11 Giue vs to day our ‡ supersubstatial bread.

12 And forgiue vs our ‖dettes, as we also forgiue our detters.

13 And ‖lead vs not into tentation. But deliuer vs from euil. Amen.

14 For ‖ if you will *forgiue men their offenses, your heauenly father will forgiue you also your offences.

15 But if you wil not forgiue men, neither wil your father forgiue you your offences.

[‡ The thirde worke of iustice.] 16 And when you ‡fast, be not as the hypocrites, sad. For they disfigure their faces, that they may appeare vnto men to fast. Amen I say to you, that thei haue receiued their reward.

[The Gospel vpon Ashwensday.] 17 But thou when thou dost fast, annoynt thy head, and wash thy face:

18 That thou appeare not to men to fast, but to thy father which is in secrete: and thy

heathen do. For they thinke that they shalbe heard, for their much babblings sake.

8 Be not ye therefore like vnto them: For your father knoweth, what things ye haue neede of, before ye aske of him.

9 After this maner therefore pray yee: *O **[Luke 11,2.]** our Father which art in heauen, halowed bee thy Name.

10 Let thy kingdome come. Thy will be done, as well in earth, as it is in heauen.

11 Giue vs this day our dayly bread.

12 And forgiue vs our debts, as wee forgiue our debters.

13 And lead vs not into temptation, * but deliuer vs from euill: for thine is the kingdome, and **[Matt. 13,19.]** the power, and the glorie, for euer, Amen.

14 For, * if yee forgiue men their trespasses, **[Mar.11,25. eccl.28,2.]** your heauenly Father shall also forgiue you.

15 But, if yee forgiue not men their trespasses: no more shall your Father forgiue you your trespasses.

16 Moreouer, when yee fast, bee not of an heauy countenance, as the hypocrites are: for they disfigure their faces, that they might appeare vnto men to fast: Verily I say vnto you, they haue their reward.

17 But thou, when thou fastest, annoynt thine head, and wash thy face:

18 That thou appeare not vnto men to fast

Fig. 7.4. The Text of the New Testament of Iesus Christ, translated out of the Vulgar Latine by the Papists of the traitorous Seminarie at Rhemes. With Arguments . . . With a Confutation . . . By William Fulke, Doctor in Divinitie. *London: Deputies of Christopher Barker, 1589. In this fiercely anti-Roman version of the Bible, the Rheims New Testament and the Bishops' Bible texts are printed side by side with the notes of the Rheims New Testament often balanced by William Fulke's vociferous refutations of them. Although the 1582 Rheims New Testament was banned in England and many copies confiscated or burned, it circulated freely in Fulke's work. And despite the negative context in which Fulke presented it, the Roman Catholic text had an impact via Fulke's edition that it never could have had alone. The translators of the King James Version knew the Rheims version – and were influenced by it – through Fulke's reprinting.*

Roman Catholic Bible also provoked other refutations, the most noteworthy are by George Wither, Edward Bulkeley, William Whitaker, Thomas Bilson, and another tract by Fulke himself.

Ironically, the popular success of Fulke's refutation made the Catholic Bible well known and it was probably due to this effort that the translators of the King James Version studied and used material in the Rheims New Testament.

Catholic Revisions

The Douai-Rheims Bible would undergo frequent and significant revision. The New Testament was reprinted some four times with only light revisions (1600, 1621, 1630, and 1633). In the early eighteenth century, Cornelius Nary (1718) and Robert Witham (1730) undertook fresh translations of the Vulgate New Testament. These efforts did not have a broad impact, except that they made the need for a complete revision of the Douai-Rheims version apparent. This was undertaken by Bishop Richard Challoner, who produced five revisions of the Rheims New Testament (1749, 1750, 1752, 1763 and 1772) and two of the Douai Old Testament (1750 and 1763). Challoner regularised (and modernised) the spelling of Martin's version and also introduced countless stylistic corrections. Hardly a verse was untouched by the editor's file. The result is a text that aims for dignity and fidelity, as did Martin's, but also for greater simplicity and clarity. Challoner's revisions enabled the Douai-Rheims version to remain the preferred basis for Catholic English Bibles until around 1950, a remarkably long life for a sixteenth-century Bible translation.

ENDNOTES TO CHAPTER SEVEN

1. Tanner 1990, 2:664.
2. Rheims New Testament 1582, fol. b3^v and b4^r.
3. Pope and Bullough 1952, 252.
4. Rheims New Testament 1582, fol. c3^r.
5. Rheims New Testament 1582, fol. b2^r-b2^v.
6. Rheims New Testament 1582, 471.
7. Rheims New Testament 1582, 71.
8. Rheims New Testament 1582, 326.

CHAPTER EIGHT
LITERARY MAJESTY

'Truly (good Christian Reader) we never thought from the beginning, that we should need to make a new Translation, nor yet to make of a bad one a good one,. . . but to make a good one better, or out of many good ones, one principal good one. . . .'

— The Translators to the Reader, *preface to the King James Version, attributed to Miles Smith*

The King James Version was an accident of history. It was an unintended outcome of a conference with King James, conservative Anglican churchmen and disgruntled Puritans. In April 1603, English Puritans presented their new king from Scotland with a petition calling for numerous changes, mostly to alter liturgical practices, although several proposals also touched on the meaning of the sacraments. Their goal was to eliminate similarities between the rituals of the Church of England and the Roman Catholic Church. More radical Puritans were also agitating against the episcopal organisation of the church, proposing instead a presbyterian structure of individual churches that would exercise a high degree of self-governance through elders. On balance, the actual proposals were modest, especially because there was hardly any force in 1603 behind the opposition to episcopacy. The document is called the *Millenary Petition* because it was said to have the endorsement of a thousand men of the cloth, a most impressive number (amounting to

about one-tenth of the English clergy of the time). Since Scotland was Presbyterian and since James I had been ruling Scotland as James VI for over 30 years, the Puritan hopes were running high that the new king might respond sympathetically to their demands.

James accepted the *Millenary Petition* as a basis for convening a religious colloquy in Hampton Court, 14-16 January, 1604. That decision, which was among his first acts of state, boded well for the Puritan faction. But once the conference began, it became painfully clear that their cause would find no advancement from the crown. The four Puritans invited, all of them handpicked as advocates of only moderate changes, were even excluded from the first day's deliberations. When finally admitted on the second day, the foursome faced a large number of Anglican churchmen. John Reynolds, president of Corpus Christi College in Oxford, spoke for the Puritans; Richard Bancroft, Bishop of London and soon to be Archbishop of Canterbury, was the chief representative of Anglican views. Along with the King, these two did most of the disputing.

From the outset, James dashed hope after hope for accommodation. He flatly rejected every single proposal the Puritans presented except for just one – and that one request seemed to slip from Reynolds' lips without much forethought.

While objecting to certain liturgical practices in the *Book of Common Prayer*, Reynolds stated 'May your Majesty be pleased to direct that the Bible be now translated, such versions as are extant not answering to the original'.[1] This matter did not appear in the *Millenary Petition* nor was it a burning issue for any known Puritan group. On the surface, it seems to have been a tangential comment. Apparently, Reynolds was using the presence of the biblical texts in the *Book of Common Prayer* as a pathway for an assault.

This plea was also unstrategic. After all, the most prominent of the various English translations available in January 1604 were the Bishops' Bible (1568; revised in 1572) and the Geneva Version (1560). The fact that the Geneva Bible dominated England must have been a source of satisfaction to Reynolds and his co-religionists because it was a partisan Calvinist work, packed full of notes that expressed Puritan views. Any threat to its continued success only ran the risk of dampening Puritan influence. Moreover, while the Bishops' Bible was not one of the great translations in the history of the Bible, it did not overtly offend Puritan views. It was essentially benign.

So why Reynolds' outburst? Was it just a rhetorical jab at the *Book of Common Prayer*? Whatever else the Puritans may have been, they were also unquestionably 'scrupulous'. Reynolds himself was a great scholar, one

who, despite his Puritanism, would be invited to sit on one of the translating committees.

It is likely that Reynolds meant what he said and that he was reacting to new biblical scholarship that had appeared since the Geneva translation of 1560. In particular, the so-called Antwerp Polyglot and a new Latin translation of Hebrew Scriptures by Immanuel Tremellius may have made him feel that the 'versions as are extant' were 'not answering to the original'. The improvements offered by the Antwerp Polyglot seem now to be slight, but its inclusion of new ancient parallel texts for the Old and New Testament was a breakthrough. These ancient versions, mostly in cognate Semitic languages, were sometimes helpful for assessing the senses of obscure places in the Hebrew and Greek. Possibly, Reynolds had slightly overestimated the importance of the Antwerp Polyglot. Nonetheless, a major task of the KJV translators would be accuracy. They carefully studied all vernacular translations made since the Antwerp Polyglot appeared (in particular, the French Genevan revision of 1587/88, the Spanish version by Cypriano de Valera of 1602 and the Italian Bible of Giovanni Diodati from 1607). They also followed Tremellius's interpretation carefully.

When Reynolds proposed the new translation, Bishop Bancroft dutifully disagreed. His famous retort was, 'If every man's humour should be followed there would be no end of translating'.[2] There is certainly much to be said for Bancroft's position!

The King silenced the inchoate wrangling with the stunning pronouncement that he 'could never yet see a Bible well translated in English, but the worst of all, his majesty thought, the Geneva to be.'[3] Bancroft backpedalled so furiously

Fig. 8.1. *Engraved portrait of King James I by Simon van de Pas, from* The Workes of the Most High and Mighty Prince, James *(London: Robert Barker and John Bill, 1616). Though not the translator of the Bible that bears his name, James I (1566-1625) was nevertheless himself a prolific writer, composing tracts on such varied topics as poetry, demonology, monarchical rule, the Gunpowder Plot – and on the evils of tobacco. His role in the making of the Bible was less direct. The idea for a new translation of the Bible came from John Reynolds (1549-1607), a Puritan minister who first proposed the idea on 15 January 1604 at the Hampton Court Conference. The king supported the project, which was undertaken by six teams of scholars at Westminster, Oxford and Cambridge. That the Bible is commonly, though not officially, named after him, was an inevitable result of his patronage and his position as head of the Church of England. Although he was the son of the Roman Catholic Mary, Queen of Scots, and was brought up in Presbyterian Scotland, he approved of the episcopal governance of the Church of England.*

that he immediately became chief overseer of the grand project.

But what moved James to take his position? The king knew that some notes in the Geneva scoffed at kings, which may have made him feel some insecurity on his new throne. James openly admitted that the Scottish Presbyterian system was not compatible with his view of monarchy. His fear was: no bishops, no monarchy. The presbyterian system of church governance, which included control of churches by members, was too democratic. His political fears are plainly seen in his statement that the Geneva Bible was 'very partial, untrue, seditious and savouring too much of dangerous and traitorous conceits'. Among

the passages he cited was a note to 2 Chronicles 15:16 complaining that King Asa should have executed his own mother for her lawlessness. It did not help matters that James's mother, Mary, Queen of Scots, had been executed. Other notes also endorsed political disobedience. A gloss of Romans 13:5, for example, stated that Christians should obey magistrates only as far as conscience allows and that 'it is better to obey God than men'.[4]

An unspoken problem was the awkwardness of having one Bible in the pulpits and another in the houses of the realm. The Bishops' Bible was used in services, whereas the Geneva Bible was dominating the market and therefore household reading.

The Church of England was generally committed to uniformity and such an inconsistency, although we take competing versions for granted nowadays, would have been viewed as a problem.

James had his share of faults but he was no intellectual slouch. He participated at Hampton Court as a scholar with a broad background in biblical studies. The text of the Bible really was an affair of the state, and James shouldered his duty in that respect admirably. He may have been the best-educated regent of his time. By the age of eight, he could translate any chapter of the Bible from Latin to French to English. He also knew Italian, Hebrew and Greek. He memorised large portions of the Bible and was a prolific writer. By 1616 his works filled a small folio volume of 569 pages and included a commentary on Revelation, a meditation on the Lord's Prayer, treatises on demonology and a *Counterblast against Tobacco*. James had a special interest in the Psalms, thirty of which he recast in English verse. Moreover, in 1601, he had secured approval from an assembly of the Scottish Church, on his initiative, for a revision of the Geneva Bible. Nothing came of that project, unless we construe the events in England as an ambitious reformulation of that Scottish goal.

Regulations for Translating

Although he was not one of the translators, James did extend his governing hand to the task of organising the project. He participated in the two crucial preliminaries — establishing a set of guidelines for the project and selecting the teams of translators. Despite his own recent counterblast, Richard Bancroft agreed to be chief overseer of the project. Although the famous fifteen rules for the translators are credited to Bancroft, James himself was a major force behind them. In a letter he sent to Bancroft on 22 July 1604, James also announced the appointment of fifty-four people to six translation teams.[5]

The guidelines were designed to ensure scholarly accuracy and to preserve as much tradition as possible.

1. The ordinary Bible read in the church, commonly called the *Bishops' Bible,* to be followed, and as little altered as the truth of the original will permit.

2. The names of the prophets, and the holy writers, with the other names of the text, to be retained, as nigh as may be, accordingly as they were vulgarly used.

3. The old ecclesiastical words to be kept, viz. the word *church* not to be translated *congregation* etc.

4. When a word hath divers significations, that to be kept which hath been most commonly used by the most of the ancient fathers, being agreeable to the propriety of the place and the analogy of the faith.

5. The division of the chapters to be altered, either not at all, or as little as may be, if necessity so require.

6. No marginal notes at all to be affixed, but only for the explanation of the Hebrew or Greek words, which cannot without some circumlocution, so briefly and fitly be expressed in the text.

7. Such quotations of places to be marginally set down as shall serve for the fit reference of one scripture to another.

8. Every particular man of each company, to take the same chapter, or chapters, and having translated or amended them severally by himself, where he thinketh good, all to meet together, confer what they have done, and agree for their parts what shall stand.

9. As any one company hath dispatched any one book in this manner they shall send it to the rest, to be considered of seriously and judiciously for his majesty is very careful in this point.

10. If any company, upon the review of the book so sent, doubt or differ upon any place, to send them word thereof; note the place, and withal send the reasons to which if they consent not the difference to be compounded at the general meeting, which is to be of the chief persons of each company, at the end of the work.

11. When any place of special obscurity is doubted of letters to be directed, by authority, to send to any learned man in the land, for his judgment of such a place.

12. Letters to be sent from every bishop to the rest of his clergy, admonishing them of this translation in hand; and to move and charge as many as being skilful in the tongues; and having taken pains in that kind, to send his particular observations to the company, either at Westminster, Cambridge or Oxford.

13. The directors in each company, to be the Deans of Westminster and Chester for that place; and the king's professors in the Hebrew or Greek in either university.

14. These translations to be used when they agree better with the text than the *Bishops' Bible*: *Tyndale's, Matthews, Coverdale's, Whitchurch's* [*The Great Bible*], *Geneva*.

15. Besides the said directors before mentioned, three or four of the most ancient and grave divines, in either of the universities, not employed in translating, to be assigned by the vice-chancellor, upon conference with the rest of the heads, to be overseers of the translations as well Hebrew as Greek, for the better observation of the fourth rule above specified.[6]

The Translators

It has been often remarked that the King James Version of the Bible is the only literary masterpiece that has ever been written by a committee. Actually, six committees pulled off the feat. The 'learned men' appointed by James I were divided into six companies – two groups met at Westminster, two at Cambridge and two at Oxford. At any earlier point in English history, it would not have been possible to assemble such a large number of people with the necessary linguistic skills. In 1525, Tyndale certainly did not have the ideal language training for his historic task. But he pushed ahead nevertheless. It was a sign of the times that by 1604 the King himself may have had better training in biblical philology than had the pioneer Tyndale. In the aftermath of Tyndale's generation biblical studies attracted the most gifted minds in England. The text of the Bible mattered. Textual studies became entrenched as the foundation for theological work at universities. Consequently, in 1604, when it came to rounding up biblical translators, one could afford the luxury of being a little choosy.

The First Westminster Company translated Genesis to 2 Kings. Among its members were Lancelot Andrewes, John Overall, Hadrian a Saravia, William Bedwell, Richard Tomson, Richard Clark, John Layfield, Robert Tighe, Francis Burleigh and Geoffrey King.

As Dean of Westminster, Lancelot Andrewes presided in name; as one of the remarkable textual scholars of his age and also a most gifted writer, Andrewes also presided in deed. At least, it is safe to assume so. Among the dozen languages he knew well were Hebrew, Greek, Latin, Syriac and Aramaic. He seemed a linguistic wonder to all who knew him. The American poet T.S. Eliot, who developed a special devotion to this scholar, gushed that Andrewes 'takes a word and derives the world from it; squeezing and squeezing the word until it yields a full juice of meaning, which we should never have supposed any word to possess'.[7] It would not be unreasonable to include Andrewes in a list of the most successful English preachers of all time. Even King James, a notoriously disrespectful church-goer, a man prone to snoring loudly during the sermon, admired Andrewes' homilies. Andrewes was opposed to oratorical ostentation. For him, a sermon should be judged by its impact. Did it cause sinners to do good deeds? If so, the sermon was admirable.

We cannot identify the specific contributions of Andrewes or those of anyone else in any group. Much indicates that Andrewes was a powerful force. Yet others also brought great gifts to the project. The scholarship of William Bedwell stood out even in this crowd of experts in Semitic languages. He had the distinction of writing the first Arabic lexicon in England.[8] Richard Clark was regius professor of Hebrew at Cambridge University. Hadrian a Saravia, formerly a pastor in Antwerp, helped draw up the Calvinistic Belgic Confession, supported the authority of bishops, and aided in translating the Bible into a language that was not his native tongue. John Overall, regius professor of divinity at Cambridge, was one of the leading Latin stylists of his age. John Layfield had excellent training in the ancient languages, especially Greek; he was also expert in the history of architecture, which must have been of some service for those knotty descriptions of the Temple. He was also the only translator who had been to the New World.

The First Westminster group had one of the most colourful translators. Richard 'Dutch' Tomson had a reputation for heavy drinking. Yet even if he had too much at night, it was said that his head was clear the next morning so that he could do his work with competence.[9] Born in Holland but educated in England, he also accepted the theology of Jacob Arminius (best known for being a Calvinist who opposed predestination). Tomson reminds us that a whole spectrum of Protestant views was represented by the translators. Moreover, even if there were no Catholics, the King James Version eschewed diatribes against Roman Catholicism.

In rough descending order of significance, Tyndale, Geneva and Coverdale exerted the greatest influence on the Pentateuch. For Joshua through to 2 Kings, Coverdale contributed nearly as much as did the Geneva. The main reason for this is that the Geneva had not needed to change very much in the smooth narrative stretches of Tyndale and Coverdale.

The Westminster companies met in the Jerusalem Chamber of Westminster Abbey. It is entered through two small rooms, the Samaria and Jericho rooms. King Henry IV died in the Jerusalem Chamber in 1483 and the roomApparently, Henry had planned to go to the Holy Land in that year but had suffered a stroke and was moved to this chamber where he recovered consciousness. It had been prophesied that he would die in Jerusalem, so when he asked where he was, and was told the 'Jerusalem Chamber' the meaning of the prophecy became clear. The Jerusalem Chamber's connection to the English Bible would extend beyond this project. It was also used for the Revised Version in 1870, the New English Bible in 1961 and the Revised English Bible in 1989.

The First Cambridge Company produced the translation of 1 Chronicles to Ecclesiastes. Among its members were Edward Lively, John Richardson, Laurence Chaderton, Francis Dillingham, Thomas Harrison, Roger Andrewes (brother of Lancelot Andrewes), Andrew Bing and Robert Spalding.

Altogether no fewer than three regius professors of Hebrew would participate in this group: Lively, Spalding and Bing. Geneva had the greatest impact, although, after 2 Chronicles, the Great Bible's impact increases. The poetic books, including the Psalms, showed much more independence, even though Geneva and especially Coverdale continues to echo in the formulations of the Psalms.

The First Oxford Company translated the rest of the Hebrew Bible, Isaiah to Malachi. Its roster of members included John Harding, John Reynolds, Thomas Holland, Richard Kilby, Miles Smith, Richard Brett and Richard Fairclough.

John Harding, regius professor of Hebrew, presided over this group. Apparently, the most dedicated leadership came from John Reynolds, the Oxford don who bravely faced Bancroft at the Hampton Court Conference. Several accounts claim that his unceasing devotion to the project hastened his death, which occurred on 21 May 1607. He even held meetings with other translators as he lay on his deathbed. He was a fine scholar but, as we saw at the Hampton Court Conference, one with openly Puritan proclivities. Elizabeth I is said to have 'scolded him for his obstinate precision'. Miles Smith, the gifted scholar and writer who would later compose the famous preface, *The Translators to the Reader*, was also an active member of this team. Geneva was their most influential source.

The Second Cambridge Company translated the Apocrypha. This group exerted the greatest independence from tradition. Among its members were John Duport, William Branthwaite, Samuel Ward, Andrew Downes, John Bois, Jeremiah Radcliffe and Robert Ward.

The earlier translations for the Apocrypha had not been on as sturdy a scholarly foundation as had other parts of the Bible. Butterworth estimates that the translators were original in some two-thirds of their renderings. John Duport, master of Jesus College, presided over this group. Andrew Downes was regius professor of Greek. The group is also noteworthy for including two members who left behind important records of the project. In 1618,

Samuel Ward attended the Synod of Dort, a historically important conference of Calvinist theologians who stamped out the teachings of Jacob Arminius against predestination. Ward gave a report there on 'the very accurate English version . . . instituted by the most Serene King James'.[10] More significantly, John Bois left notes for meetings at Stationers' Hall in London among the twelve representatives from the six teams who hammered out a final version. The notes, which only cover discussions of Romans to Revelation, do not give a clear sense of how difficulties were resolved, but they do document the meticulousness of the process. The twelve representatives painstakingly considered many options for rendering passages under review.

Andrew Downes must have played a major role in this group. As regius professor of Greek, he was a formidable scholar. In Bois's notes on the meetings at Stationers' Hall, Downes emerges as a powerful contributor to the final analysis of the New Testament text (no notes on the Old Testament or Apocrypha deliberations are known to have survived). He led the way with multiple proposals for alternatives for difficult passages in the New Testament. Downes was a testy, self-possessed professor, who would not always appear at meetings voluntarily – he may have been protesting the slight remuneration. The king's constables were sent on several occasions to escort the recalcitrant academic to the meetings and Downes even managed to secure extra pay from the king, a singular accomplishment.

The Second Oxford Company, which was led by Thomas Ravis, dean of Christ Church, translated the Gospels, Acts and Revelation. Among its members were George Abbot (1562-1633), the future

Archbishop of Canterbury (1611-33), Sir Henry Saville, John Harmer, John Perrin, Giles Thomson, Richard Edes, John Aglionby and James Montague. Abbot would later suffer the ignominy of having killed another human being in a hunting accident. Though deeply remorseful all his life, he was technically disqualified from church service as a 'man of blood'. However, when a council of bishops could not decide whether to make an exception and restore him, King James came to the rescue and granted Abbot a pardon. In 1604, however, Abbot was known as a powerful biblical exegete, having published a massive study of Jonah in 1600. He also corresponded voluminously with the king on theological subjects. Some of their letters run to over one thousand words.

Tyndale, who made his finest contributions in the Gospels, gave the second Oxford group a good basis for its work.

The Second Westminster Company translated Romans to Jude. William Barlow, John Spenser, Roger Fenton, Michael Rabbett, Thomas Sanderson, Ralph Hutchinson and Williams Dakins are the known members of this group.

The New Testament epistles present some of the greatest challenges to the biblical translator. The meaning of the letters is almost always clear enough, but the style of some passages is rough; some passages appear to have been composed in considerable haste, perhaps without adequate care. An uneven original text makes for dreary work on the part of translators. This group rose to the occasion with quite innovative style. It used the Bishops' Bible more than had any other group. It also freely incorporated suggestions from the Rheims New Testament of 1582, especially in its use of Latinate vocabulary.

This group allowed itself great liberty in varying the English equivalents for the same Greek words, making the English version in some ways smoother than the Greek. Butterworth stressed the example of the Greek *katargeo* or *katargeomai*, which was translated fifteen different ways in Romans and the two letters to the Corinthians. This variety in diction noticeably brightens the text. The group included William Barlow, who is also important as the author of *The Sum and Substance of the Conference* (1604), the best historical source for the proceedings at the Hampton Court Conference.

Creating the Fair Copy and Printing the Book

The reader of the KJV will not detect stylistic differences between the various groups. One reason for this is that two men from each company met in a final committee to determine the final form of the text. The names of three members are known for sure: Andrew Downes, John Harmer and John Bois. This last phase of editing occurred in 1609 at Stationers' Hall in London. Thereafter, two men, Miles Smith and Bishop Thomas Bilson, took responsibility for preparing the final manuscript – the fair copy – for the printer.

King James was notoriously impecunious. Apparently, he spent none of his own resources on the Bible. In July 1604 Bancroft had to propose that the clergy underwrite the cost of the new Bible. There was no zeal on the part of the clergy to come up with the money even though Bancroft threatened to inform the King how much each gave. It seems the scheme came to naught. The scholars had to struggle living on their own resources, although free room and board were provided. Each member of the final revision committee of twelve, which met daily for nine months, was given a weekly stipend of thirty shillings – but from the King's printer! It is, however, known that the reluctant and plaintive Downes did manage to squeeze a sizable bonus out of James for the work – fifty pounds.

The king's printer was Robert Barker, and he paid 3,500 pounds for the exclusive rights to print the new Bible. What happened to the original manuscript is not known. However, a pamphlet circulating in London in 1660 complained that certain printers had in their possession that original manuscript. Perhaps it was destroyed in the Great Fire of 1666. Perhaps because Barker was the King's authorised printer to publish this Bible, the Bible was said to be 'authorised'. In fact, no official sanction survives, though King James obviously supported and endorsed the project. The title page, after all, identifies it as the Bible which was 'appointed to be read in the churches'. Approximately 20,000 copies were printed, although not all of these were bound at once. Thus, pages left over from one folio printing could be used in subsequent ones.

This accounts for the 'he/she' controversy, as well as several other less celebrated differences. Two 1611 editions had different translations of Ruth 3:15. One reads 'he went into the city' and the other 'she went into the city'. Although the Hebrew could be translated either way, even today English translations waver as to how that verse should be interpreted. The current King James reads 'she' while the New International Version has 'he' in the text and 'she' in a note. Most believe that the 'he' Bible of 1611 represents the first edition, while the 'she' Bible is a second issue of the first edition (dated 1613 on the Old Testament title page and 1611 on

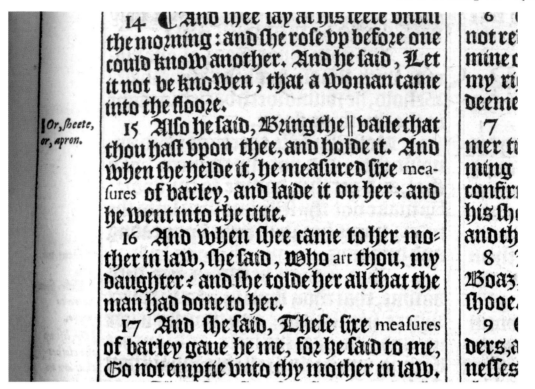

Fig. 8.2. The first edition of the King James Bible seems to have been printed in two versions – perhaps at two separate presses – that both appeared at the same time in 1611. We know this because there are slight differences in the text of copies of the 1611 edition. The variants are known as the 'He' and the 'She' Bible because of their renderings of Ruth 3:15. One, probably the first issue, reads 'he went into the citie', while the other claims that 'she went into the citie'. Though Ruth 3:15 is the most famous difference, there are, in fact, over two hundred variations between the two issues of 1611. Because the 1611 Bible was often used as copy text for subsequent Bibles, the variant also occurs in many later printings of the KJV, with the result that bibliographers speak of 'He Bibles' and 'She Bibles'. Both versions of the 1611 edition are also riddled with typographical and editorial errors, including faulty psalm references and in one place a disconcertingly mistaken 'Judas' where the text should read 'Jesus' (Matthew 26:36). The 1613 printing corrected some of these errors, but the first conscious attempt at revision would not be undertaken until 1629.

the New). The first quarto and octavo editions (1612) have 'he', but another octavo edition of 1612 reads 'she'.

There are several other oddities. Matthew 26:36 of the 1613/11 substitutes 'Judas' for 'Jesus' in the phrase 'then commeth Judas with them unto a place called Gethsemane'. The paragraph symbol (¶) does not appear after Acts 10:36. Perhaps Barker simply ran out of them. Matthew 23:24 reads (and still mistakenly

does) 'strain at a gnat' rather than 'strain out a gnat'. Luke 23:32 implies that Jesus was also a malefactor by saying 'two other malefactors'. Later, this was corrected by placing commas around the word 'malefactors'.

The page-designs for the first edition are stately. The reverential student approaching the first edition of the KJV for the first time will not be disappointed. Based on the Bishops' Bible, the pages display large,

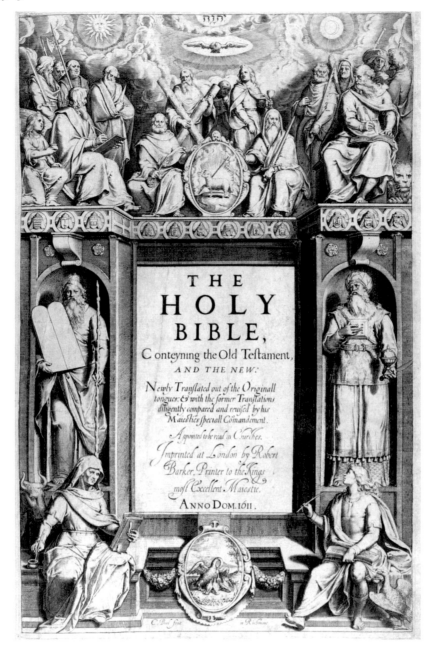

Fig. 8.3. Title page of the first edition of the King James Bible, 1611, by the engraver Cornelius Boel († after 1616). Symbols represent the Trinity at the top (the Hebrew letters for Yahweh, the dove of the Holy Spirit and the Lamb of God). In the upper panel, the apostles are gathered with Matthew and Mark, shown writing. Luke and John sit at the bottom of the architectural frame with their symbols of bull and eagle. In the frame itself, as if statues in niches, stand Moses with the tablets of the Law on the left and Aaron representing the priesthood on the right. The lengthy title emphasises the translation's roots in the original languages without denying the role of earlier English translations that were 'diligently compared'. Almost fifty translators, in six committees, used the Bishops' Bible as their basis, revising as necessary to reflect the Hebrew and Greek most truthfully.

decorative, elegant and lucid gothic letters. Thin lines form rectangles around the columns of text, giving the text a sense of permanence and also serving to delineate the text from marginal notes. Most verses begin on a new line, with the verse number displayed. This lavish layout is relatively easy to manage because the double-columns reduce the line length. The designers, again inspired by the earlier practices of the Geneva and Bishops' Bible, carefully distinguished scholarly insertions from sacred text. They used roman font for words with a shaky textual status. For example, words that do not literally render words of the original are set in roman or glossed. Also, it often happens because of different idioms and different syntax that words must be added to the English rendering in order to create complete sentences in English. The most common example is the verb 'to be', which is frequently omitted in biblical Hebrew. These words are also put in roman font. In later editions that used roman as the main font, these words and phrases are set in italics.

The general title is a fine copperplate engraving by Cornelius Boel. It is a noble image, certainly the most recognisable title page of the entire seventeenth century. The New Testament title page is a wood engraving. A few copies have the general title with a woodcut border dated 1611 instead of the copperplate engraving.

The design of the title page represents an important modification over previous English Bible title pages. For one thing, the vulgarity of the king's image authorising scripture has disappeared. Images of Henry VIII, Edward VI and Elizabeth I had adorned many title pages, propagating the concept of the monarch's headship over the church in England.

Boel's design conveys the sense of the material and spiritual worlds converging in the monumentality of the Bible to form an architecture for Christian life and faith. The law and the gospel, by now the venerable mainstays of Protestant iconography, are still present in the statues of Moses and Aaron on the entablature niches, as well as in the images of the four evangelists in the four corners. The sequence of evangelists, going clockwise and beginning with the upper left, is Matthew (with the angel), Mark (with the lion), Luke (with the ox) and John (with the eagle). The overall look, however, is not distinctively Protestant. Unlike Lutheran title pages, as we saw in the example of the Matthew's Bible (see Chapter Three), the law and gospel are not oppositional. Rather, in combination, they form the substance of Christian life. The symbols for the Trinity dominate the upper centre of the composition: the tetragrammaton (four letters designating God's name), the dove designating the Holy Spirit and the lamb representing Christ. Even more than the Trinity, it is the unity of scripture that the engraving stresses. The twelve tents represent the twelve tribes (and patriarchs) of Israel, the history of the Old Testament, whereas the twelve martyrs of the top segment are the Apostles, the witnesses to faith in Christ, as articulated in the New Testament.

This depiction of the twelve Apostles brings us to a noticeable feature – the compatibility with Catholic sensibilities. The Apostles appear as martyrs, carrying the symbols of their martyrdoms, most of which are drawn from extra-biblical sources, very much a part of the Catholic tradition. Similarly, the eucharistic symbol of the pelican at the base is a common Catholic emblem. It designates Christ's sacrifice and also the

Fig. 8.4. The New Testament title page of the King James Bible, 1611.

This unsigned woodcut exudes symbolism, from the heavenly authority of Hebrew letters for God at the top to the more worldly printers' rights clause of 'cum privilegio' at the very bottom of the page. The dove and the Lamb of God complete the Trinity, and the symbols for the twelve tribes of Israel run down the left border, while those of the twelve Apostles balance them on the right.

In addition, representations of the four evangelists are shown with their various emblems: Matthew (with an angel) and Mark (with a lion) at the top and Luke (with an ox) and John (with an eagle) at the bottom. The whole sends a clear message that the writings of the New Testament are not only to be considered inspired, but also rooted in authority and tradition.

presence of Christ in the Eucharist. There is nothing in the engraving that would seem alien to a traditional Catholic sensibility.

Doctrinal Neutrality

Unlike the fiery Bibles of protest (Tyndale, Geneva and Rheims), the KJV tries to avoid giving offence. In fact, the KJV conveys the impression that, on the whole, the text of the Bible is without controversy. The only partisanship of importance is a stray comment or two in *The Translators to the Readers*, cavilling against the scrupulosity of the Puritans and ranting, briefly, against the turgidity of the 'papists'.[11] Scholars of the English Bible are familiar with many laments in older studies that the preface has long since been dropped from KJV publications. Those older laments are all from Anglicans, insensitive to these exceptions. It is only without the preface that the KJV can be used by all Christians; its absence is one reason why so many Christians of a most unepiscopal stripe still accept no other translation.

Still, there are many notes in the KJV. None of them promote theological or creedal stances. Instead, they include references to parallel passages, alternative manuscript readings, and, above all, possible alternative translations of words or phrases. Not counting the references to parallel scriptures, the Old Testament has 6,637 philological notes. This far exceeds the number of textual notes in the Geneva Bible (which, however, bulk larger because they also offer historical and theological information). Over 4,000 of these notes give literal renderings of Hebrew idioms and some 2,156 offer alternative manuscript readings for the text. The New Testament has 765 notes, of which 35 give manuscript variants, 112 literal renderings of Greek idioms and 582 possible alternative translations.[12]

The only sensitive issue that could not be answered by silence was the question of ecclesiastical words. Ever since Tyndale, more radical Bibles have tried to jettison some of the traditional terminology – 'congregation' instead of 'church', 'senior' or 'elder' instead of 'priest', even 'washing' instead of 'baptism'. These changes aim to lower the prestige of the hierarchy and also to challenge traditional views on the sacraments. Obviously, a decision had to be made. The KJV, as enshrined in its regulation (rule 3), opted for the traditional terminology of 'church' and 'baptism', a decision that indicates moderation more than a rebuff to radicals.

Earlier Versions and Originality

One element that stands out in the fifteen regulations is the deference shown the previous translations. The sixteenth-century Bibles had indeed accomplished so much that deserved to be retained. The translators were aware of their dependence on the earlier English Bibles. As quoted in the epigraph to this chapter, they sought to improve ('to make a good one better') and to make one standard version out of the many different Bibles in circulation ('or out of many good ones' to make 'one principal good one'). *The Translators to the Reader* acknowledges the contributions of previous translations and reminds the reader that the history of Bible translation is a history of continuous revision and correction. The authors do, however, betray confidence that they have finally done it – they have produced a standard, one 'principal' and 'good' version.

The companies display slight variances in their relationships to the earlier versions. One reason for this is that the different segments of the earlier versions had varying degrees of success. The Psalms, for example, were Miles Coverdale's most powerful contribution. Tyndale hadn't touched them; nor could Tyndale be a source for the final books of the Old Testament or for the Apocrypha because he did not get that far before his execution. The Geneva, generally, exerted the greatest influence in those segments. In accord with the rules, the Bishops' Bible, apparently the imprint of 1602, was the basis for the deliberation of all groups. Robert Barker, it is said, provided forty unbound copies of the Bishops' Bible for the groups to use in their deliberations. Nonetheless, of the earlier translations, the Bishops' Bible certainly did not make the largest contribution. The earlier translations were closely consulted. Also, the Bishops' Bible itself depended on earlier versions.

An implicit goal was to create a version that would sound as familiar and traditional as possible. Individual idiosyncrasy – even if that meant verve – was not desired. A Tyndalian 'tush, tush' would have to go. The new version tried to create the illusion that the text had always sounded precisely this way. This is one of the reasons that the language of the KJV was slightly archaic even in 1611.

In fact, the earlier versions, especially Tyndale, Geneva and those by Coverdale (the Bible of 1535 and the Great Bible), did make substantial contributions. Measuring the influence of the precursors is an inexact science. One way to approach the question is to count the first occurrences of the words that appeared in the KJV. Another, rather more telling way, is to count the first appearances of complete phrases in the KJV. Charles Butterworth conducted some studies according to this second method, although his statistics are derived only from analyses of samples, not the entirety, of the text. Of the phrases in the KJV, 39% were original to it; 19% were from the Geneva Bible; 18% from Tyndale (including the Matthew Bible); 13% from Coverdale Bibles and 4% from the Bishops' Bible (including the revision of 1572).[13]

The high percentage of originality in KJV is debatable. Butterworth recorded the first occurrences of the exact phrasing of the KJV. Even the slightest change would score a phrase as being original to the KJV. Nonetheless, slight changes are important and it is often in light editing that a merely adequate phrase becomes a classic. Tyndale would score a much higher percentage, if one calculated the number of individual words or even 'almost final' wording of phrases. Indeed, Butterworth's approach will not please Tyndale admirers. Nonetheless, when one looks closely at the individual cases, there really is something important in the slight alterations made by the KJV scholars. They did bring stability and completeness to the phrases. It is rare to find a revised phrase that does not make a noticeable improvement.

In many ways, Tyndale is the opposite of the KJV. Although Tyndale has found many champions among modern readers, a few who even argue his literary superiority over KJV, there is something idiosyncratic in his nervous, energetic style that makes the Bible seem the work of an individual translator. Tyndale's English has the electrical charge of a protestor. Martin Luther said that a Bible translation should be in fresh colloquial language and that readers should feel as though 'it had been written only yesterday'. Even if his theology would deviate slightly from the Wittenbergers, Tyndale would remain very much under the influence of Luther's approach to style.

The KJV did not give the impression of having just been written, even in the seventeenth century. It presented itself as the ancient word of God in formulations hallowed by the patina of age.

An Audible Bible – Listen for the Word of God!

Whatever its gait, nearly every sentence in the KJV moves smoothly and with a natural dignity. Similarly, nearly every passage sounds complete and finished. Often there is a palpable grandiloquence, for the primary purpose of this translation was public reading aloud. That was also the primary method in its composition. The committees tested every phrase audibly – they read it to each other, probably again and again, until it sounded right. One thinks of a troupe of actors and a dramatist going over a new play until every line works as it should. In this process, many phrasings were rejected, but, finally, one stood the test. It is no wonder that it took so many years to complete the task.

Over the centuries, many readers have commented on the cadences of the phrasing. Some scholars have tried to describe the prose rhythms, identifying passages that use different combinations of poetic meters. F.F. Bruce offered some examples of anapestic and dactylic feet in a few verses. On the whole, his approach makes the impression of forcing a Latin pattern for poetry on English. The important point is that, while the phrases do not wear Bruce's tags very easily, the cadences are both beautiful and constantly shifting. It is arbitrary to identify anapests (a sequence of three syllables that run not-stressed, not-stressed, stressed) in 'Who hath believed our report, and to whom is the arm of the Lord revealed?' (Isaiah 53:1) and in 'My doctrine shall drop as the rain, my speech shall distil as the dew' (Deuteronomy 32:2), or even the combination of dactyls (stressed, not-stressed, not-stressed) and spondees (a sequence of two stressed syllables) as in the classical dactylic hexameter line, as in 'Bind their kings with chains, their nobles with fetters of iron' (Psalms 149:8) and 'How art thou fallen from heaven, O Lucifer, son of the morning' (Isaiah 14:2). The patterns Bruce identifies emerge only briefly, scanning but for a few words. But the prose, taken as a whole, has an unmistakable and appealing cadence, as is most evident in his excellent examples.[14]

The overall tone has gravitas. Occasionally, the rhetoric flies rather high. In other stretches, the literary flights are more poetic and even enigmatic. But even where the substance is weighty, the phrasing is never stodgy. One of the amazing accomplishments is that there is so much vigour and freedom in such carefully measured sentences. Fifty or so of the most erudite scholars of the early seventeenth century poring over a book for years on end? Most

people would predict stiffness akin to rigor mortis. One reason for the literary suppleness is the liberty all the groups exercised in their search for English equivalents. In some respects, one could argue that the KJV is the freest translation of the English Renaissance. The texture of the KJV is so finely worked that it introduces many literary sensations – especially in the form of subtle metaphors – that are not necessarily present in the original languages. A typical translation, especially one with legal or sacred ramification, needs to be, whatever else, accurate. For the KJV authors, the result also needed to be fluent and effective.

Above all, the translators did not equate accuracy with uniformity. Many people have wondered about the amazing variety shown by the translators in rendering the same words and phrases in the original. For example, the Hebrew original is identical in Isaiah 35:10 and 51:11. The translators put the identical passages in beautiful – but starkly divergent – variations:

> 35:10 And the ransomed of the Lord shall return and come to Zion with songs, and everlasting joy upon their heads. They shall obtain joy and gladness, and sorrow and sighing shall flee away.

> 51:11 Therefore the redeemed of the Lord shall return and come with singing unto Zion, and everlasting joy shall be upon their heads. They shall obtain gladness and joy, and sorrow and mourning shall flee away.[15]

Each of the companies exercised a similar degree of freedom, especially in renderings of the New Testament. The prefatory essay, *The Translators to the Reader*,

❧ December hath xxxj. dayes.

¶ The Moone xxx.

Sunne { riseth / falleth } houre { 8.mi.12 / 3.mi.48 }					Psalmes	¶ Morning Prayer		¶ Euening Prayer	
						1.Leſſon.	2.Leſſon.	1.Leſſon.	2.Leſſon.
	1	f		Kalend.	i	Eſa.xiiij.	Actes ij.	Eſa.xv.	Heb2.7.
xviij	2	g	iiii	No.	ii	xvj	iii	xvij	viij
vij	3	A	iii	No.	iii	xviij	iiii	xix	ix
	4	b	p2d.No.		iiii	xx.xxi.	v	xxii	x
xv	5	c	Nonas.		v	xxiij	vi	xxiiii	xi
iiii	6	d	viii	Jd.	Nicolas biſh.	vi	xxv	di.vii.	xxvi	xij
	7	e	vii	Jd.	vij	xxvij	di.vij.	xxviij	xiii
xij	8	f	vi	Jd.	Conc. of Mary.	viii	xxix	viii	xxx	Joh.i.d.
i	9	g	v	Jd.	ix	xxxj	ix	xxxij	ii
	10	A	iiii	Jd.	x	xxxiij	x	xxxiiii	iii
ix	11	b	iii	Jd.	xi	xxxv	xi	xxxvi	iiii
	12	c	p2d.Jd.	Sol in Capricor.	xij	xxxvij	xii	xxxviij	v
xvij	13	d	Idus.	Luci virgin.	xiij	xxxix	xiii	xl	1.Pet.i.
	14	e	xix	Kl.	Januarii	xiiii	xlj	xiiii	xlii	ii
vi	15	f	xviii	Kl.	xv	xliij	xv	xliiii	iii
xiiii	16	g	xvii	Kl.	O ſapientia.	xvi	xlv	xvi	xlvi	iiii
iii	17	A	xvi	Kl.	xvii	xlvij	xvij	xlviii	v
	18	b	xv	Kl.	xviii	xlix	xviij	l	2.Pet.i.
xi	19	c	xiiii	Kl.	xix	li	xix	lij	ii
xix	20	d	xiii	Kl.	Faſt.	xx	liij	xx	liiii	iii
	21	e	xii	Kl.	Thomas Apoſt.	xxi	P2o.xxiij.	xxi	P2ou.24.	1. John.
viij	22	f	xi	Kl.	xxii	Eſa.lv.	xxii	Eſa.56.	ii
	23	g	x	Kl.	xxiij	lvij	xxiii	lviii	iii.
xvi	24	A	ix	Kl.	Faſt.	xxiiii	lix	xxiiii	lx	iiii
v	25	b	viii	Kl.	Chriſtmas.	xxv	Eſa.ix.	Luke ij.	Eſa.7.	Titus.iii.
	26	c	vii	Kl.	S Steuen.	xxvi	P2ou.28.	Acts 6,7.	Ecclel.4.	Acts.7.
xiii	27	d	vi	Kl.	S.John.	xxvii	Ecclef.v.	Reuel.i.	Eccle.6.	Reuel.22.
ii	28	e	v	Kl.	Inn cents.	xxviii	Jerem.31.	Acts 25.	Wiſd.i.	1.Joh.iij.
	29	f	iiii	Kl.	xxix	Eſa.lxi.	xxvi	Eſa.62.	2.Joh.iij.
x	30	g	iii	Kl.	xxx	lxiij	xxvii	lxiiii	3.John.
	31	A	p2d.	Kl.	Silueſter biſh.	xxx	lxv	xxviii	lxvi	Jude.

Fig. 8.5. *The King James Bible followed the tradition of medieval manuscript Bibles in its inclusion of a calendar in the prefatory material. This handy reference records holy days and gives 'the order of Psalms and Lessons to be said at Morning and Evening prayer throughout the year'. The two-colour printing also harks back to the look of a manuscript.*

also celebrated that freedom in a deservedly famous passage:

> Another thing we think good to admonish thee of, gentle Reader, that we have not tied ourselves to a uniformity of phrasing, or to an identity of words, as some peradventure would wish that we had done, because they observe that some learned men somewhere have been as exact as they could that way. Truly, that we might not vary from the sense of that which we had translated before, if the word signified the same thing in both phrases (for there be some words that be not of the same sense everywhere) we were especially careful, and made a conscience, according to our duty. But that we should express the same option in the same particular word – as for example, if we translate the Hebrew or Greek word once by *Purpose*, never to call it *Intent*; if one were *Journeying*, never *Travelling*; if one were *Think*, never *Suppose*; if one were *Pain*, never *Ache*; if one were *Joy*, never *Gladness*, etc. – Thus to mince the matter, we thought to savour more of curiosity than wisdom. . . .[16] Is the kingdom of God become words and syllables? Why should we be in bondage then, if we may be free?

A major change in the Revised Version of 1881, the first attempt to supersede the KJV, was to bring uniformity to the renderings of identical phrases. The whole undertaking produced a wooden and pedantic version. Perhaps one could argue that the Revised Version was somewhat more literal but it was certainly not as effective as the KJV, which continued to be the dominant version for many decades thereafter.

A Hebrew Bible in English

In some respects, however, the KJV is the least free of the translations. A major component is its Hebraic structure. For the Old Testament, this is the quintessence of the KJV. Tyndale enthusiasts give their man credit for enriching the English language with its first literary contact with the Hebrew language. The most momentous encounter, however, comes with the KJV. Moreover, in this respect, the KJV's most important precursor is Geneva, not Tyndale. While there is a degree of subjectivity in these views and while assigning 'credit' for this development matters little, it is certainly true that Hebraisms are a major component of the KJV's sound. The KJV sounds different. It sounds ancient, ritualistic, even formulaic. A major reason for this difference is that the translators tuned their English instruments, as much as possible, to the scale of the original Greek and, especially, Hebrew syntax.

More than their predecessors, the translators tried to replicate the style of Hebrew syntax and they tried to do this systematically. We can see this in one of the most distinctive basic features of biblical Hebrew, the frequent use of the conjunction *waw*. Its primary sense is the concessive 'and', but it connotes causal and temporal senses, also. Most translators use different conjunctions and adverbs to render *waw*. But the KJV repeats 'and' after 'and' after 'and' to the extent that the reader now associates this structure of serial sentences beginning with 'and' with biblical English. In one stretch of fourteen verses (Genesis 25:21-34), the Hebrew Bible uses *waw* forty times. KJV renders thirty-six as 'and', while

---

HEBREW IDIOMS FROM THE KING JAMES BIBLE

The King James Bible translated many Hebrew phrases quite literally, thereby introducing a number of Hebraic idioms into standard English usage. We include a small sampling of this phenomenon that so enriched the English language. For more examples, see Rosenau 1902.

'to put words in his mouth'
[Exodus 4:15, etc.]

'to pour out one's heart'
[Psalm 62:8]

'to fall flat on his face'
[Numbers 22:31]

'pride goes before a fall'
[Proverbs 16:18]

'a man after his own heart'
[1 Samuel 13:14]

'like a lamb to the slaughter'
[Isaiah 53:7]

'the skin of my teeth'
[Job 19:20]

'sour grapes'
[Ezekiel 18:2]

'the land of the living'
[Job 28:13, etc.]

'from time to time'
[Ezekiel 4:10]

Geneva does this only twenty-four times.[17]

When someone says 'And it came to pass' or 'And it shall come to pass', we know immediately that that person is trying to sound 'biblical'. The phrase is a distinctive formula in biblical Hebrew *wayʰhî*, which is the 'and it came to pass' and *nʰhâyâh*, which means 'and it shall come to pass'. Earlier biblical translators thought that this flourish was usually unnecessary, a Hebrew idiom that sounded foreign in English. They almost always left it out. Yet it unquestionably stresses narrative continuity and it gives the narration a confident sense of formulaic certitude. Unlike their predecessors, the KJV translators were faithful to the original and truly created this distinctive ring for the English Bible. In the first twenty-two chapters of Genesis the formula appears eighteen times in the KJV, but only twice in the Geneva Version (and the Geneva Bible was the predecessor with the greatest fidelity to the

Hebrew).[18]

Among the distinctive elements of biblical Hebrew usage are several devices for giving emphasis to a phrase. One of these is the use of the same root twice in a sentence. Specifically, biblical Hebrew sometimes adds the infinitive of the same verb used as the main verb (finite verb) to stress the point. This infinitive structure is usually called the 'infinitive absolute' and it cannot really be translated into English. For example, *shâmôr shâmer* means something like 'he indeed kept'. (Literally, *shâmer* means 'he kept' and *shâmôr* means 'to keep'.) An early example of this usage is in Genesis 2:17, where God stresses to Adam that all will not go well if Adam eats of the tree of knowledge. Literally, God says 'you shall die to die'. The Geneva translators put this as 'Thou shalt die the death'. The KJV translators developed a systematic approach to conveying the emphatic repetition of the finite verb in the absolute infinitive construction. It uses adverbial intensifiers, in particular 'surely', 'verily' and 'utterly', which have become hallmarks of a biblical style. Thus, God says to Adam, 'thou shalt surely die'.

There are several other Hebrew structures for which the translators developed a formula. The *casus pendens*, which means 'the hanging case', is quite distinctive, for it stresses a noun and then repeats a pronominal reference to it in the normal word position of the sentence. Gerald Hammond defines it as 'the separation of the principal subject or object from the main body of the sentence, and then its repetition in the form of a retrospective pronoun or pronominal suffix'.[19] It is an emphatic structure that gives a unit of speech two separate insertions in the same sentence. Perhaps the closest thing we have in English is the placement of one word in apposition to another. But we cannot separate these words for emphasis. What is a translator to do? The precursors to the KJV ignored the structure! This blindness to the original does yield smoother sentences in English, but it misses the thrust and often even the rhythm of the phrase. The parallelisms of Hebrew are not always elegantly simple; they can be circular and bluntly stylised. The Geneva rendering of Psalms 10:5, 'Therefore defieth he all his enemies', seems unobjectionable until it is measured against the KJV's close following of the Hebrew structure, 'As for his enemies, he puffeth at them'. Thus, the formula is to use the prepositional phrase 'as for' plus the noun that will be re-expressed in the pronoun of the main clause. Among other advantages, this allowed the translators to adhere to the Hebrew word order quite closely. The literal rendering is both powerful and distinctive. It not only leaps off the page but also rings

in one's ear. Repetition is memorable. The same is true of other examples, even though in each case one might say the Geneva gives a more natural English phrase. However, natural can be bland and is certainly not true to the original: for example, Geneva's Psalms 147:20, 'He hath not dealt so with every nation, neither have they known his judgments,' became 'He hath not dealt so with any nation: and as for his judgments, they have not known them'.[20]

Sample Passages, Including Examples from Each Company

The statistics provided above from Butterworth's study do not give a real measure of the artistry of the KJV.

As Mark Twain once noted (attributing the statement to Benjamin Disraeli), 'There are three kinds of lies: lies, damn lies and statistics.' Rather than using statistics on phrases, the best way to appreciate the accomplishment of the KJV is to read a few of its passages in comparison to their closest precursors.

Often, in fact, the translators changed very little. But that very little made a very large difference. The beginning of Genesis, a translation carried out by the First Westminster Company, illustrates this point. Almost every syllable is taken from the Geneva version.

1 In the beginning God created the Heaven, and the Earth.
2 And the earth was without form, and void, and darkness *was* upon the face of the deep; and the Spirit of God moved upon the face of the waters.

The Geneva Bible had rendered most of this:

1 In the beginning God created the heaven and the earth.

2 And the earth was without form and void, and darkness *was* upon the deep, and the Spirit of God moved upon the waters.

Obviously, the Geneva Version contributed mightily to this auspicious beginning, and this close similarity is not atypical for the entire Bible. Frequently the credit we assign Tyndale or Coverdale is, in fact, an echo of their voices bouncing off the Geneva Version (or sometimes off the Bishops' Bible). The only difference between Geneva and the KJV is 'the face of', which appears twice in the latter. Is this important? In essence, it makes the translation more exact and makes it correspond more closely to the Hebrew. Earlier translators had simply left out the two occurrences of *p*ᵉ*nt* ('the face of'), assuming that it was not necessary for the sense. Yet the concept of surface adds meaningfully to the physical presence of God in this passage and the slightly elliptical formulation 'face' gives the prose a poetic ambiguity.

Similarly, not many individual words separate one of the best-known Psalms in the KJV from its precursors. For Psalm 23, the First Cambridge Company drew mostly on the melodic renderings of Coverdale, lightly edited in the Geneva version. The KJV reads as follows:

1 The Lord *is* my shepherd, I shall not want.
2 He maketh me to lie down in green pastures: he leadeth me beside the still waters.
3 He restoreth my soul: he leadeth me in the paths of righteousness, for his name's sake.
4 Yea though I walk through the valley of the shadow of death, I will fear no evil: for thou *art* with me, thy rod

and thy staff, they comfort me.
5 Thou preparest a table before me, in the presence of mine enemies: thou anointest my head with oil, my cup runneth over.
6 Surely goodness and mercy shall follow me all the days of my life: and I will dwell in the house of the Lord forever.

Once again, the differences from the Geneva version can be counted up quickly:

1 The Lord *is* my shepherd, I shall not want.
2 He maketh me to rest in green pasture, and leadeth me by the still waters.
3 He restoreth my soul, and leadeth me in the paths of righteousness for his name's sake.
4 Yea, though I should walk through the valley of the shadow of death, I will fear no evil: for thou art with me: thy rod and thy staff, they comfort me.
5 Thou doest prepare a table before me in the sight of mine adversaries: thou doest anoint my head with oil, *and* my cup runneth over.
6 Doubtless kindness, and mercy shall follow me all the days of my life, and I shall remain a long season in the house of the Lord.

The Geneva's refinement of Coverdale was impressive but the further improvements in the KJV are fine illustrations of the artistry that springs from its rigorous scholarship. In verse 2, the KJV renders the Hebrew more correctly (and more effectively) with 'lie down'. Geneva's use of the singular 'pasture' in that same verse contradicts the Hebrew; the singular also lessens the general sense of *all* that God provides. The use of 'beside' instead of 'by' might seem rather minor but 'beside' appreciably improves the rhythm by adding a stress to break up what had been five unstressed syllables in a row, a weak cadence typical for the Geneva. 'In the presence of' and 'enemies' are also closer to the original than were Geneva's 'in the sight of' and 'adversaries'. The two instances of the auxiliary 'doest' in Geneva's verse 5 bloat the sentences unnecessarily. The finale, 'for a long season', is a disastrous blunder, something that almost never happens in the KJV. However, the Hebrew idiom, 'for the length of days', is a little tricky, but it does mean exactly what the KJV gives — 'forever'. This correction also places the key concept of the entire Psalm at the end, which corresponds to the word order of the Hebrew as well. Psalm 23 was lovely in Coverdale, spirited and fairly reliable in Geneva, but it became eternal in the King James Version: 'I will dwell in the house of the Lord forever.'

Other passages are profoundly different from the precursors. With Isaiah 2:4, the First Oxford Company turned a moderately obscure sentence into one of the Bible's best-known winged words:

> 4 And he shall judge among the nations, and shall rebuke many people: and they shall beat their swords into plow-shares, and their spears into pruning hooks; nation shall not lift up sword against nation, neither shall they learn war any more.

The closest antecedent is the Geneva version: 'They shall break their swords also into mattocks, and their spears into scythes; nation shall not lift up a sword against nation, neither shall they learn to fight any more.' It is hard to imagine that this passage could ever have garnered its present popularity in any formulation other than that of the KJV. 'Breaking swords into mattocks' is a perfectly correct way to render the Hebrew, but does it capture the mind as does the smithing metaphor introduced in the KJV? Also, the Hebrew does say that they shall learn not 'to fight' anymore, but obviously 'war' is what this means and it was only the KJV that made this so plain and thus so profoundly hopeful.

The King James Version brought literary respectability to the Apocrypha. The Apocrypha were accepted by the early Christian church as Greek portions of the Old Testament but were eventually excluded from the Hebrew canon of the Jewish Bible. They are writings that exist primarily in Greek originals (not Hebrew originals). The medieval manuscripts of the Vulgate even mixed several of these books in with the translations of the Hebrew canon without making distinction. Typically, Protestants viewed them as being 'non-canonical' (i.e. not part of the inspired scripture) but edifying; Catholics labelled them as 'deutero-canonical,' which means canonical but in a secondary status. In earlier English Bibles, the apocryphal books were neglected children, wearing woefully tattered clothes. Many passages were so badly done as to be unsightly. In one respect, the Geneva Bible elevated the status of the Apocrypha: it grounded its translation in the latest scholarship on the original texts. Because of its approach to the Apocrypha, Geneva is in fact the first English Bible translated in its entirety according to the original languages. Nonetheless, the Apocrypha is the Geneva Bible at its most stilted. It often leaves the unmistakable impression of a translation of scholarly conjectures rather than of the text of God's word. The KJV, on the other hand, devoted equal energy to the Apocrypha, assigning a company of distinguished scholars solely to those books.

The acknowledged masterpieces are the Wisdom of Solomon and Sirach (the latter entitled Ecclesiasticus in the KJV). The following quote, Ecclesiasticus 24:1-5, from the KJV, restores simplicity to the highly poetic (and also allusively enigmatic) pronouncements of the personification of 'Wisdom':

1 Wisdom shall praise herself, and
shall glory in the midst of her people.
2 In the congregation of the most
high, shall she open her mouth, and
triumph before his power.
3 I came out of the mouth of the
most High, and covered the earth as
a cloud.
4 I dwelt in high places, and my throne
is in a cloudy pillar.
5 I alone compassed the circuit of
heaven, and walked in the bottom
of the deep.

The Geneva Version of this passage — and others — is a near total disaster. Obviously, the KJV translators consulted Geneva. But what they found was a sedimented text that needed to be distilled. Incidentally, this is a segment where the versification in the KJV differs from its predecessors':

1 Wisdom shall praise herself, [and
be honoured in God,] and rejoice in
the midst of her people.
2 In the congregation of the most
high shall she open her mouth, and
triumph before his power.
3 [In the midst of her people, shall
she be exalted, and wondered at in
the holy assembly.

4 In the multitude of the chosen she
shall be commended, and among
such as be blessed, she shall be praised,
and shall say,]
5 I am come out of the mouth of
the most high, [first born before all
creatures.
6 I caused the light that faileth not,
to arise in the heaven,] and covered
the earth as a cloud.
7 My dwelling is above in the height,
and my throne is in the pillar of the
cloud.
8 I alone have gone round about the
compass of heaven and have walked
in the bottom of the depth.

It is, however, only fair to say that the Geneva did give the KJV some beautiful lines in the Apocrypha, such as the classic phrase, just a few verses after this, 'Come unto me all ye that be desirous of me, and fill yourselves with my fruits' (Ecclesiasticus 24:19 in the KJV; 24:22 in the Geneva Version).

When it came to translating the New Testament, the KJV had much more than a foundation to build on. A century of English Bible production had erected a new temple of literary splendour for the Christian testament. Indeed, very little had to be altered in some cases, yet the slight modifications to the syntax, ornament, or tone could be decisive.

The Lord's Prayer, the work of the Second Oxford Company, is the same as in the Geneva Bible, with one slight change:

9 . . . Our Father which art in heaven,
hallowed be thy name.
10 Thy kingdom come. Thy will be
done, in earth, as it is in Heaven.
11 Give us this day our daily bread.
12 And forgive us our debts, as we
forgive our debtors.

13 And lead us not into temptation, but deliver us from evil: For thine is the kingdom, and the power, and the glory, for ever, Amen.

The only difference is in verse 12, where the KJV deleted 'also' from the Geneva Bible's 'as we also forgive our debtors'. In this instance the Geneva is the more literal version because its 'also' is the rendering of the original Greek's *kai*. The reason for the change is mysterious. Does the deletion make verse 12 more nearly parallel to verse 10? The 'also' does seem to weaken any stress on 'we,' and does soften the sound of the phrase. But there is nothing particularly wrong with that, especially since it is in the original. The bottom line is that the Geneva's Lord's Prayer brought Tyndale's version to its zenith. There was really nothing more to do.

Matthew 11:28-30, also the work of the Second Oxford Company, is another good example of the KJV putting the final touches to the Geneva New Testament, and everything they touched did turn to gold, it seems. In the Geneva, Christ speaks as follows:

28 Come unto me all ye that are weary and laden, and I will ease you.
29 Take my yoke on you, and learn of me, that I am meek and lowly in heart: and ye shall find rest unto your souls.
30 For my yoke is easy, and my burden is light.

King James has:

28 Come unto me all ye that labour, and are heavy laden, and I will give you rest.
29 Take my yoke upon you, and learn of me, for I am meek and lowly in heart: and ye shall find rest unto your souls.
30 For my yoke is easy, and my burden is light.

Except for verse 28, Geneva had already captured the full beauty of Christ's invitation. From a literal perspective, the translation 'ye that are weary' for the Greek 'hoi kopiôntes' is unobjectionable, as is the KJV change to 'ye that labour'. But from a literary perspective, the KJV phrasing has many advantages. The light alliteration between 'labour' and 'laden' is pleasing, as is the use of the active verb. 'Labour' also avoids the hint of redundancy that clings to the combination of 'weary' and 'laden'. The KJV rendering of 'pephotimenoi' as 'heavy laden' is a mark of finesse. It is what the Greek means and says. In 1525, Tyndale had been seduced by Luther's German word 'beladen', which is, however, not as neutral as its English cognate laden. But 'laden' seemed good enough to all of Tyndale's followers until 1611, even though the word by itself just does not express the onerousness connoted by the Greek original. The one phrase in the Geneva passage that cries out loudest for change is 'I will ease you,' a translation of the Greek 'anapauso'. The phrase is so awkward that it doesn't even seem to be a possible English usage. Moreover, this translation obliterates the echo of 'anapauso' in the noun 'anapausis' (rest) in verse 29. The KJV's brilliant solution – 'I will give you rest' – gracefully restores the full force of that significant repetition.

The verb tenses and moods in the original Greek caused intermittent difficulties in the history of the English Bible. Sometimes, translators undertook quite complex approaches. In his revision of the New Testament for the 1534 edition, Tyndale simplified the Greek verbs, using the argument that they were only intended to render original Semitic verb structures. This caused a good deal of refuse to enter the stream of English Bibles. The KJV purified the verbal system, which, though not really such a difficult task, was important. Even the highly reliable Geneva Bible used verb forms that were quite questionable. For example, Geneva translates the first two verses of 1 Corinthians 13, as follows:

> 1 Though I speak with the tongues of men and angels, and have not love, I am *as* sounding brass, or a tinkling cymbal.
> 2 And though I had the *gift* of prophecy, and knew all secrets and all knowledge, yea, if I had all faith, so that I could remove mountains and had not love, I were nothing.

Despite their obvious reliance on the diction of their precursors, the Second Westminster Company delivered a quite different text:

> 1 Though I speak with the tongues of men and of angels, and have not charity, I am become as sounding brass, or a tinkling cymbal.
> 2 And though I have the gift of prophecy, and understand all mysteries and all knowledge; and though I have faith, so that I could remove mountains, and have no charity, I am nothing.

A good place to start thinking about the treatment of verbs is with the italicised 'as' in the Geneva version. Those italics, as always, signal a departure from the original text. The Geneva does not explain what

that departure is, but a comparison with the Greek immediately shows us that the Genevans decided to omit the verb 'gegona,' which means, as the KJV says, 'I am become'. Certainly the awkward result in English is why the Genevans omitted this. There is no sense in being judgmental on these issues of taste, but, for this one, an ordinary sensibility would seem to favour the Genevans' side. Why did the KJV introduce this literal but clumsy phrase? Probably because the Westminster Company was so sensitive to the verbs in this section. The Genevans translated the present tense indicative in this section as a present tense subjunctive ('I were nothing' would nowadays be more commonly rendered as 'I would be nothing'). Throughout verse 2, the Greek is unequivocally present indicative, a tense that the Greeks used in order to make a conditional statement vivid or real (as opposed to contrary-to-fact or potential). Indeed, the KJV version 'I am nothing' is not only a word-for-word equivalent of the Greek ('outhen eimi') but also a more powerful statement, by far. It is a major improvement.

The other major difference – 'love' as opposed to 'charity' – harks back to the regulations for the translation. Charity stresses the moral responsibility of the individual believer and strengthens the possible implication that someone's good works contribute to redemption. That was an issue that divided Protestants and Catholics and something about which the Church of England typically sought a middle way. Obviously we are speaking of nuance here and, of course, the KJV does not have a theological note at this point.

Ultimately, it is the King James Version that is the source of the phrases that have come to inform our consciousness of

Christian faith and history. To illustrate this, we have decided to quote the narrative of Christ's birth, as recorded in the second chapter of Luke's Gospel. The following words are the ones that echo in our minds when we think of the saviour's birth:

1 And it came to pass in those days, that there went out a decree from Caesar Augustus, that all the world should be taxed.

2 (And this taxing was first made when Cyrenius was governor of Syria.)

3 And all went to be taxed, everyone to his own city.

4 And Joseph also went up from Galilee, out of the city of Nazareth, into Judea, unto the city of David, which is called Bethlehem, (because he was of the house and lineage of David,)

5 To be taxed with Mary his espoused wife, being great with child.

6 And so it was, that while they were there, the days were accomplished that she should be delivered.

7 And she brought forth her first born son, and wrapped him in swaddling clothes, and laid him in a manger, because there was no room for them in the inn.

These phrases owe much to the Geneva version and the other versions that the Geneva Bible had absorbed, particularly Tyndale's. But, once again, the small changes accomplish everything.

1 And it came to pass in those days, that there came a commandment from Augustus Caesar, that all the world should be taxed.

2 (This first taxing was made when Cyrenius was governor of Syria.)

3 Therefore went all to be taxed every man to his own city.

4 And Joseph also went up from Galilee out of a city called Nazareth, into Judea, unto the city of David, which is called Beth-lehem (because he was of the house and lineage of David,)

5 To be taxed with Marie that was given him to wife, which was with child.

6 And so it was, that while they were there, the days were accomplished that she should be delivered,

7 And she brought forth her first begotten son, and wrapped him in swaddling clothes and laid him in a cratche, because there was no room for them in the inn.

Every change does indeed seem justified. 'commandment' is so wrong as to cause a reader to stumble. Verse 3 is nearly a jumble in the Geneva version. The KJV's 'great with child' has given us yet another idiom and it conjures up an image totally lacking in Geneva's 'was with child'. 'First born' is both more literal and more poetic than 'first begotten'. And what is a 'cratche'? The Greek uses a very simple word for that humble, makeshift crib – 'phatnē', a manger.

The Revisions of the King James Bible

Subsequent editions of the King James Bible corrected errors in previous printings, although naturally they also introduced new slips on occasion. The small folio of 1616 revised the text in many places. In 1629 two of the original translators, Samuel Ward and John Bois, undertook a revision of the entire Bible. This revision, the first to omit the Apocrypha, was printed in 1629 by two Cambridge printers, Thomas and John Buck. In 1638, a group of Cambridge scholars produced another revision, which

THE GREAT POLYGLOT BIBLES

1514-17/1520 The Complutensian Polyglot.

Produced at the University of Alcalá ('Complutum' in Latin) under the editorship of Cardinal Francisco de Cisneros Ximénes. The six-volume work provides accurate texts of the Old Testament in Hebrew, Greek and Latin, and of the New Testament in Greek and Latin (the Vulgate). Also included is the Chaldaic Targum of the Pentateuch and interlinear translations of the Greek Septuagint in the Old Testament. The final volume contains Greek, Hebrew, and Chaldaic dictionaries, as well as a Hebrew grammar. Ximénes used the best manuscripts available from the Vatican Library and in Spain.

1569-72 The Plantin Polyglot.

Also called the 'Antwerp' or 'Royal' Polyglot, this eight-volume work was printed by Christopher Plantin, the largest and most important printer in Europe at the time. Edited by Benedictus Arias Montanus, the Plantin Polyglot corrects and revises the Complutensian text, adding an interlinear Latin translation of the Hebrew text and the Chaldaic Targums, as well as the Peshitta text of the Syriac New Testament with a Latin translation. The last two volumes contain dictionaries, grammatical analyses and a critical apparatus. The work was dedicated to Philip II of Spain.

1629-45 The Paris Polyglot.

A ten-volume polyglot edition of the Bible that builds upon the Plantin Polyglot texts, but adds the Syriac Old Testament and Antilegomena of the New Testament, the Arabic version of the Old Testament, and the Samaritan Pentateuch (an Old Hebrew consonantal text that differs somewhat from the Masoretic text), all with Latin translations. The text is largely dependent on the Plantin edition. It is also sometimes called 'Le Jay's Polyglot' after Guy Michel le Jay, the financial backer of the production.

1654-57 The London Polyglot.

This is the most scholarly of the four great polyglots. Brian Walton (1600-61), an Oxford scholar of Oriental languages, led the editorial project. John Lightfoot and James Ussher, among others, also contributed to the work. Volumes 1 to 3 contain the Old Testament in Hebrew with an interlinear Latin translation (Pagnini's version), the Latin Vulgate, the Greek Septuagint with Latin translation, the Chaldaic Targums with Latin translation, the Syriac Old Testament and the Arabic text, both with their own Latin translations. Volume 4 contains the Apocryphal books in four languages, and the New Testament appears in volume 5 in Greek, Latin (Vulgate), Syriac, Arabic, Ethiopic and Persian. All non-Latin texts appear with Latin translations, and all the texts, sometimes in as many as nine languages, are laid out in parallel or interlinear fashion across the folio pages for comparison. In 1669 two companion volumes appeared with lexicons, grammatical information and indexes.

they printed in a stately folio. Greater care was taken in rendering italics uniformly.

Over time, several reprints became famous for their misprints. In 1631, the 'Wicked Bible' appeared with its commandment 'thou shalt commit adultery' (Exodus 20:14), apparently a deliberate sabotage on the part of a rival printer (the edition was recalled and a heavy fine imposed). In 1653, 20,000 copies of the 'Unrighteous Bible' were released, in which Romans 6:13 read 'Neither yield your members as instruments of righteousness [instead of 'unrighteousness'] unto sin,' and 1 Corinthians 6:9 read 'Know ye not that the unrighteous shall inherit [instead of 'shall not inherit'] the kingdom of God.' In a 1717 Bible, the heading over the parable of the vineyard in Luke 20 read 'Parable of the Vinegar'.

In 1762 another serious effort was undertaken to correct errors, regularise spelling and punctuation, add marginal references and modernise the language. It became known as the Cambridge Standard Edition. Modernisation was carried further in an Oxford Standard Edition of 1769 in the spelling, italics, and by adding 30,495 marginal references.[21] These two editions, 1762 and 1769, became the basis of modern editions of the King James Version.

Although important manuscripts have been discovered since 1611, language has changed, and biblical scholarship has made important advances (especially in textual criticism), the King James Bible still endures.

It is distinctive that the KJV has lasted so long, but perhaps even more distinctive that it took so long for a standard English version to come into existence. The KJV's lateness, relative to Bibles in the other major European cultures, is emblematic of the entire history of the English Bible. Before the KJV, the outstanding English Bibles

were profoundly dependent for their greatness on translations into other European languages. In every stage of Renaissance history, the English Bible follows developments elsewhere. Even the medieval English Bible lagged behind the European scene – it was late and illegal, while other cultures, especially German and Italian, were promoting vernacular Bibles in the late Middle Ages, especially after the invention of printing. The first German Bible was printed in 1466 (a complete Bible) and the first English not until 1526 (a New Testament only). The date of the first Roman Catholic Bible in English is also a shock. Germans and Italians had printed dozens of vernacular Bibles even before there had been such a thing as a 'Protestant Bible'. In Germany there would be several new translations in response to Luther's version, the first of which was brought out in 1527. The Douai-Rheims, the first Roman Catholic Bible in English, was not to be printed in its entirety until 1610.

The English did take advantage of their lateness. There would have been no Tyndale without Luther. The Geneva Bible would not have achieved its brilliance without the foundation in biblical research in Geneva, including the revisions of the French Geneva Bible that Calvin directed. The KJV translators consulted virtually the entire library of Continental vernacular Bibles. They are best known for their careful scrutiny of the history of English Bibles, which they studied word by word in version by version. They are equally renowned for their superb scholarship, which, similarly, depended in part on the entire history of Renaissance biblical philology, and especially on the new contributions by Tremmelius, Junius and Arias Montanus. But they also studied the old and new European translations. Among the latter, they singled out the French Genevan version (1587-8), the Italian version by Giovanni Diodati (Geneva, 1607) and the Spanish versions by Cassiodoro de Reyna (Basel, 1569) and by Cipriano de Valera (Amsterdam, 1602). The KJV has always been seen as a culmination of a rich English literary development. It is also a culmination of the European Bible in general.

From this point on, English scholars would never again be among the laggards – with the KJV project they moved to the vanguard of historical and philological research. Indeed, in the aftermath of creating the KJV, the English accomplished what is perhaps the greatest feat in biblical scholarship, the best-equipped and most accurate Polyglot Bible of all time – the London Polyglot of 1654-7.[22] It is vastly superior to its noble precursors – the Complutensian (1514-17), the Antwerp (1569-72) and the Paris polyglots (1629-45). The London Polyglot, which appeared in six massive volumes and also featured two additional volumes of grammars and lexicons, was the work of Brian Walton and many English scholars of enormous erudition, including John Lightfoot and James Ussher. It would print the text in some nine languages – Hebrew, Greek, Samaritan, Aramaic, Syriac, Ethiopic, Persian, Arabic and Latin. Its accuracy and its coverage of the ancient versions would never be equalled. It is a stunning coda to the King James Version, a translation that in many ways would also never be equalled.

ENDNOTES TO CHAPTER EIGHT

1. Barlow [1604] 1965, 45.
2. Barlow [1604] 1965, 46.
3. Barlow [1604] 1965, 46.
4. Hill 1993, 60.
5. Pollard 1911, 331, and Butterworth 1941, 207.
6. Isaacs in Robinson 1940, 199-200.
7. Eliot 1951, 347-8; Opfell 1982, 27.
8. Daiches 1941, 162.
9. Paine 1959, 40, 58.
10. Pollard 1911, 338.
11. Pollard 1911, 373.
12. Figures are taken from Isaacs in Robinson 1940, 206.
13. Butterworth 1941, 231.
14. Bruce 1978, 109-10.
15. See discussion in Butterworth 1941, 220.
16. Isaacs in Robinson 1940, 212.
17. Hammond 1983, 211-12.
18. Genesis 4:3, 4:8, 6:1, 8:6, 8:13, 9:14, 12:11, 12:12, 12:14, 14:1, 15:17, 19:17, 19:29, 19:34, 20:13, 21:22, 22:1, 22:20. The formula appears in the Geneva only in Genesis 4:3 and 12:12. See also Hammond 1983, 194, on this phenomenon.
19. Hammond 1983, 225.
20. Examples are from Hammond 1983, 227.
21. Lewis 1981, 39.
22. See Darlow and Moule [1903] 1963, no. 1446.

Appendix 1
Revising the King James Bible

Modern readers of the King James Bible may not realise that the venerable text has undergone some revisions over the years. Indeed, the King James Version currently in print includes hundreds of changes and 'modernisations' that have been introduced since 1611. Fredrick Henry Ambrose Scrivener's list of variations from the original edition includes about 850 alterations or corrections introduced from 1613 to 1873[1] – and editors of the last 130 years have further revised the text to lesser and greater extents.

1613   Oxford: Oxford University Press. This small, black-letter folio edition includes 412 variations from the 'He' Bible (only 70 of which also appear in the 'She' Bible). Most of these changes are corrections of obvious misprints. In four places, however, an unknown reviser offers improvements to the text (Ezra 3:5; Ezekiel 24:7; 1 Maccabees 4:29; 2 Thessalonians 2:15).

1616   London: Robert Barker. The first edition of the KJV to undergo real revision. This small folio was printed in roman type, many of its corrections were overlooked by printers of the black-letter KJV, who continued to set their texts from either the 'He' or 'She' Bible of 1611.

1629   Cambridge: Thomas and John Buck and Roger Daniel, Printers to the University of Cambridge. A complete revision by unknown scholars at Cambridge University. The revision corrects errors of the 1611 and the subsequent printings that perpetuated them or created new ones.

1638   Cambridge: Thomas Buck and Roger Daniel, Printers to the University of Cambridge. A second, and further revised Cambridge edition with corrections, particularly on making uniform the KJV's use of italic and roman typefaces to reflect the relation of the translation to the original text. New readings were also introduced in this edition, which clearly builds upon the work of the 1629 revisers. A manuscript note in the Jesus College copy of this edition credits Dr Goad of Hadley, Dr Ward, Mr Boyce (John Bois, who had been a translator of the original 1611 text), and Mr (Joseph) Mede. The Cambridge revisions are the first to include parallel textual references in the margins.

1755   London: William Bowyer. John Wesley presented a modified version of the New Testament text of the KJV in his *Notes on the New Testament* and many of his changes appear in subsequent, and more official, revisions of the Authorised Version.

1762   Cambridge: J. Bentham. A thorough revision undertaken by Dr F.S. Paris and H. Therold, two scholars at the University of Cambridge. Though carefully done and influential in the making of our KJV text because of Blayney's use of this revision (see 1769 below), this edition is extremely rare because most copies were burned in a fire before they could be circulated.

The revisers not only corrected printers' errors and punctuation and 'modernised' some of the language, but also added marginal annotations and accepted many other marginal notes and references that had crept into printings of the KJV since 1611.

1769 Oxford: T. Wright and W. Gil. Relying heavily on Paris's 1762 edition, Benjamin Blayney of Oxford further revised the KJV to produce the standard Oxford edition. In a report to the Clarendon Press, Blayney says he compared the 1611 text with later printings, reviewed the punctuation, added marginal notes when appropriate, and had 'frequent recourse . . . to the Hebrew and Greek originals'. Blayney also introduced a few errors of his own, mostly minor, that were slowly and almost completely corrected by the mid-nineteenth century in printings from Cambridge and Oxford. This corrected Blayney edition is the 'standard' edition most people read today when they pick up a King James Bible.

1833 New Haven: Hezekiah Howe and Co. for Durrie and Peck. Noah Webster (of dictionary fame) published a revision of the KJV that claims to correct mistranslations and errors in grammar and to modernise the language where necessary. The revision is a dead end for KJV recension. Few if any of his changes were incorporated into later editions.

1873 Cambridge: Cambridge University Press. The Cambridge Paragraph Bible is a carefully revised text of the KJV printed in paragraph form. Edited by F.H.A. Scrivener, the textual revision is scrupulous, based on careful collation with earlier editions. The use of italics is corrected throughout. Though the format is off-putting to the average Bible reader, the text itself is remarkably free from error.

1881-85 Cambridge: Cambridge University Press. The Revised Version (RV). The first revision authorised by the Church of England. In 1870, the Convocation of Canterbury appointed 52 scholars to review the KJV and suggest revisions to improve the text. An American committee of Old and New Testament scholars was later invited to participate. The revisers were enjoined to make as few changes to the KJV as possible, and to make any alterations to the text in a style befitting the original language of the text. They incorporated many of the corrections found in earlier revisions. The American committee published its preferred readings in 1901, thus creating an American Standard Version as opposed to the English Revised Version.

1982 Nashville: Thomas Nelson. A revision of the King James by over 130 evangelical scholars updated archaic language and expressions to reflect current English style.

ENDNOTE

1. Scrivener 1884, 148-202.

APPENDIX 2
THE POST-KING JAMES ERA

In the twentieth century alone, nearly fifty new English translations of both testaments appeared in print. When one adds translations of the New Testament, paraphrases, partial translations and versions for special audiences, the number easily triples. Translations vary depending on the base text, intended audience and approach to translating. Most translators since the sixteenth century, however, have worked from the Hebrew and Greek texts, but even in this regard, there are differences. In the sixteenth and seventeenth centuries, for example, the textus receptus for the Greek New Testament was Estienne's 1550 edition, whereas more recent translations use as their base text newer critical editions, such as Nestlé-Aland, as well as manuscripts and papyri.

In addition to the fundamental difference between a literal 'word-for-word' approach and a 'sense-for-sense' rendering, the act of translating itself involves interpretation. In the transferral of the meaning and sense of the original into English, translators often express – intentionally or not – their own doctrinal allegiances and theological views. A sample comparison of a passage from English Bibles over the past 400 years should suffice to illustrate the idiosyncratic nature of Bible translating. In the various renditions of Job 15:20 below, one senses interpretative as well as stylistic differences:

King James Version – 'The wicked man travaileth with pain all his days, and the number of years is hidden to the oppressor.'

Moffat Bible – 'The bad man suffers torment all his life, through all the years he has to work his will.'

New Jerusalem Bible – 'The life of the wicked is unceasing torment, the years allotted to the tyrant are numbered.'

New International Version – 'All his days the wicked man suffers torment, the ruthless through all the years stored up for him.'

The Good News Bible – 'A wicked man who oppresses others will be in torment as long as he lives.'

The Message – 'Those who live by their own rules, not God's, can expect nothing but trouble, and the longer they live, the worse it gets.'

New Revised Standard Version – 'The wicked writhe in pain all their days, through all the years that are laid up for the ruthless.'

Though the King James Version was revised after 1611, most notably in the English Revised Version of 1881-5 and the American Standard Version of 1901, new translations based on the original sources are really a phenomenon of the twentieth century (and one that shows no signs of slowing down in the twenty-first century).[1] Our annotated list gives an overview of some of the more significant modern English translations.

1876 Translation of Julia Evelina Smith
A literal version by one of the few women ever to translate the Bible. Smith carefully translated each occurrence of the same Greek or Hebrew word with the same English equivalent, making for a rather wooden translation, but an excellent 'crib' for Bible students.

1913-24 The Moffatt Bible
The first 'modern language' version that attempts an informal or more colloquial style. James Moffatt (1870-1944) used the Greek edition of Hermann Freiherr von Soden, a 1913 critical edition based on the Koine, Hesychian and Jerusalem recensions as his base text for the New Testament and the various Masoretic editions for the Old Testament. His approach to translation – and the reasons for the criticism it received – is clear in his introduction: 'When the choice lay between a guess and a gap, I inclined to prefer the former, feeling that the ordinary reader for whom this version was designed would have a proper dislike for gaps.'

1923-27 Smith-Goodspeed Bible
An early attempt at a popular or 'dynamic equivalence' version (that is, a sense for sense, rather than a word-for-word translation). Whereas Moffatt's modern version spoke to a British audience, or more specifically a Scottish one, the Smith-Goodspeed Bible was tuned to the ear of American readers. J.M. Powis Smith (1866-1932) was responsible for the Old Testament and Edgar Johnson Goodspeed (1871-1962) for the New Testament.

1941 The Confraternity Version (CV)
A thorough revision of the New Testament of the Douai-Rheims Bible, based on both the Vulgate and Greek originals. The Old Testament was also revised and appeared in 1948-59. This version was authorised by the Catholic Church until a new translation based on the original language texts was completed after the Second Vatican Council (The New American Bible, 1970).

1945 The Berkeley New Testament
A new translation by twenty scholars, headed by Gerrit Verkuyl. The text is accurate, but the notes are rather conservative and moralistic. The entire Bible was issued in 1959 as the New Berkeley Version in Modern English. A revision was done in 1969 and was released as the Modern Language Bible.

1949 The Bible in Basic English
Using a vocabulary of only one thousand words that C.K. Ogden established as 'Basic English', a committee of scholars in Cambridge translated the Bible from the original languages. More of a linguistic curiosity than a useful Bible translation.

1946-57 Revised Standard Version (RSV)
In 1937 the International Council of Religious Education authorised a thorough revision of the 1901 American Standard Version (an American variant of the Revised Version) in order that the translation 'should embody the best results of modern scholarship as to the meaning of the Scriptures, and express this meaning in English diction which is designed for use in public and private worship'. More than a revision, however, this is a new translation based on original sources. Translated by a committee of American scholars, the RSV version of the New Testament was published in 1946; the Old Testament in 1952; and the Apocrypha in 1957. Since 1950 the RSV has been authorised by the National Council of Churches. It became the version of choice for most Protestants and was also approved for use by Roman Catholic and Orthodox Christians (with the books, however, arranged in a different order).

1962-71 The Living Bible Paraphrased (LB)
A popular, conservative paraphrase of the Bible. The LB has also been sold as the Reach Out Version (NT), The Way: Catholic Edition and Soul Food. The use of paraphrase has evoked both praise and criticism, but it has motivated many to read the Bible. In 1996 the New Living Translation was issued which is more a dynamic equivalent translation than a paraphrase.

1966 The Jerusalem Bible (JB)
An English edition of a Roman Catholic translation produced by French Dominican scholars (La Bible de Jérusalem), the JB makes a good study Bible not only because of careful scholarship behind the translation, but also because of its copious notes, indices and tables.

1970 New American Standard Bible (NASB)

This is not an official revision of the American Standard Version (1901), though the preface claims to 'follow the principles used in the ASV'. The NASB was produced by an anonymous group of conservative biblical scholars. This translation aimed to combine literalness and readability. It achieved the former more successfully than the latter. The 1995 update removed 'thees' and 'thous' and generally modernised the language.

1970 New American Bible (NAB)

Sponsored by the Catholic Biblical Association of America, the NAB is a revision of the Confraternity Version of the Old Testament and a new translation of the New Testament based on the Greek. It is the first Catholic Bible in English translated directly from the original Hebrew and Greek texts rather than from the Latin Vulgate. The notes reflect liberal, higher criticism views (J,E,D,P sources for the Pentateuch, two Isaiahs, John may not have written the Gospel of John, etc.).

1978 The New International Version (NIV)

Under the auspices of the New York Bible Society International (now the International Bible Society), this is the work of over 100 conservative and evangelical Protestant scholars. The translation was a response to the perceived liberal interpretation/translation of the RSV, often carrying its own doctrinal views into the English rendering. The bibliographers Gorman and Gorman suggest it 'lacks the critical scholarly acceptance afforded other modern translations and so has little active place in advanced biblical studies'.[2] The translators, however, claim that their goal is to be accurate, idiomatic and readable. When the NIV appeared, the publicity ambitiously proclaimed that its goal was to do for its day what the King James had done for its age. It did not achieve this, but has been very successful and appears in a variety of formats including study Bibles and age-specific Bibles.

1966/79 The Good News Bible (Today's English Version)

The New Testament of this Bible is well-known as the Good News for Modern Man (1966). Translations of the Old Testament and Apocrypha were completed in 1979. Written in everyday English, the GNB uses a simple and limited vocabulary to translate the original. 'Unleavened bread', for example, becomes 'bread made without yeast'. The language is not colloquial, but rather an attempt at an English *koine*. It attempts to make the Bible 'read like a newspaper'.

1982 New King James Version (NKJV)

A committee of over 130 evangelical scholars is responsible for this revision of the KJV, which was commissioned by Thomas Nelson Publishers and issued in 1982. The language has been updated and archaic formulations have been altered to reflect current English style. The NKJV is available in several forms, including, the NKJV Scofield Reference Bible; the Businessman's Bible; the Businesswoman's Bible; and even the NKJV Precious Moments Baby Bible.

1985 The New Jerusalem Bible (NJB)

A revision of the JB, the NJB attempts to be more literal than its predecessor. Though not a colloquial translation, its strength is its comprehensible style. Like the NRSV, this version reads very well in liturgical settings. The language is inclusive whenever possible. The NJB also includes useful annotations and notes at the bottom of the page.

1985 The Five Books of Moses

The work of Everett Fox, who spent twenty-five years translating the Pentateuch, basing his work on principles developed by Martin Buber and Franz Rosenzweig to capture in English the poetics of the Hebrew original, including word-plays, rhythm, alliterations and dialectal differences. The version is praised most often for its beauty as a text to be read aloud.

1989 New Revised Standard Version (NRSV)

The NRSV has been described as 'another step in the long, continual process of making the Bible available in the form of the English language that is most widely current in our day'. The steps leading up to this version were the KJV, the American Standard Version and the RSV. In this latest revision, an ecumenical committee of scholars used the most recent editions of the Biblia Hebraica Stuttgartensia and the Greek New Testament (United Bible Societies) as their base texts. The NRSV is a scholarly translation that is 'as literal as possible and as free as necessary'. The English tendency to use male-oriented language when referring to a larger group has been changed and androcentric passages have been rephrased, unless the original reflected a particular bias. The NRSV has replaced the RSV for most mainline Protestants. Bruce M. Metzger chaired the translation committee.

1989 Revised English Bible (REB)

A revision of the New English Bible (1970). The REB represents the work of the Joint Committee of the British Churches, a multi-denominational group including major Protestant churches in England, Scotland and Ireland, as well as Roman Catholic representatives. The idea was to produce a literary translation, with a richer vocabulary than one finds in more popular versions, while keeping readability a primary goal. Gender-specific language is avoided when possible.

1991 Contemporary English Version

Issued on 9 May 1991 (New Testament portion only) by the American Bible Society (Thomas Nelson Publishers), the CEV is a new translation by some of the same scholars that produced the Good News New Testament. A major concern of the translators was 'oral readability and oral comprehension'; liberties and paraphrases are apparent throughout. The entire CEV, with both Testaments, was published in 1995.

1993 The Message

A popular paraphrase of the Bible by Eugene H. Peterson. The language is colloquial and somewhat jarring to readers more familiar with a formal sound. Peterson argues, however, that the originals were written in the common language, so our translations should reflect that.

1996 New Living Translation

A new modern language version that nonetheless tries to avoid paraphrase. Produced by ninety evangelical scholars, their goal was to revise and make The Living Bible (1970) more accurate.

1994-98 Twenty-first Century King James Version/Third Millennium Bible

A 1994 translation that claims to be 'an accurate updating of the King James Version of 1611', published with the Apocrypha in 1998 as the Third Millennium Bible. Obsolete words have been changed, spelling updated and capitalisation normalised. The goal is to make the KJV 'easier to read and understand'. Though designed for a conservative audience, the work annoyed many Protestants because of the inclusion of the apocryphal books that have been left out of most English Bibles since 1825.

2001 English Standard Version

Published by Crossway Bibles, a division of Good News Publishers, this new version attempts a word-for-word translation from the original languages (Biblia Hebraica Stuttgartensia, 1983 and Nestlé/Aland, 27th ed.). It is clear, however, that the translators are largely revising the Revised Standard Version to rid it of what they consider 'liberal' interpretations or translation choices. The translation team was made up of over one hundred Bible scholars and the readings and notes reflect an evangelical theology.

2002 Today's New International Version 2002, New Testament

A revision of the NIV that has caused much controversy in conservative circles because of its decision to use gender-neutral language when possible. The complete Bible is scheduled for publication in 2005.

ENDNOTES

1. For the twentieth century alone, Kubo and Specht 1983, 345-75, list over 155 different translations through 1982.
2. Gorman and Gorman 1984, 1:351.

BIBLIOGRAPHY OF WORKS CONSULTED

Allen, Ward, ed. and trans. 1969. *Translating for King James: Being a True Copy of the Only Notes Made By a Translator of King James's Bible*. Nashville: Vanderbilt UP.

Amram, David Werner. 1909. *Makers of Hebrew Books in Italy*. Philadelphia: J.H. Greenstone.

Armstrong, Elizabeth Tyler. 1954. *Robert Estienne, Royal Printer: An Historical Study of the Elder Stephanus*. Cambridge: Cambridge UP.

Aston, Margaret. 1992. 'The Bishops' Bible Illustrations'. *The Church and the Arts*, 267-85. Edited by Diana Wood. Oxford: Blackwell.

Avis, Frederick C. 1973. 'England's Use of Antwerp Printers, 1500-1540'. *Gutenberg-Jahrbuch 1973*, 234-40. Mainz: Verlag der Gutenberg-Gesellschaft.

Backus, Irena D. 1980. *The Reformed Roots of the English New Testament: The Influence of Theodore Beza on the English New Testament*. Pittsburgh: Pickwick Press.

Bainton, Roland Herbert. 1969. *Erasmus of Christendom*. New York: Scribner.

Ballinger, John, and James Ifano Jones. 1906. *The Bible in Wales: A Study in the History of the Welsh People, with an Introductory Address and a Bibliography*. London: H. Sotheran.

Barlow, William. [1604] 1965. *The Summe and Substance of the Conference which It Pleased His Excellent Majestie to Have with the Lords, Bishops, and Other of His Clergie at Hampton Court, January 14, 1603*. A facsimile reproduction with an introduction by William T. Costello and Charles Kennan. Gainesville, Florida: Scholars' Facsimiles and Reprints.

Bartlett, Kenneth R. 1996. 'Marian Exiles'. *Oxford Encyclopedia of the Reformation* 3:8-10.

Bentley, Jerry H. 1983. *Humanists and Holy Writ: New Testament Scholarship in the Renaissance*. Princeton: Princeton UP.

Berkowitz, David Sandler. 1968. *In Remembrance of Creation: Evolution of Art and Scholarship in the Medieval and Renaissance Bible*. Waltham, Massachusetts: Brandeis UP.

Betteridge, Maurice S. 1983. 'The Bitter Notes: The Geneva Bible and its Annotations'. *Sixteenth Century Journal* 14:41-62.

Bloch, Joshua. [1933] 1976. 'Venetian Printers of Hebrew Books'. Reprinted in *Hebrew Printing and Bibliography*, 65–88. Edited by Charles Berlin. New York: New York Public Library and KTAV Publishing House.

Blumenthal, Joseph. 1977. *The Printed Book in America*. Boston: D.R. Godine.

Bobrick, Benson. 2001. *Wide as the Waters: The Story of the English Bible and the Revolution It Inspired*. New York: Simon and Schuster.

Boyle, Marjorie O'Rourke. 1977. *Erasmus on Language and Method in Theology*. Toronto: University of Toronto Press.

Bray, Gerald, ed. 1994. *Documents of the English Reformation*. Cambridge: James Clarke.

Brook, V.J.K. 1962. *A Life of Archbishop Parker*. Oxford: Clarendon Press.

Bruce, Frederick Fyvie. 1978. *History of the Bible in English: From the Earliest Versions*. 4th edition. Cambridge: Lutterworth Press.

Butterworth, Charles C. 1941. *The Literary Lineage of the King James Bible, 1340-1611*. Philadelphia: University of Pennsylvania Press.

Cambridge History of the Bible. [1963-70] 1978-80. 3 volumes. Volume 1 edited by P.R. Ackroyd and

C.F. Evans; Volume 2 edited by G.W.H. Lampe; Volume 3 edited by S.L. Greensalde. New York: Cambridge UP.

Carleton, James George. 1902. *The Part of Rheims in the Making of the English Bible*. Oxford: Clarendon Press.

Chadwick, Owen. [1964] 1990. *The Reformation*. New York: Penguin Books.

Chambers, Bettye Thomas. 1983. *Bibliography of French Bibles: Fifteenth- and Sixteenth-Century French-Language Editions of the Scriptures*. Geneva: Droz.

Cohn, Joseph Hoffman. 1952. *The Revised Standard Version: A Sad Travesty*. New York: American Board of Missions to the Jews, Inc.

Collected Works of Erasmus. 1974-. Toronto; Buffalo: University of Toronto Press.

Collinson, Patrick. 1967. *The Elizabethan Puritan Movement*. London: Jonathan Cape.

——. 1983. *The Religion of Protestants*. Oxford: Clarendon Press.

Cook, Albert S. 1903. *Biblical Quotations in Old English Prose Writers*. New York: Charles Scribner; London Edward Arnold.

Copinger, Walter Arthur. 1897. *The Bible and Its Transmission: Being an Historical and Bibliographical View of the Hebrew and Greek Texts, and the Greek, Latin, and Other Versions of the Bible (both Manuscript and Printed) Prior to the Reformation*. London: Henry Sotheran.

Coverdale Bible, 1535. 1975. With an Introduction by S.L. Greenslade. Facsimile, Kent: Dawson.

Daiches, David. 1941. *The King James Version of the English Bible: An Account of the Development and Sources of the English Bible of 1911 with Special Reference to the Hebrew Tradition*. Chicago: University of Chicago Press.

Daniell, David, ed. 1989. *Tyndale's New Testament*. Translated from the Greek by William Tyndale in 1534. New Haven: Yale UP.

——. 1992. *Tyndale's Old Testament: Being the Pentateuch of 1530, Joshua to 2 Chronicles of 1537, and Jonah Translated by William Tyndale; in a Modern Spelling Edition*. New Haven: Yale UP.

——. 1994. *William Tyndale: A Biography*. New Haven: Yale UP.

Darlow, Thomas Herbert, and Horace Frederick Moule. [1903] 1963. *Historical Catalogue of the Printed Editions of Holy Scripture in the Library of the British and Foreign Bible Society*. 4 volumes. New York: Kraus.

Deansley, Margaret. 1920. *The Lollard Bible and Other Medieval Biblical Versions*. Cambridge: Cambridge UP.

De Hamel, Christopher. 1984. *Glossed Books of the Bible and the Origins of the Paris Booktrade*. Woodbridge: D.S. Brewer.

——. 1986. *A History of Illuminated Manuscripts*. Boston: David C. Godine.

——. 2001. *The Book: A History of the Bible*. New York: Phaidon.

De Jonge, Henk Jan. 1980. 'Erasmus and the Comma Johanneum'. *Ephemerides Theologicae Lovanienses* 56:381–9.

Devereux, E.J. 1969. 'The Publication of the English *Paraphrases* of Erasmus'. *Bulletin of the John Rylands Library* 51:348-67.

Dickens, A. G. [1964] 1989. *The English Reformation*. 2nd Edition. University Park, Pennsylvania: Pennsylvania State UP.

Dictionary of National Biography: From the Earliest Times to 1900. 1921–2. Edited by Leslie Stephen and Sydney Lee. 22 volumes. London: Oxford UP.

Douglas, James Dixon, ed. 1974. *The New International Dictionary of the Christian Church*. Grand Rapids: Zondervan.

Eichenberger, Walter, and Henning Wendland. 1977. *Deutsche Bibeln vor Luther: Die Buchkunst der achtzehn deutschen Bibeln zwischen 1466 und 1522*. Hamburg: Friedrich Wittig.

Eliot, T.S. 1951. *Selected Essays*. London: Faber and Faber.

Engammare, Max. 1991. 'Cinquante ans de révisions de la traduction biblique d'Olivétan: Les

Bibles réformées genevoises en français au XVIème siècle'. *Bibliothèque d'Humanisme et Renaissance* 53(2):347–77.

English Hexapla. [1848]. London: Samuel Bagster and Sons.

Erasmus, Desiderius. 1548. *The first tome or volume of the paraphrase of Erasmus vpon the newe testamente.* London: Edward Whitchurch.

Fogarty, Gerald P. 1988. 'American Catholic Translations of the Bible'. *The Bible and Bibles in America*, 117–18. Edited by Ernest S. Frerichs. Atlanta: Scholars Press.

Forshall, Josiah, and Frederic Madden, eds. 1850. *The Holy Bible, Containing the Old and New Testaments, with Apocryphal Books, in the Earliest English Versions Made from the Latin Vulgate by John Wycliffe and His Followers.* 4 volumes. Oxford: Oxford UP.

Frere, W.H., and C.E. Douglas. 1954. *Puritan Manifestoes*. London: S.P.C.K.

Froelich, Karlfried, and Margaret T. Gibson, eds. 1992. *Biblia latina cum Glossa ordinaria*. Turnhout: Brepols.

Fry, Francis. 1867. *The Bible by Coverdale, MDXXXV. Remarks on the Titles; the Year of Publication; the Preliminary, the Water Marks, etc., with Facsimiles.* London: Willis and Sotheran.

——. 1878. *The Editions of the New Testament. Tyndale's Version, 1525–1566.* London: Henry Sotheran.

Fry, Theodore. 1887. *A Brief Memoir of Francis Fry.* London: Barclay and Fry.

Garrett, Christina H. 1938. *The Marian Exiles.* Cambridge: Cambridge UP.

Geneva Bible. 1969. A Facsimile of the 1560 Edition. With an Introduction by Lloyd E. Berry. Madison: University of Wisconsin Press.

Geneva Bible. 1989. The Annotated New Testament, 1602 Edition. Edited by Gerald T. Sheppard. New York: Pilgrim Press.

Goodspeed, Edgar Johnson, ed. 1935. *The Translators to the Reader: Preface to the King James Version, 1611.* Chicago: University of Chicago Press.

Gorman, G.E., and Lyn Gorman. 1984. *Theological and Religious Reference Materials.* Westport, CT: Greenwood Press.

Goshen-Gottstein, Moshe, ed. 1972. *Biblia Rabbinica: A Reprint of the 1525 Venice Edition.* 4 volumes. Jerusalem: Makor.

Hall, Basil. 1966. *The Great Polyglot Bibles: Including a Leaf from the Complutensian of Alcalá, 1514–17.* San Francisco: Book Club of California.

——. 1995. 'The Geneva Version of the English Bible: Its Aims and Achievements'. *The Bible, the Reformation and the Church. Essays in Honour of James Atkinson*, 124-49. Edited by W.P. Stephens. Sheffield: Sheffield Academic Press.

Hall, Isaac Hollister. 1883. *American Greek Testaments. A Critical Bibliography of the Greek New Testament as Published in America.* Philadelphia: Pickwick.

Hammond, Gerald S. 1980. 'William Tyndale's Pentateuch: Its Relation to Luther's German Bible and the Hebrew Original'. *Renaissance Quarterly* 33:351–85.

——. 1983. *The Making of the English Bible.* New York: Philosophical Library.

Handover, P.M. 1960. *Printing in London from 1476 to Modern Times.* Cambridge: Harvard UP.

Hargreaves, Henry. 1979. 'Popularizing Biblical Scholarship: The Role of the Wycliffite Glossed Gospels'. In *The Bible and Medieval Culture*, 171–89. Edited by W. Lourdaux and D. Verhelst. Leuven: Leuven UP.

Hatch, Henry Paine. 1951. *Facsimiles and Descriptions of Minuscule Manuscripts of the New Testament.* Cambridge: Harvard UP.

Hefele, Carl Joseph. [1851] 1968. *Der Cardinal Ximenes.* Frankfurt: Minerva.

Herbert, Arthur Sumner. 1968. *Historical Catalogue of Printed Editions of the English Bibles, 1525-1961.* Revised and expanded from the edition of T.H. Darlow and H.F. Moule, 1903. London: British and Foreign Bible Society.

Hill, Christopher. 1993. *The English Bible and the Seventeenth-Century Revolution*. London: Allen Lane; New York: Penguin Press.

Holy Bible, 1611. 1965. Facsimile of 1611 edition of the King James Bible. Cleveland: World Publishing Co.

Hotchkiss, Valerie R., and Charles C. Ryrie. 1998. *Formatting the Word of God*. Dallas: Bridwell Library.

Howell, John, comp. 1974. *A Leaf from the First Edition of the First Complete Bible in English, the Coverdale Bible, 1535: With an Historical Introduction by Allen P. Wikgren and a Census of Copies Recorded in the British Isles and North America Compiled by John Howell*. San Francisco: Book Club of California.

Hudson, Anne. 1988. *The Premature Reformation: Wycliffite Texts and Lollard History*. Oxford: Clarendon Press; New York: Oxford UP.

Ing, Janet Thompson. 1988. *Johann Gutenberg and his Bible: A Historical Study*. Preface by Paul Needham. New York: Typophiles.

Irwin, William Andrew. [1952]. 'Method and Procedure of the Revision'. *An Introduction to the Revised Standard Version of the Old Testament*. New York: Thomas Nelson and Sons.

King, John N. 1989. *Tudor Royal Iconography: Literature and Art in an Age of Religious Crisis*. Princeton: Princeton UP.

Kingdon, John Abernethy, et al. 1895. *Incidents in the Lives of Thomas Poyntz and Richard Grafton, Two Citizens and Grocers of London, Who Suffered Loss and Incurred Danger in Common with Tyndale, Coverdale, and Rogers, in Bringing out the Bible in the Vulgar Tongue*. London: Rixon and Arnold.

———. 1901. *Richard Grafton, Citizen and Grocer of London and One Time Master of his Company, Servant and Printer to Edward Prince and King and First Treasurer General of Christ's Hospital: A Sequel to 'Poyntz and Grafton'*. London: Rixon and Arnold.

Kubo, Sakae, and Walter Specht. 1983. *So Many Versions?: Twentieth Century English Versions of the Bible*. Revised and enlarged edition. Grand Rapids: Zondervan.

Larue, Gerald A. 1963. 'Another Chapter in the History of Bible Translation'. *Journal of Bible and Religion* 31(1):301–10.

The Letters and Memorials of William, Cardinal Allen (1532-1594). [1882] 1965. Edited by the Fathers of the London Oratory. Reprint, Ridgewood, N.J.: The Gregg Press.

Lewis, Jack P. 1981. *The English Bible from KJV to NIV: A History and Evaluation*. Grand Rapids: Baker Book House.

Life of Mr. William Whittingham, Dean of Durham. 1871. Edited by Mary Anne Everett Green. Westminster: J.B. Nichols and Sons for the Camden Society.

Light, Laura. 1988. *The Bible in the Twelfth Century: An Exhibition of Manuscripts at the Houghton Library*. Cambridge: Harvard College Library.

Lowry, Martin. 1979. *The World of Aldus Manutius: Business and Scholarship in Renaissance Venice*. Ithaca: Cornell UP.

Lyell, James Patrick Ronaldson. 1917. *Cardinal Ximenes: Statesman, Ecclesiastic, Soldier, and Man of Letters; with an Account of the Complutensian Polyglot Bible*. London: Grafton.

MacCulloch, Diarmaid. 1990. *The Later Reformation in England, 1547-1603*. New York: St Martin's Press.

———. 1996. *Thomas Cranmer: A Life*. New Haven: Yale UP.

———. 2001. *The Boy King: Edward VI and the Protestant Reformation*. New York: Palgrave.

MacGregor, Geddes. 1968. *A Literary History of the Bible*. Nashville: Abingdon Press.

Martin, Ira Jay. 1961. 'The Geneva Bible'. *Andover Newton Quarterly* 1:46-51.

McGrath, Alister E. 2001. *In the Beginning: The Story of the King James Bible*. New York: Doubleday.

McMurtrie, Douglas Crawford. 1943. *The Book*. London: Oxford UP.

McNally, Robert E. 1966. 'The Council of Trent and Vernacular Bibles'. *Theological Studies* 27:204–27.

Merton, Reginald. 1934. *Cardinal Ximenes and the Making of Spain.* London: Kegan Paul, Trench, and Trübner.

Metzger, Bruce Manning. 1960. 'The Geneva Bible of 1560'. *Theology Today* 17:339-52.

———. 1961. 'The Influence of the Codex Bezae upon the Geneva Bible of 1560'. *New Testament Studies* 8:72-7.

———. 1981. *Manuscripts of the Greek Bible.* New York: Oxford UP.

———. 1992. *The Text of the New Testament: Its Transmission, Corruption, and Restoration.* 3rd enlarged edition. Oxford: Oxford UP.

Milne, Herbert John Mansfield, and Theodore Cressy Skeat. 1955. *The Codex Sinaiticus and the Codex Alexandrinus.* 2nd edition. London: British Museum.

Mombert, Jacob Isidor. [1884]. *William Tyndale's Five Books of Moses, Called the Pentateuch, Being a Verbatim Reprint of the Edition of M.CCCCC.XXX. Compared with Tyndale's Genesis of 1534, and the Pentateuch in the Vulgate, Luther, and Matthew's Bible, with Various Collations and Prolegomena.* New York: Anson D.F. Randolph and Co.; London: S. Bagster.

More, Thomas. 1927. *The Dialogue Concerning Tyndale by Sir Thomas More.* Edited by W.E. Campbell. London: Eyre and Spottiswoode.

Morrell, Minnie Cate. 1965. *A Manual of Old English Bible Materials.* Knoxville: University of Tennessee Press.

Moynahan, Brian. 2002. *If God Spare My Life: William Tyndale, the English Bible and Sir Thomas More.* London: Little, Brown.

Mozley, James Frederic. 1937. *William Tyndale.* London: S.P.C.K.

———. 1953. *Coverdale and His Bibles.* London: Lutterworth Press.

Murphy, Lawrence. 1983. 'An 'Authorized' American Bible?' *American Book Collector* 4(1):3–9.

Needham, Paul. 1985. 'The Paper Supply of the Gutenberg Bible'. *Papers of the Bibliographical Society of America* 79:303–74.

New Testament Octapla. 1962. Edited by Luther A. Weigle. New York: Thomas Nelson and Sons.

Noble, Richmond. [1935] 1970. *Shakespeare's Biblical Knowledge.* New York: Octagon.

Norton, David. 2000. *A History of the English Bible as Literature.* Cambridge: Cambridge UP.

O'Callaghan, Edmund Bailey. [1861] 1966. *A List of Editions of the Holy Scriptures and Parts thereof Printed in America Previous to 1860.* Detroit: Gale Research Co.

Ohly, Friedrich. 1985. *Gesetz und Evangelium: Zur Typologie bei Luther und Lucas Cranach. Zum Blutstrahl der Gnade in der Kunst.* Münster: Aschendorff.

Olin, John C., ed. 1975. *Christian Humanism and the Reformation: Selected Writings of Erasmus, with the Life of Erasmus by Beatus Rhenanus.* New York: Fordham UP.

———. 1990. *Catholic Reform: From Cardinal Ximenes to the Council of Trent, 1495–1563: An Essay with Illustrative Documents and a Brief Study of St Ignatius Loyola.* New York: Fordham UP.

Opfell, Olga S. 1982. *The King James Bible Translators.* Jefferson, North Carolina: McFarland.

Oswald, John Clyde. 1937. *Printing in the Americas.* New York and Chicago: Gregg Publishing Co.

Oxford Dictionary of the Christian Church. 1997. 3rd edition. Edited by Elizabeth A. Livingstone and Frank Leslie Cross. New York: Oxford UP.

Ozment, Steven. 1980. *The Age of Reform.* New Haven: Yale UP.

Paine, Gustavus Swift. 1959. *The Learned Men.* New York: Crowell.

Parker, Matthew. 1853. *Correspondence of Matthew Parker.* Edited by John Bruce and Thomas Thomason Perowne. Cambridge: Cambridge UP.

Pelikan, Jaroslav, with Valerie R. Hotchkiss and David Price. 1996. *The Reformation of the Bible/The Bible of the Reformation.* New Haven: Yale UP.

Pollard, Alfred W., ed. 1911. *Records of the English Bible: The Documents Relating to the Translation and Publication of the Bible in English, 1525-1611.* London: Oxford UP.

Pope, Hugh, and Sebastian Bullough. 1952. *English Versions of the Bible.* St Louis: B. Herder Book Co.

Reinitzer, Heimo. 1983. *Biblia deutsch: Luthers Bibelübersetzung und ihre Tradition.* Wolfenbüttel: Herzog August Bibliothek.

Renouard, Antoine Augustin. 1825. *Annales de l'imprimerie des Alde.* 2nd edition. Paris: Antoine Augustin Renouard.

Rheims New Testament. 1975. *The New Testament of Jesus Christ, 1582.* Facsimile of the Rheims New Testament. *English Recusant Literature, 1558–1640*, vol. 267. Ilkley: Scholar Press.

Robinson, Fred C. 1999. *Wycliffite Manuscript: The New Testament.* Palo Alto: Octavo.

Robinson, Henry Wheeler, ed. 1940. *The Bible in Its Ancient and English Versions.* Oxford: Clarendon Press.

Rosenau, William. 1902. *Hebraisms in the Authorized Version of the Bible.* Baltimore: Johns Hopkins UP.

Rummel, Erika. 1986. *Erasmus' 'Annotations' on the New Testament: From Philologist to Theologian.* Toronto: University of Toronto Press.

Ruppel, Aloys. 1937. *Peter Schöffer aus Gernsheim.* Mainz: Gutenberg-Gesellschaft.

Ryrie, Charles Caldwell. 1965. 'Calvinistic Emphases in the Geneva and Bishops' Bible'. *Bibliotheca Sacra* 122:23-30.

———. 1969. *The Bible of the Middle Way.* Fort Worth: Brite Divinity School.

———. 1981. 'The Notes of the Geneva Bible'. *Fine Books and Collecting.* Edited by Christopher de Hamel and Richard A. Linenthal, 54-6. Leamington Spa: James Hall.

Schmidt, Philipp. 1962. *Die Illustration der Lutherbibel, 1522–1700: Ein Stück abendländischer Kultur- und Kirchengeschichte mit Verzeichnissen der Bibeln, Bilder, und Künstler.* Basel: F. Reinhardt.

Schreiber, Fred. 1982. *The Estiennes: An Annotated Catalogue of Three Hundred Highlights of their Various Presses.* New York: E.K. Schreiber.

Schwarz, W. 1955. *Principles and Problems of Biblical Translation: Some Reformation Controversies and their Background.* Cambridge: Cambridge UP.

Scribner, Robert W. 1994. *For the Sake of Simple Folk: Popular Propaganda for the German Reformation.* 2nd edition. Oxford: Clarendon Press; New York: Oxford UP.

Scrivener, Fredrick Henry Ambrose. 1884. *The Authorized Edition of the English Bible (1611), Its Subsequent Reprints and Modern Representations.* Cambridge: Cambridge UP.

Sider, Robert Dick, ed. 1994. *Erasmus' Annotations on Romans.* Translated and annotated by John Barton Payne. Toronto: University of Toronto Press.

Simms, Paris Marion. 1936. *The Bible in America: Versions that Have Played their Part in the Making of the Republic.* New York: Wilson-Erikson, Inc.

Slater, John Rothwell. 1906. *The Sources of Tyndale's Version of the Pentateuch.* Chicago: University of Chicago Press.

Smalley, Beryl. 1964. *The Study of the Bible in the Middle Ages.* Notre Dame: University of Notre Dame Press.

Spinka, Matthew. 1953. *Advocates of Reform, from Wyclif to Erasmus.* Philadelphia: Westminster Press.

Strachan, James. 1957. *Early Bible Illustrations.* Cambridge: Cambridge UP.

Strype, John. 1711. *The Life and Acts of Matthew Parker.* 3 parts. London: J. Wyat.

Tanner, Norman P., ed. 1990. *Decrees of the Ecumenical Councils.* London: Sheed and Ward.

Thomas, Isaiah, et al. 1964. *The History of Printing in America.* New York: Burt Franklin.

Warnicke, Retha M. 1989. *The Rise and Fall of Anne Boleyn: Family Politics at the Court of Henry VIII.* Cambridge: Cambridge UP.

Westcott, Brooke Foss. 1905. *A General View of the History of the English Bible.* 3rd edition; revised by W.A. Wright. New York: Macmillan.

Index